Introduction to the New Testament

Introduction to the New Testament

Copyright 2017 Lexham Press

Lexham Press, 1313 Commercial St., Bellingham, WA 98225
LexhamPress.com

Originally published as *New Testament Introduction (or Special Canonics)*, Eerdmans-Sevensma Co., Grand Rapids, Michigan, 1915.

ISBN 9781577997948

Cover art: Vincent van Gogh, *Stillleben mit Bibel*, 1885. Public domain.

Introduction to the New Testament

Louis Berkhof

LEXHAM PRESS

— Preface

This little work on New Testament Introduction is the result of labor done in and for the class-room, and is primarily intended for my own students. It is not and does not pretend to be a work of original research, but depends in a large measure on the labors of such men as Davidson, Reuss, Weiss, Westcott, Lightfoot, Godet, Holtzmann, Jülicher, Zahn, e. a. The indebtedness to these will be evident from its pages.

In method of treatment I have partly gone my own way, both in virtue of principles that are not generally recognized in works of Introduction and for practical considerations. As far as the limits of the work allowed, the directions given by Dr. Kuyper in his Encyclopaedia of Sacred Theology have been followed; not only the human but also the divine side of the Sacred Scriptures has been treated.

It has been my constant endeavor in writing this book, to make it a work that would introduce the students to the books of the New Testament, as they have in fact been transmitted to the Church, and not as some critic or other would have them be. Hence critical questions, though not disregarded, do not loom as large on its pages as they often do in works on Introduction; the positive constructive element has a decided precedence over the apologetic; and the human factor that operated in the origin and composition of the Scriptures, is not studied to the neglect of the divine.

A limited number of copies was printed, partly in deference to the expressed wish of some of my present and past students, and partly because I desire to use it as a text-book in the future, there being none of the smaller works on Introduction, such as those of Dods, Pullan, Kerr, Barth, Peake e. a., however excellent some of them may be in their own way, that gave me what I desired. If the book may in some small measure be instrumental in leading others to a greater appreciation and an ever better understanding of the New Testament writings, I shall be very grateful indeed.

—L. Berkhof

Grand Rapids, Mich., November 30, 1915

Contents

Preface...iii

Prolegomena 1

The Gospels in General 15

The Gospel of Luke...64

The Gospel of John 74

The Acts of the Apostles..86

The Epistles in General 96

The Epistles of Paul...104

The Epistle to the Romans...109

The First Epistle to the Corinthians 119

The Second Epistle to the Corinthians 128

The Epistle to the Galatians..135

The Epistle to the Ephesians 145

The Epistle to the Philippians 154

The Epistle to the Colossians 162

The First Epistle to the Thessalonians 169

The Second Epistle to the Thessalonians 176

The Pastoral Epistles 182

The First Epistle to Timothy...190

The Second Epistle to Timothy...196

The Epistle to Titus 200

The Epistle to Philemon 204

The Epistle to the Hebrews 207

The General Epistle of James..218

The First General Epistle of Peter 228

The Second General Epistle of Peter 239

The First General Epistle of John 247

The Second and Third General Epistles of John 254

The General Epistle of Jude 260

The Revelation of John 266

1

Prolegomena

NAME AND IDEA

The name Introduction or Isagogics (from the Greek εἰσαγωγή) did not always denote what it does today. As it is used by the monk Adrianus (circa 440) and by Cassiodorus (circa 570), it designates a conglomeration of linguistic, rhetorical, archæological, geographical and historical matter such as might be helpful in the interpretation of Scripture. In course of time the connotation of the word changed. Michaelis (1750) was the first one to employ it in something like its present sense, when he entitled his work, devoted to the literary historical questions of the New Testament, Einleitung in die göttlichen Schriften des neuen Bundes. The study of Introduction was gradually limited to an investigation of the origin, the composition, the history, and the significance of the Bible as a whole (General Introduction), or of its separate books (Special Introduction). But as a designation of this discipline the name Introduction did not meet with general approval. It was pointed out—and correctly so—that the name is too comprehensive, since there are other disciplinæ that introduce to the study of the Bible; and that it does not express the essential character of the discipline, but only one of its practical uses.

Several attempts have been made to supply a name that is more in harmony with the central contents and the unifying principle of this study. But opinions differed as to the essential character of the discipline. Some scholars, as Reuss, Credner and Hupfeld, emphasizing its historical nature, would designate it by a name something like that already employed by Richard Simon in 1678, when he styled his work, "Critical History of the Old Testament. Thus Hupfeld says: "Der eigentliche und allein richtige Name der Wissenschaft in ihrem heutigen Sinn ist demnach Geschichte der heiligen Schriften Alten und Neuen Testaments." Begriff und Methode des sogenannten biblischen Einleitung p. 12. Reuss arranged his work entirely on this principle. It was objected however, by several scholars that a history of the Biblical literature is now, and perhaps for all time an impossibility and that such a treatment necessarily leads to a co-ordination of the canonical and the apocryphal books. And this is just what we find in the History of Reuss. Hence the great majority of New Testament scholars, as Bleek, Weiss, Davidson, Holtzmann, Jülicher, Zahn e. a. prefer to retain the old name, either with or without the qualification, "historical-critical."

Another and important stricture on the name suggested by Hupfeld, is that it loses sight of the theological character of this discipline. Holtzmann correctly says: "Als Glied des Organismus der theologischen Wissenschaften ist die biblische Einleitung allerdings nur vom Begriffe des Kanons aus zu begreifen, nur in ihm findet sie ihre innere Einheit," Historisch-critische Einleitung in das Neue Testament p. 11. This consideration also leads Kuyper to prefer the name, Special Canonics. Encyclopaedie der Heilige Godgeleerdheid III p. 22 ff. Ideally this name is probably the best; it is certainly better than the others, but for practical reasons it seems preferable to abide by the generally recognized name Introduction. There is no serious objection to this, if we but remember its deficiency, and bear in mind that verba valent usu.

FUNCTION

What is the proper function of this discipline? According to De Wette it must answer the questions: "Was ist die Bibel, und wie ist sie geworden was sie ist?" Hupfeld objects to the first question that it has no place in a historical inquiry; hence he would change it a little and state the problem as follows: "Was waren die unter den Namen des Bibel vereinigten Schriften ursprünglich, und wie sind sie geworden was sie jetzt sind?" Begriff u. Meth. p. 13. It is now generally understood and admitted that the study must investigate the questions of the authorship, the composition, the history, the purpose and the canonicity of the different books of the Bible.

A difference of opinion becomes apparent, however, as soon as we ask, whether the investigation should be limited to the canonical books, or should include the Apocrypha as well. The answer to that question will necessarily depend on one's standpoint. They who regard Introduction as a purely historical study of Hebrew and Old Christian literature, will hold with Räbiger and Reuss that the apocryphal books must also receive due consideration. On the other hand, they who desire to maintain the theological character of this discipline and believe that it finds its unity in the idea of the canon, will exclude the Apocrypha from the investigation.

A similar difference obtains with reference to the question, whether it is only the human or also the divine side of the canonical books that should be the object of study. It is perfectly obvious that, if the discipline be regarded as a purely historical one, the divine factor that operated in the composition of the books of the Bible and that gives them their permanent canonical significance, cannot come in consideration. The Word of God must then be treated like all purely human compositions. This is the stand taken by nearly all writers on Introduction, and Hupfeld believes that even so it is possible to maintain the theological character of the discipline. Begriff u. Meth. p. 17. It appears to us, however, that this is impossible, and with Kuyper we hold that we should not only study the human, but should also have regard to the divine side of the Biblical books, notably to their inspiration and canonical significance.

Lastly the conception of the final aim of this study also varies. Many scholars are of the opinion that it is the final purpose of Introduction to determine in a historico-critical way what part of the Biblical writings are credible and therefore really constitute the Word of God. Human reason is placed as an arbiter over the divine Revelation. This, of course, cannot be the position of those who believe that the Bible is the Word of God. This belief is our starting point and not our goal in the study of Introduction. Thus we begin with a theological postulate, and our aim is to set forth the true character of Scripture, in order to explain, why the Church universal honors it as the Word of God; to strengthen the faith of believers; and to vindicate the claims of the canonical books over against the assaults of Rationalism.

To define: Introduction is that Bibliological discipline that investigates the origin, composition, history and purpose of the Scriptural writings, on their human side; and their inspiration and canonical significance, on the divine side.

LEADING PRINCIPLES

There are certain fundamental principles that guide us in our investigation, which it is desirable to state at the outset, in order that our position may be perfectly clear. For the sake of brevity we do not seek to establish them argumentatively.

1. For us the Bible as a whole and in all its parts is the very Word of God, written by men indeed, but organically inspired by the Holy Spirit; and not the natural product of the religious development of men, not merely the expression of the subjective religious consciousness of believers. Resting, as it ultimately does, on the testimony of the Holy Spirit, no amount of historical investigation can shake this conviction.

2. This being our position, we unflinchingly accept all that the various books of the Bible tell us concerning their authorship, destination, composition, inspiration, etc. Only in cases where the text is evidently corrupt, will we hesitate to accept their dicta as final. This applies equally to all parts of the Word of God.

3. Since we do not believe that the Bible is the result of a purely natural development, but regard it as the product of supernatural revelation, a revelation that often looks beyond the immediate present, we cannot allow the so-called zeitgeschichtliche arguments the force which they are often supposed to have.

4. While it is the prevailing habit of many New Testament scholars to discredit what the early Church fathers say respecting the books of the Bible, because of the uncritical character of their work, we accept those early traditions as trustworthy until they are clearly proven unreliable. The character of those first witnesses warrants this position.

5. We regard the use of working-hypotheses as perfectly legitimate within certain limits. They may render good service, when historical evidence fails, but even then may not go contrary to the data at hand, and the problematic character of the results to which they lead must always be borne in mind.

6. It is not assumed that the problems of New Testament Introduction are insignificant, and that all the difficulties that present themselves can easily be cleared up. Whatever our standpoint, whatever our method of procedure in studying these problems, we shall sometimes have to admit our ignorance, and often find reason to confess that we know but in part.

ENCYCLOPAEDIC PLACE

There is little uniformity in Theological Encyclopædias with respect to the proper place of this discipline. They all correctly place it among the Exegetical (Bibliological) group of Theological disciplinæ, but its relation to the other studies of that group is a matter of dispute. The most usual arrangement is that of Hagenbach, followed in our country by Schaff,

Crooks and Hurst and Weidner, viz.: Biblical Philology, dealing with the words, and Biblical Archæology, in its broadest sense, with the things of the Bible; Biblical Introduction, treating of the fortunes, and Biblical Criticism, supplying the test of Scripture; Biblical Hermeneutics, relating to the theory, and Biblical Exegesis, pertaining to the practice of interpretation. The order of Räbiger is unusual: Hermeneutics, Linguistics, Criticism, Antiquities, Biblical History, Isagogics, Exegesis, and Biblical theology. The disposition of Kuyper and Cave is preferable to either one of these. They place Introduction (Canonics) first, as pertaining to the formal side of Scripture as a book, and then let the studies follow that have reference to the formal and material side of the contents of the Bible.

HISTORICAL REVIEW

Although the beginnings of New Testament Isagogics are already found in Origen, Dionysius and Eusebius; and in the time of the Reformation some attention was devoted to it by Pagninus, Sixtus of Siene and Serarius among the Roman Catholics; by Walther of the Lutherans; and by the Reformed scholars Rivetus and Heidegger;—Richard Simon is generally regarded as the father of this study. His works were epoch-making in this respect, though they had reference primarily to the language of the New Testament. He minimized the divine element in Scripture. Michaelis, who in his, Einleitung in die göttlichen Schriften des neuen Bundes, 1750, produced the first Introduction in the modern sense, though somewhat dependent on Simon, did not altogether share his rationalistic views. Yet in the succeeding editions of his work he gradually relaxed on the doctrine of inspiration, and attached no value to the Testimonium Spiritus Sancti.

The next significant contribution to the science was made by Semler in his, Abhandlung von freier Untersuchung des Kanons, 1771–75. He broke with the doctrine of inspiration and held that the Bible was not, but contained the Word of God, which could be discovered only by the inner light. All questions of authenticity and credibility had to be investigated voraussetzungslos. Eichhorn also departed decidedly from traditional views and was the first to fix attention on the Synoptic problem, for which he sought the solution in his Urevangelium, 1804–27. At the same time the Johannine problem was placed in the foreground by several scholars, especially by Bretschneider, 1820. An acute defender of the traditional views arose in the Roman Catholic scholar Hug, who fought the rationalistic critics with their own weapons.

Meanwhile the Mediating school made its appearance under the leadership of Schleiermacher. The critics belonging to that school sought a mean between the positions of Rationalism and the traditional views. They were naturally divided into two sections, the naturalistic wing, inclining towards the position of Semler and Eichhorn; and the evangelical wing, leaning decidedly toward traditionalism. Of the first class De Wette was the ablest exponent, though his work was disappointing as to positive results; while Credner, following in general the same line, emphasized the historical idea in the study of Introduction. The other wing was represented by Guericke, Olshausen and Neander.

The Tübingen school of New Testament criticism took its rise with F. C. Baur, 1792–1860 who applied the Hegelian principle of development to the literature of the New Testament. According to him the origin of the New Testament, too, finds its explanation in the three-fold process of thesis, antithesis and synthesis. There was action, reaction and compromise. Paul defended his position in the four great epistles (Romans, I and II Corinthians and Galatians), the only genuine productions of the apostle. This position is assailed by the Apocalypse, the sole work of John. And all the other writings of the New Testament were written by others than their reputed authors in the interest of reconciliation, the fourth Gospel and the first Epistle of John issuing in the blending of the different parties. Among the immediate followers of Baur we have especially Zeller, Schwegler and Köstlin. The further adherents of the school, such as Hilgenfeld, Holsten and Davidson, modified the views of Baur considerably; while later German scholars, as Pfleiderer, Hausrath, Holtzmann, Weizsäcker and Jülicher, broke with the distinctive Tübingen theory and indulged independently in rationalistic criticism. The wildest offshoot of the Tübingen school was Bruno Bauer, who rejected even the four epistles regarded as genuine by F. C. Baur. He had no followers in Germany, but of late his views found support in the writings of the Dutch school of Pierson, Naber, Loman and Van Manen, and in the criticism of the Swiss scholar Steck.

Opposition to the radicalism of the Tübingen school became apparent in two directions. Some scholars, as Bleek, Ewald Reuss, without intending a return to the traditional standpoint discarded the subjective element of the Tübingen theory, the Hegelian principle of thesis, antithesis and synthesis, in connection with the supposed second century struggle between Petrine and Pauline factions. Ritschl also broke away from the Tübingen tendency, but substituted an equally subjective principle of criticism by applying his favorite Werthurtheile to the authentication of the books of the Bible. He had, as he claimed, no interest in saving mere objective statements. What had for him the value of a divine revelation was regarded as authentic. Some of his most prominent followers are Harnack, Schürer and Wendt.

An evangelical reaction against the subjective Tübingen vagaries also made its appearance in Ebrard, Dietlein, Thiersch, Lechler and the school of Hofmann, who himself defended the genuineness of all the New Testament books. His disciples are Luthardt, Grau, Nösgen and Th. Zahn. The works of Beischlag and B. Weiss are also quite conservative. Moreover the writings of such men as Lightfoot, Westcott, Ellicott, Godet, Dods, Pullan e. a. maintain with great ability the traditional position respecting the books of the New Testament.

SELECT LITERATURE
Including the Works referred to in the Text. In order that the list may serve as a guide for students, both the edition and the value of the books are indicated.

I. BOOKS ON INTRODUCTION, BIBLE DICTIONARIES AND RELATED WORKS

Alexander, The Canon of the Old and New Testaments, Philadelphia 1851. Conservative.

Andrews, The Life of our Lord upon the Earth, New York 1894. Excellent for chronological and historical discussions.

Baljon, Geschiedenis van de Boeken des Nieuwen Verbonds, Groningen 1901. Scholarly with a liberal point of view.

Barth, Einleitung in das Neue Testament, Gütersloh 1908; 2d edit. since published. Conservative and good.

Baur, Church History of the first three Centuries, London 1878-79. Brilliant but written with a rationalistic tendency.

Bernard, The Progress of Doctrine in the New Testament, New York 1864; 4th edit. 1878. A conservative and valuable work.

Blass, Crammatik des neutestamentlichen Griechisch, Göttingen 1911. Supercedes Winer and Buttmann, but does not render them worthless. An excellent work.

Bleek, Einleitung in das Neue Testament, 4th edit. by Mangold, Berlin 1886. Eng. transl. by W. Urwick, London 1870. One of the best works on N. T. Introd. Standpoint, moderately liberal.

Buckley, Introduction to the Synoptic Problem, London 1912. Proceeds on the Combinations-hypothese.

Clark, Geo. W., Harmony of the Acts of the Apostles, Philadelphia 1897. A very useful work.

Davidson, S., Introduction to the Study of the New Testament, London 1894. Scholarly, but extremely rationalistic and verbose.

Davis, A Dictionary of the Bible, Philadelphia 1903. The best one volume Dictionary of the Bible.

Deissmann, Light from the Ancient East, London 1911. Very valuable for the new light it sheds on the language of the N. T.

Deissmann, St. Paul, a Study in Social and Religious History, London 1912. A vivid and delightful portrayal of Paul and his world.

Dods, An Introduction to the New Testament, London. A useful manual.

Farrar, The Life and Work of St. Paul, London 1879. Instructive and written in a beautiful style, but not always characterized by sobriety.

Godet, Introduction to the New Testament, I Pauline Epistles, Edinburgh 1894; II The Collection of the Four Gospels and the Gospel of St. Matthew, Edinburgh 1899. Scholarly and conservative; devotes much space to the contents of the books.

Godet, Bijbelstudiën over het Nieuwe Testament, Amsterdam. Contains introductions to the Gospels and the Apocalypse.

Gregory, D. S., Why Four Gospels, New York 1907. The work of a conservative scholar, valuable in differentiating the Gospels.

Gregory, C. R., Canon and Text of the New Testament, New York 1907. A scholarly and moderately conservative work.

Hastings, Dictionary of the Bible, dealing with its Language, Literature and Contents, New York 1900–04. Contains valuable introductions to the books of the Bible. Those pertaining to the New Testament are characterized by greater moderation than those relating to the Old; the latter are often extremely rationalistic, the former usually moderately conservative.

Hausrath, History of New Testament Times: The Life of Jesus 2 vols., Edinburgh 1878–80; The Life of the Apostles 4 vols., Edinburgh 1895. A learned work, full of information, but extremely rationalistic.

Hill, Introduction to the Life of Christ, New York 1911. A concise statement of the problems that enter into a study of the Life of Christ.

Holdsworth, Gospel Origins. New York 1913. Though differing somewhat from the work of Buckley, it also advocates the Combinations-hypothese.

Holtzmann, Historisch-critische Einleitung in das Neue Testament, Freiburg 1892. Perhaps the most important representative of the rationalistic position in New Testament study. Very learned, and rich in historical matter.

Jülicher, Einleitung in des Neue Testament, Leipzig 1906. A scholarly work, written from the rationalistic point of view.

King, The Theology of Christ's Teaching, New York 1903. Conservative and very instructive; weak in genetic treatment.

Kerr, Introduction to New Testament Study, New York 1892. A conservative manual.

Kuyper, Encyclopaedie der Heilige Godgeleerdheid, Amsterdam 1894.

Luthardt, St. John the Author of the Fourth Gospel, Edinburgh 1875. An able conservative defense, containing a large Bibliography by C. R. Gregory.

McGiffert, The Apostolic Age, New York 1910. A scholarly but rationalizing work.

Moffat, An Introduction to the Literature of the New Testament. New York 1911. Very able, but vitiated by rationalistic principles.

Norton, Genuineness of the Gospels (abridged), Boston 1890. An able defense of the Gospels. The author adheres to the Traditions-hypothese.

Peake, A Critical Introduction to the New Testament, New York 1910. Well written, able, but following the line of negative criticism.

Pullan, The Books of the New Testament, London 1901. A very useful manual; conservative.

Purves, Christianity in the Apostolic Age, New York 1900. The work of a scholar. In point of view the antipode of McGiffert's book.

Ramsay, Historical Commentary on the Galatians, London 1899.

Ramsay, St. Paul the Traveler and the Roman Citizen, London 1903.

Ramsay, The Church in the Roman Empire, London 1893.

Ramsay, Luke the Physician (and other Studies), New York 1908. The works of Ramsay have a charm of their own: they are original and informing, based on large historical and archæological knowledge, and, on the whole, written in a conservative spirit.

Real-EncyolopÆdie, Hauck, Leipzig 1896–1909. Contains very valuable material for New Testament study, but many of its articles are marred by their destructive tendency.

Reuss, History of the New Testament, Boston 1884. The work of a great scholar; its method is peculiar; its standpoint moderately rationalistic.

Salmon, Historical Introduction to the Books of the New Testament, New York 1889. The antipode of Davidson's Introduction; very able, but suffering from want of method.

Schürer, Geschichte des Jüdischen Volkes im Zeitalter Jesu Christi, Leipzig 1901–1911. The greatest work on the subject, but, on account of its liberal tendency, to be used with care.

Simcox, Writers of the New Testament, London 1890. Contains a lucid discussion of the style of the N. T. writers.

Stevens, Johannine Theology, New York 1894.

Stevens, Pauline Theology, New York 1903. Both works are stimulating and helpful, but must be used with discrimination.

Urquhart, The Bible, its Structure and Purpose, New York 1904.

Urquhart, The New Biblical Guide, London. Written by a staunch defender of the Bible, in popular style. Often helpful, especially the last work, in clearing up difficulties; but sometimes too confident and fanciful.

Van Melle, Inleiding tot het Nieuwe Testament, Utrecht 1908. A very good manual; conservative in spirit.

Von Soden, Urchristliche Literaturgeschichte, Berlin 1905. Rationalistic.

Weiss, Manual of Introduction to the New Testament, London 1888. One of the best Introductions to the New Testament. Moderately conservative.

Weiss, Theology of the New Testament, Edinburgh 1892-3. On the whole the best work on the subject.

Westcott, Introduction to the Study of the Gospels, Boston 1902. Very helpful in differentiating the Gospels; defends the Traditions-hypothese.

Westcott, The Canon of the New Testament, London 1881. One of the best works on the Canon of the N. T.

Westcott and Hort, The New Testament in the original Greek; Introduction and Appendix, New York 1882. The indispensible companion to the Greek Testament, if one desires the reasons for the readings adopted.

Wrede, The Origin of the New Testament, London 1909. Very brief and radical.

Wright, A Synopsis of the Gospels in Greek, London 1903. The most able presentation of the Traditions- hypothese.

Zahn, Einleitung in das Neue Testament, Leipzig 1900; 3. Aufl. 1906; Eng. transl. Edinburgh 1909. A work of immense learning; the best on N. T. Introduction from the conservative side.

II. COMMENTARIES

Alexander, Commentaries on Matthew, New York 1867; Mark, New York 1870; Acts 4th edit. New York 1884. Valuable works, containing sound learning and thoroughly conservative.

Alford, The Greek Testament, Cambridge 1894; Vol I, 7th edit.; Vol. II, 7th edit.; Vol. III, 5th edit.; Vol. IV, 5th edit. A truly great work; brief, lucid, scholarly, conservative, embodying the results of German scholarship, yet with a measure of independence, though in some parts leaning rather much on Meyer. Still very useful, though not up to date. Contains valuable Prolegomena.

Barde, Kommentaar op de Handelingen der Apostelen, Kampen 1910. A good commentary, written in a conservative spirit.

Beet, Commentaries on Romans, 10th edit.; I and II Corinthians, 7th edit.; Galatians, 6th edit.; and Ephesians, Philippians, Colossians, 3d edit., all London 1891–1903. Good commentaries by a Methodist scholar; conservative, but must be used with care, especially in passages pertaining to election, the doctrine of the last things, e. a.

Biesterveld, De Brief van Paulus aan de Colossensen, Kampen 1908. An excellent work.

Brown, J., Expositions of Galatians, Edinburgh 1853; Hebrews, Edinburgh 1862; and I Peter, Edinburgh 1866. Sound works of a Puritan divine, learned but somewhat diffuse.

Calvin, Commentaries in Opera, Vols. 24–55. There is a fairly good English translation of the Calvin Translation Society. Calvin was undoubtedly the greatest exegete among the Reformers. The value of his exegetical work is generally recoguized by present day scholars.

Eadie, Commentaries on Galatians, 1869; Ephesians, 1883; Colossians, 1884; Philippians, 1884; Thessalonians, 1877, all at Edinburgh. Able and reliable works of a Presbyterian scholar.

Edwards T. C., Commentary on I Corinthians, 3d edit. London 1897. A good and learned commentary, though sometimes a little overstrained.

Ellicott, Commentaries on I Corinthians, Andover 1889; Galatians, 1867; Ephesians, 1884; Philippians and Colossians, 1861; Thessalonians, 1866; Pastoral Epistles, 1869, all at London. Very able grammatical commentaries; conservative.

Expositor's Greek Testament, London 1912. A very scholarly work on the order of Alford's Greek Testament; being more recent, it supersedes the latter. Standpoint is on the whole moderately conservative; it contains valuable introductions.

Godet, Commentaries on Luke, 1875; John, 1877; Romans, 1886; I Corinthians, 1886–7, all at Edinburgh. Very able and reliable.

Greydanus, De Openbaring des Heeren aan Johannes, Doesburg. A good popular commentary.

Hodge, Commentaries on Romans, 2d edit. 1886; I Corinthians, 1860; II Corinthians, 1860; Ephesians, 1886. Admirable commentaries, especialy the one on Romans.

International Critical Commentary, New York, in course of publication. Some volumes of exceptional value; others of inferior merit. Characterized by a rationalistic tendency, especially the volumes on the O. T.

Lange, A Commentary on the Holy Scriptures, Critical, Doctrinal and Homiletical. On the whole a useful work; New Testament far better than the Old. Often suffers for want of clearness, and sometimes loses itself in mystical speculations. Its Homiletical material has little value.

Lightfoot, Commentaries on Galatians, 1895; Philippians, 1895; Colossians and Philemon, 1895, all at London. Very able commentaries, containing valuable dissertations. Conservative.

Meyer (Lünemann, Huther and Düsterdieck), Commentary on the New Testament, New York 1890. Meyer is recoguized as the prince of grammatical commentators. Parts of Vol. 8 and Vols. 9, 10, 11, contain the work of Lunemann, Huther and Dusterdieck, which though good, is not up to the standard of Meyer's work. Standpoint: moderately conservative. Last German edition by Weiss, Haupt e. a. is no more the work of Meyer.

Olshausen, Commentary on the New Testament, New York 1860–72. Quite good. Excells in organic interpretation of Scripture; but its mysticism often runs wild.

Pulpit Commentary, London 1880 sqq. This, as its name indicates, is far more homiletical than exegetical; yet it contains some real exposition.

Stier, The Words of the Lord Jesus, New York 1864. Very useful, but often fanciful and diffuse; devout, but frequently characterized by too great a desire to find a deeper meaning in Scripture.

Strack Und Zöckler, Kurzgefasster Commentar zu den Schriften des

Alten und Neuen Testaments, sowie zu den Apokryphen, Munchen 1886–93. One of the best recent German commentaries. Moderately conservative.

Vincent, Word Studies in the New Testament, New York 1887–91. Contains some useful material.

Westcott, Commentaries on the Gospel of John, 1890; the Epistle to the Hebrews, 1892; and the Epistles of John, 1905, all at London. All very scholarly and reliable.

Zahn, Kommentar zum Neuen Testament (several co-laborators), Erlangen 1903 sqq., still in course of publication. Will constitute one of the best conservative commentaries of the New Testament.

2

The Gospels in General

THE TITLE OF THE GOSPELS

The shortest form of the title is κατὰ Ματθᾶιον, κατὰ Μάρχον, etc. The Textus Receptus and some of the Mnn. have τὸ κατὰ Ματθᾶιον εὐαγγέλιον; but the greater part of the Mjj. read εὐαγγέλιον κατὰ Ματθᾶιον, etc.

The word εὐαγγέλιον passed through three stages in the history of its use. In the older Greek authors it signified a reward for bringing good tidings; also, a thankoffering for good tidings brought. Next in later Greek it indicated the good news itself. And finally it was employed to denote the books in which the gospel of Jesus Christ is presented in historic form. It is used very extensively in the New Testament, and always in the second sense, signifying the good news of God, the message of salvation. This meaning is also retained in the title of the gospels. The first trace of the word as indicating a written gospel is found in the Didache, the Teaching of the Twelve Apostles, discovered in 1873 and in all probability composed between the years 90 and 100 A. D. This contains the following exhortation in 15:3: "And reprove one another not in wrath but in peace, as ye have it in the Gospel. Here the word εὐαγγέλιον evidently refers to a written record. It is very explicitly and repeatedly applied to a written account of the life of Christ about the middle of the second century. The plural εὐαγγελία, signifying the four Gospels, is first found in Justin Martyr, about 152 A. D.

The expression κατὰ Ματθᾶιον, κατὰ Μάρχον, etc., has often been misinterpreted. Some maintained that κατὰ simply indicated a genitive relation, so that we should read: the Gospel of Matthew, the Gospel of Mark, etc. But if this is the idea intended, why was not the simple genitive used, just as it is employed by Paul, when he expresses a similar idea, τὸ εὐαγγέλιόν μου, Rom. 2:16; 16:25? Moreover, it cannot be maintained that the preposition κατὰ is equivalent to the Hebrew Lamedh of possession, for the Septuagint never renders this by κατὰ. Others inferred from the use of this expression that the Gospels were not written by the persons named, but were shaped after the Gospel as they preached it. But on this interpretation it seems very peculiar that the second and third Gospels were not called κατὰ Πέτρον and κατὰ Παῦλον, seeing that they were fashioned after their type of preaching. The expression must be explained from the Church's consciousness that there is but one Gospel of Jesus Christ, and indicates that in these writings we have that Gospel, as it was shaped (i. e. in writing) by the persons whose names they bear.

That the early Church caught the idea of the unity of the Gospel is quite evident. It is true, the plural of εὐαγγέλιον is sometimes employed, but the singular prevails. Justin Martyr speaks of the Memoirs that are called Gospels, but he also expresses himself thus: "the precepts in what is called the Gospel," "it is written in the Gospel." Irenaeus in one of his writings states his theme as: "The Gospel is essentially fourfold." Clement of Alexandria speaks of "the Law, the Prophets and the Gospel," and Augustine, of "the four Gospels, or rather, the four books of the one Gospel."

The English word Gospel is derived from the Anglo Saxon gŏdspell, composed of gŏd=God and spel=story, thus indicating the story of the life of God in human flesh. It is not improbable, however, that the original form of the Anglo-Saxon word was gōdspell, from gōd=good and spel=story, this being a literal translation of the Greek εὐαγγέλιον. It denotes the good tidings of salvation in Christ for a perishing world.

THE NUMBER OF THE GOSPELS
RECOGNIZED BY THE EARLY CHURCH

In view of the fact that the first Christian century produced many Gospels besides those which are included in our canon, and that many at the present day deny the authority of some or all of our Gospels, it is important to know, how many the early Church received as canonic. The apostolic fathers, though often quoting the Gospels do not mention their authors, nor do they enumerate them. They testify to the substance and canonicity of the Gospels therefore, but not, except indirectly, to their authenticity and number. In all probability the earliest evidence that the Church of the first ages accepted the four Gospels that we now possess as canonic, is furnished by the Peshito, which most likey dates from the first half of the second century. And being a translation, it points to the fact that even before its origin our four Gospels were received into the canon, while all others were left out. Another early witness is found in the Muratorian

Fragment, a mutilated work of which the real character cannot now be determined, and that was probably written about 170 A. D. It commences with the last words of a sentence that seemingly belongs to a description of Mark's Gospel, and then tells us that "Luke's Gospel stands third in order, having been written by Luke, the physician, the companion of Paul." After making this statement it proceeds to assign the fourth place to "the Gospel of John, a disciple of the Lord." The conclusion seems perfectly warranted that the first two Gospels, of which the description is lost, are those of Matthew and Mark. An important witness, really the first one to a fourfold Gospel, i. e. to a Gospel that is four and yet one, is Tatian, the Assyrian. His Diatessaron was the first harmony of the Gospels. The exact date of its composition is not known; the meaning of its name is obviously [the Gospel] by the Four. This, no doubt, points to the fact that it was based on four Gospels, and also implies that these four were our canonical Gospels, since they constituted the only collection in existence that needed no other description than "the Four." The testimony of Eusebius is in harmony with this, when he says: "Tatian, the former leader of the Encratites, having put together in some strange fashion a combination and collection of the Gospels, gave it the name of the Diatessaron, and the work is still partially current." Church History, IV, 29. Very important testimony to our four Gospels is found in the writings of Irenaeus (c. 120–200) and of Tertullian (c. 150–130). The former was a disciple of Polycarp, who in turn had enjoyed the personal instruction of the apostle John. He preached the Gospel to the Gauls and in 178 succeeded Pothinus as bishop of Lyons. In one of his books he has a long chapter entitled: "Proofs that there can be neither more nor fewer than four Evangelists." Looking at the Gospels as a unit, he called them "the Gospel with four Faces." And he searched to find mystic reasons for this quadruple form, thus showing how strongly he and his age were persuaded that there were but four canonical Gospels. He compares the quadriform Gospel (τετράμορφον) to the four regions of the earth, to the four universal spirits, to the cherubim with four faces, etc. The testimony of Tertullian is equally explicit. This famous church father received a liberal education at Rome, lived on in heathen darkness until about his thirtieth or fortieth year, when he converted and entered the ministry. Embittered by the treatment he received at the hands of the Church, he went into the fold of the Montanists about the beginning of the third century. He wrote numerous works in defense of the Christian religion. In his work against Marcion he says, after stating that the Gospel of Luke had been maintained from its first publication: "The same authority of the apostolic churches will uphold the other Gospels which we have in due succession through them and according to their usage, I mean those of [the apostles] Matthew and John; although that which was published by Mark may also be maintained to be Peter's, whose interpreter Mark was: for the narrative of Luke also is generally ascribed to Paul: since it is allowable that that which scholars publish should be regarded as their master's work." Just as those that went before him Tertullian appealed to the testimony of antiquity as proving the canonicity of our four Gospels and the other Scriptural books; and his appeal was never gainsaid. Another significant testimony is that of Origin, the great teacher of Alexandria, of whom Eusebius records that in the first book of his commentaries on the Gospel of Matthew he asserts that he knows of only four Gospels, as follows: "I have learnt by tradition concerning the four Gospels, which alone are uncontroverted in the Church of God spread under heaven, that according to Matthew, who was once a publican but afterwards an apostle of Jesus Christ, was written first; ... that according to Mark second; ... that according to Luke third; ... that according to John last of all." Church History VI, 25. Eusebius himself, who was the first historian of the Christian Church, in giving a catalogue of the New Testament writings, says: "First then we must place the holy quaternion of the Gospels."

From the testimony which we have now reviewed the conclusion seems perfectly warranted that the Church from the earliest times knew four and only four canonical Gospels; and that these four are the same that she has recognized ever since. It is true that the heretic Marcion acknowledged only the Gospel of Luke, and this in mutilated form, but his attitude toward the Gospels finds a ready explanation in his dogmatic bias.

THE LITERARY CHARACTER OF THE GOSPELS

The Gospels have a literary character all their own; they are sui generis. There is not another book or group of books in the Bible to which they can be compared. They are four and yet one in a very essential sense; they express four sides of the one εὐαγγέλιον of Jesus Christ. In studying them the question naturally arises, how we must conceive of them. Now we need not argue that they are not mere collections of myths and fables, with or without a historical basis, as many Rationalists would have us believe. Nor is it necessary to show at length that they are not four biographies of Jesus. If their authors intended them to be such, they would be very disappointing indeed. There is, however, another misconception against which we must warn, because it is quite prevalent in the circles of those who accept these writings unquestionably as a part of the Word of God, and since it is a positive hindrance to a true understanding of these priceless records. We refer to the conviction that the writers of the Gospels were minded to prepare for following generations more or less complete histories of the life of Christ. In reading these writings we soon find that, looked at as histories, they leave a great deal to be desired. In the first place they tell us comparatively little of that rich and varied life of Christ, of which they knew so much, Cf. John 20:30; 21:25. The historical facts narrated by John f. i. only represent the work of a few days. His Gospel would thus be a life of Jesus with yawning gaps. The same is true of the other Gospels. In the second place the materials, except those at the beginning and at the end of Christ's life, are not arranged in chronological order. Any possible doubt that we may have on this point is soon dispelled, when we compare the Gospels. The same facts are often narrated in altogether different connections. Closely allied with this is a third feature that deserves attention. The casual relation of the important events that are narrated is not traced, except in a few instances, and yet this is just what one expects in histories. And finally if they were really meant to be histories, why was it necessary that we should have four of them?

The harmonists generally proceeded on the erroneous conception to which we refer. They were aware indeed that there were great lacunæ in all the Gospels, but thought they might remedy matters by supplying from one Gospel what was wanting in the other. Thus the relation of the Gospels to one another was conceived of as supplemental. But their work was doomed to failure; it did violence to the exquisite compositions on which they operated, and marred the characteristic beauty of those literary productions. They were always uncertain as to the true order of events, and did not know which one of the evangelists was the best chronological guide. Some preferred Matthew, others chose Mark, and still others followed Luke. And after all their efforts to combine the four Gospels into one continuous narrative with the facts arranged in the exact order in which they occurred, their work must be pronounced a failure. The Gospels are not histories of the life of Christ, nor do they, taken together, form one history.

But what are they, if they are neither biographies nor histories? They are four pen-pictures, or better, a fourfold portraiture of the Saviour; a fourfold representation of the apostolic κήρυγμα; fourfold witness regarding our Lord. It is said that the great artist Van Dyke prepared a threefold portrait of Charles I for the sculptor, that the latter might fashion an absolutely faithful likeness of the king. These three portraits were necessary; their differences and agreements were all required to give a true representation of the monarch. So it is in the case of the Gospels. Each one of them gives us a certain view of the Lord, and only the four taken together present to us his perfect likeness, revealing him as the Saviour of the world. The apostolic κήρυγμα had taken a wide flight. Its central content was the cross and the resurrection. But in connection with this the words and deeds of the Saviour and his history also formed the subject of the apostles, preaching. And when this apostolic κήρυγμα was reduced to writing, it was found necessary to give it a fourfold form, that it might answer to the needs of four classes of people, viz. to those of the Jews, to those of the Romans, to those of the Greeks and to those of the people who confessed Christ as Lord; needs that were typical of the spiritual requirements of all future ages. Matthew wrote for the Jews and characterized Christ as the great King of the house of David. Mark composed his Gospel for the Romans and pictured the Saviour as the mighty Worker, triumphing over sin and evil. Luke in writing his Gospel had in mind the needs of the Greeks and portrayed Christ as the perfect man, the universal Saviour. And John, composing his Gospel for those who already had a saving knowledge of the Lord and stood in need of a more profound understanding of the essential character of Jesus, emphasized the divinity of Christ, the glory that was manifested in his works. Each Gospel is complete in itself and acquaints us with a certain aspect of the Lord's life. Yet it is only the fourfold Gospel that furnishes us with a complete, a perfect image of him whom to know is life eternal. And it is only, when we grasp the different features that are mirrored in the Gospels and see how they blend harmoniously in that noblest of all lives, the life of Christ, that we have found the true harmony of the Gospels.

THE SYNOPTIC PROBLEM

The first three Gospels are known as the Synoptics, and their authors are called the Synoptists. The name is derived from the Greek σύν and ὄψις, and is applied to these Gospels, since they, as distinguished from the fourth, give us a common view of the life of our Lord. But notwithstanding the great similarity by which these Gospels are characterized, they also reveal very striking differences. This remarkable agreement on the one hand, and these manifest dissimilarities on the other, constitute one of the most difficult literary problems of the New Testament. The question is, whether we can account for the origin of these Gospels in such a manner that we can explain both the close resemblances and the often surprising differences.

In the first place the general plan of these Gospels exhibits a remarkable agreement. Only Matthew and Luke contain a narrative of the infancy of our Lord and their accounts of it are quite distinct; but the history of Christ's public ministry follows very much the same order in all the Synoptics. They treat successively of the Lord's preparation for the ministry, John the Baptist, the baptism, the temptation, the return to Galilee, the preaching in its villages and cities, the journey to Jerusalem, the entrance into the Holy City, the preaching there, the passion and the resurrection. The details that fit into this general plan are also arranged in quite a uniform manner, except in some places, especially of the first Gospel. The most striking differences in the arrangement of the material results from the narrative of a long series of events connected with the Galilean ministry, which is peculiar to Matthew and Mark, Matt. 14:22–16:12; Mark 6:45–8:26; and from the history of another series of events related to the journey to Jerusalem that is found only in Luke 9:51–18:14.

But there is not only similarity in the broad outlines of those Gospels; the particular incidents that are narrated are also in many cases the same in substance and similar if not identical in form. The amount of agreement that we find in this respect is represented by Norton, Genuineness of the Gospels p. 373, and by Westcott, Introduction to the Study of the Gospels p. 201, in the following manner: If the total contents of the Gospel is represented by 100, the following result is obtained:

Mark has	7 peculiarities and—93 coincidences
Matthew has	42 peculiarities and—58 coincidences
Luke has	59 peculiarities and—41 coincidences

If the extent of all the coincidences be represented by 100 their proportionate distribution will be:

| Matthew, Mark, and Luke | 53 |
| Matthew and Luke | 21 |

Matthew and Mark	20
Mark and Luke	6

Still another estimate, viz. that by verses, is suggested by Reuss, History of the New Testament, I p. 177:

Matthew out of a total of 971 verses has 330 peculiar to him.
Mark out of a total of 478 verses has 68 peculiar to him.
Luke out of a total of 1151 verses has 541 peculiar to him.

The first two have 170 to 180 verses that are lacking in Luke; Matthew and Luke, 230 to 240 wanting in Mark; Mark and Luke about 50 wanting in Matthew. The number common to all three is 330 to 370.

The preceding statements refer to the subject-matter of the Synoptics. Taken by itself this might give us an exaggerated idea of the similarity of these Gospels. As a corrective it is necessary to bear in mind that the verbal coincidences, though they are remarkable indeed, are nevertheless considerably less than one would expect. Dr. Schaff and his son, after some calculations based on Rushbrooke's Synopticon, get the following results:

"The proportion of words peculiar to the Synoptics is 28,000 out of 48,000, more than one-half.

In Matthew 56 words out of every 100 are peculiar.

In Mark 40 words out of every 100 are peculiar.

In Luke 67 words out of every 100 are peculiar.

The number of coincidences common to all three is less than the number of divergences.

Matthew agrees with the other two gospels in 1 word out of 7.

Mark agrees with the other two gospels in 1 word out of 4½.

Luke agrees with the other two gospels in 1 word out of 8.

But comparing the Gospels two by two, it is evident that Matthew and Mark have most in common, and Matthew and Luke are most divergent.

One-half of Mark is found in Matthew.

One-fourth of Luke is found in Matthew.

One-third of Mark is found in Luke.

The general conclusion from these figures is that all three Gospels widely diverge from the common matter, or triple tradition, Mark the least so and Luke the most (almost twice as much as Mark). On the other hand, both Matthew and Luke are nearer Mark than Luke and Matthew to each other."[1]

In connection with the preceding we should bear in mind that these verbal agreements are greatest, not in the narrative, but in the recitative parts of the Gospels. About one-fifth of them is found in the narrative portion of the Gospel, and four-fifths in the recital of the words of our Lord and others. This statement will create a false impression, however, unless we bear in mind the proportion in which the narrative parts stand to the recitative element, which is as follows:

	Narrative	Recitative
Matthew	25	75
Mark	50	50
Luke	34	66

From what has now been said it is perfectly clear that the Synoptics present an intricate literary problem. Is it possible to explain the origin in such a manner that both the resemblances and differences are accounted for? During the last century many scholars have applied themselves with painstaking diligence to the arduous task of solving this problem. The solution has been sought along different lines; several hypotheses have been broached, of which we shall name only the four most important ones.

In the first place there is what has been called (though not altogether correctly) the mutual dependence theory (Benützungshypothese, Augustine, Bengel, Bleek, Storr). According to this theory the one Gospel is dependent on the other, so that the second borrowed from the first and the third from both the first and the second. On this theory, of course, six permutations are possible viz.:

- Matthew, Mark, Luke
- Matthew, Luke, Mark
- Mark, Matthew, Luke
- Mark, Luke, Matthew
- Luke, Matthew, Mark
- Luke, Mark, Matthew

In every possible form this theory has found defenders, but it does not meet with great favor at present. True, it seems to account for the general

---

1   Church History, I p. 597.

agreement in a very simple manner, but serious difficulties arise, when one seeks to determine which one of the Gospels was first, which second and which third. This is perfectly evident from the difference of opinion among the adherents of this hypothesis. Again it fails to account for the divergencies; it does not explain why one writer adopts the language of his predecessor(s) up to a certain point, and then suddenly abandons it. Of late it is tacitly admitted, however, that it does contain an element of truth.

In the second place the hypothesis of oral tradition (Traditions-hypothese, Gieseler, Westcott, Wright), should be mentioned. This theory starts from the supposition that the Gospel existed first of all in an unwritten form. It is assumed that the apostles repeatedly told the story of Christ's life, dwelling especially on the most important incidents of his career, and often reiterating the very words of their blessed Lord. These narratives and words were eagerly caught up by willing ears and treasured in faithful and retentive memories, the Jews making it a practice to retain whatever they learnt in the exact form in which they received it. Thus a stereotyped tradition arose which served as the basis for our present Gospels. Several objections have been urged against this theory. It is said that, as a result of the apostles' preaching in the vernacular, the oral tradition was embodied in the Aramaic language, and hence cannot account for the verbal coincidences in the Greek Gospels. Again it is urged that the more stereotyped the tradition was, the harder it becomes to account for the differences between the Synoptics. Would anyone be apt to alter such a tradition on his own authority? Moreover this hypothesis offers no explanation of the existence of the two-fold, the triple and the double tradition, i. e. the tradition that is embodied in all three of the Gospels and that which is found only in two of them. The majority of scholars have now abandoned this theory, although it has ardent defenders even at present. And no doubt, it must be taken into account in the solution of this problem.

In the third place we have the hypothesis of one primitive Gospel (Urevangeliums-hypothese), from which all three of the Synoptists drew their material. According to G. E. Lessing this Gospel, containing a short account of the life of Jesus for the use of traveling missionaries, was written in the popular language of Palestine. Eichhorn, however, following him, held that it was translated into Greek, worked over and enriched in various ways, and soon took shape in several redactions, which became the source of our present Gospels. There is very little agreement among the defenders of this theory regarding the exact character of this original source. At present it finds little favor in scientific circles, but has been discarded for various reasons. There is absolutely no trace of such an original Gospel, nor any historical reference to it, which seems peculiar in view of its unique significance. And if the existence of such a source be postulated, how must the arbitrary alteration of it be explained, how did these different recensions come into existence. It is evident that by this theory the problem is not solved, but simply shifted to another place. Moreover while in its original form this hypothesis accounted very well for the agreement, but not for the differences found in the Synoptics, in its final form it was too artificial and too complicated to inspire confidence and to seem anything like a natural solution of the Synoptic problem.

In the fourth place the so-called double source, or two document theory (Combinations-hypothese, Weisse, Wilke, Holtzmann, Wendt) deserves mention, since it is the favorite theory of New Testament scholars today. This hypothesis holds that, in order to explain the phenomena of the Gospels, it is necessary to postulate the existence of at least two primitive documents, and recognizes the use of one Gospel in the composition of the others. The form in which this theory is most widely accepted at present is the following: The Gospel of Mark was the first one to be written and, either in the form in which we now have it, or in a slightly different form was the source of the triple tradition. For the double tradition, which is common to Matthew and Luke, these writers used a second source that, for want of definite knowledge regarding it, is simply called Q (from the German Quelle). This Q may have been the λόγια of Matthew mentioned by Papias, and was probably a collection of the sayings of our Lord. The differences between Matthew and Luke in the matter of the double tradition finds its explanation in the assumption that, while Matthew drew directly from Q, Luke derived the corresponding matter from Q and other sources, or from a primitive Gospel based on Q. On the last supposition the relation of Matthew and Luke to Q would be as follows:

But even so the use of some inferior sources by both Matthew and Luke must be assumed. The double source theory presupposes the existence of a rather large precanonical literature.

There are some evident objections to this theory also. The assumption that the λόγια of Matthew was anything else than the Hebrew or Aramaic original of our Greek Matthew is a baseless supposition; it has no historical foundation whatever. Furthermore the theory offers no explanation of the fact that the writers in some cases faithfully copied their original and in others altered the text rather freely or even departed from it entirely. And by postulating the development of a somewhat extensive Gospel literature previous to the composition of Matthew and Luke, it has naturally led to the position that our Gospels were written late, and therefore in all probability not by their reputed authors. Moreover it also requires us to believe that Luke included the Gospel of Mark in the number of the attempted Gospel stories which his Gospel was meant to supercede.

None of the theories broached up to the present time has proved satisfactory. There is still a great deal of uncertainty and confusion in the study of the Synoptic problem; we do not seem to be nearer to its solution now than we were fifty years ago. The great aim has always been to explain the origin of the Synoptics without taking into account the supernatural factor that entered into their composition. Now we do not doubt the value of these studies; they have already taught us a good many things regarding the origin of these Gospels; but they have proven themselves insufficient to lead to a final solution of the problem. It is, of course, folly to rule this problem out of existence by simply appealing to the supernatural agency of the Holy Spirit. It is true, if one believes in the mechanical inspiration of the Bible, there is no Synoptic problem. This is quite different, however, for those who believe that the Scriptures have been inspired in an organic way. The more naturally we conceive of the origin of these writings, the better it is, if we only do not lose sight of the operation of the divine factor, of the directing, the guiding influence of the Holy Spirit. Cf. Kuyper, Encyclopedie III p. 51 f. It is hardly sufficient to say with Urquhart, New Biblical Guide VII p. 357, that the key to the problem is found in the fact that the Synoptic Gospels are all the work of one author, and that each book is serving a distinct purpose. Yet this statement contains two important truths that we should continually bear in mind.

In any attempt to account for the similarities of the synoptics great allowance should be made for the influence of oral tradition. It is very natural to suppose that, since the apostles for some time labored together at Jerusalem with Peter at the head, a particular, perhaps Petrine type of tradition became the common property of these early preachers and of their first hearers. And because the life of Christ entered as a very important element into the life of his apostles, and they felt the supreme significance of his words, it is also reasonable to assume that they aimed at inculcating the teachings of our Lord on their hearers in the exact form in which He gave it. It is equally rational to suppose that, at a comparatively early time, the desire to escape the uncertainty that always attends oral transmission, led to the composition of brief gospel narratives, containing especially the sayings and discourses of our Lord. These suppositions are entirely in harmony too with the opening verses of the Gospel of Luke: "Forasmuch as many have taken in hand to draw up a narrative concerning those matters which have been fulfilled among us, even as they delivered them unto us, who from the beginning were eyewitnesses and ministers of the word, it seemed good to me also, etc." Some of these early documents may have been written in Aramaic and others in Greek. The groundwork thus furnished and drawn upon by the writers of our Gospels, explains in a very natural way most of the agreements that are found in the Synoptics. And those that cannot be accounted for in that manner may have resulted directly from the guiding influence of the Holy Spirit, who led the writers also in the choice of their words. These three Gospels are in a very real sense the work of one Author.

In seeking to explain the differences that are found in the Synoptical Gospels, we should bear in mind first of all that they are no histories, but memoirs, historical arguments. In composing them each one of the writers had his own purpose. Matthew, writing for the Jews, made it his aim to present Christ as the King, the great Son of David; Mark, intending his Gospel for the Romans, endeavored to draw a vivid picture of the powerful Worker, conquering the forces of evil; and Luke, addressing the Greeks and adjusting his Gospel to their needs, sought to describe Christ as the universal Saviour, as a person with wide sympathies. This diversity of aim accounts to a great extent for the variations exhibited in the Gospels, i. e. for omissions on the one hand and additions on the other, for differences in the distribution and arrangement of the material, etc. The writers of the Gospels selected from the great mass of early traditions the material that was suited to their purpose and used it to advantage. The difference between the Synoptics is not accidental, is not the result of the chance use of certain sources. And where the identical teachings of Christ are sometimes found in different forms, we should remember, first, that the Lord may have uttered the same truth at different times in varying forms; and secondly, that the Synoptists do not always give the identical words of the Saviour, but were so guided by the Holy Spirit that they do give an exact representation of the Lord's teachings, perhaps in a form better adapted to their purpose than the original would have been. Cf. Kuyper, Dict. Dogm., Locus de Sacra Scriptura II p. 131 f.; Gregory, Why Four Gospels;

Van Leeuwen, Literatuur en Schriftuur p. 14 ff.; Urquhart, New Biblical Guide VII p. 328–428.

For further study of the Synoptic Problem we refer to: Norton, Genuineness of the Gospels; Westcott, Introduction to the Study of the Gospels; Arthur Wright, A Synopsis of the Gospels in Greek; Holdsworth, Gospel Origins; Buckley, Introduction to the Synoptic Problem; Hill, Introduction to the Life of Christ; Reuss, History of the New Testament I p. 163–218 (where the most important German literature is referred to); and the various Introductions of Davidson, Weiss, Zahn, Jülicher, Salmon, e. a.

THE RELATION OF THE GOSPEL OF JOHN TO THE SYNOPTICS

After pointing out the remarkable agreement between the synoptic Gospels and referring to some of the attempted explanations of this feature, we must consider the equally striking difference that exists between the Synoptics on the one hand and the Gospel of John on the other. This difference is so great that even untrained minds immediately feel it. Hence the question naturally arises: How can we account for it? This is in substance the Johannine problem. The differences that are found may conveniently be arranged under two heads: 1. Differences touching the external course of events in the Lord's ministry; and 2. Differences in regard to the form and contents of Christ's teaching.

I. Differences touching the external course of events in the Lord's ministry

a. According to the Synoptics the principal scene of the Lord's activity is Galilee. He repairs to this Northern province soon after the imprisonment of John the Baptist, and apparently does not return to Judea until the last Passover. The representation that is found in the Gospel of John is quite different. Very little is said about the Galilean ministry, while the activity of Christ in Judea looms large on his pages. Most of the work of which John speaks was done at Jerusalem.

b. The first three Gospels mention but one Passover in their narrative of Christ's public ministry, viz. that at the end of his life. This led many to the conviction that the Lord's public ministry was limited to a period of one year. In the Gospel of John, on the other hand, we find three Passovers definitely mentioned, while a fourth is probably referred to in 5:1. Judging by this the length of the Lord's ministry was at least two and possibly three years.

c. The people with whom Jesus deals primarily are not the same in the Synoptics and in the Gospel of John. In the first three Gospels we see Jesus moving along the Galilean peasantry and preaching to them the gospel of the Kingdom, while in the fourth the Jews (by which John means the leaders of the people, i. e. Chief Priests, Scribes and Pharisees) are generally in the foreground, and certain individuals, that are not named, or are merely names, in the Synoptics, are very prominent, such as Philip, Nathanael, the Samaritan woman, Mary Magdalena and Thomas.

d. The attitude of the Jews towards Jesus appears to be quite different in the synoptic Gospels and in the Gospel of John. According to the Synoptics Jesus meets with great success at first. The multitudes flock unto him, are delighted to hear him and marvel at his teachings and work. And it is only after He has clearly shown that He had not come to establish an earthly kingdom that their enthusiasm dies away, and that He begins to prepare his disciples for his coming suffering and death. The Gospel of John makes it appear that from the beginning of Christ's ministry at Jerusalem the hearts of the Jews were filled with a hatred that gradually grew, reaching its highest pitch after the raising of Lazarus, and that finally issued in the crucifixion of the Lord of glory.

e. There are also several details in which the Gospel of John does not agree with the Synoptics. We shall only mention a couple of the most important examples. In the synoptic Gospels we find the cleansing of the temple at the end of Christ's public ministry, while John places this at the very beginning. Then there is also a difference in the representation of the time of the Lord's death. The Synoptics convey the impression that Christ ate the Passover in the evening of the 14th of Nisan, and was therefore crucified on the 15th; while the Gospel of John seems to say with equal explicitness that He ate it a day in advance of the regular time and died at the very hour, when the symbolic Paschal lamb was slain.

II. Differences in respect to the form and contents of our Lord's teaching.

a. There is a striking diversity in the form in which the teaching of Jesus is cast. In the Synoptics we have short incisive sayings of the Lord, which in some cases are and in others are not connected with what immediately precedes or follows. In the Gospel of John, on the other hand, we find long and labored discourses, closely connected with the signs, the miracles of our Lord. The first three Gospels contain a goodly number of parables, which are strangely absent from the fourth Gospel, where we have have instead a few allegories, such as the Door of the Sheepfold, the good Shepherd, and the true Vine. The style of the Gospel of John too is quite different from that of the Synoptics. It is a more Hebraic style, in which the statements are brief, the construction is simple and the sentences are usually connected with the conjunction and. This style is carried through also in the discourses of Christ, so that in some cases it is very hard, if not impossible, to tell just where the words of the Lord come to an end and those of the evangelist begin, or vice versa. Notice this especially in the third chapter.

b. There is an equally great difference in the contents of the Lord's teaching. In the Synoptics the central theme on which Christ dwells is the Kingdom of God. He speaks of its origin, its nature, its subjects, its King, its requirements, its righteousness, its enemies and its future glory. In vain do we turn to the fourth Gospel for a corresponding line of thought. The Kingdom of God is mentioned but once there, viz. in the conversation of our Lord with Nicodemus. Christ himself is the main theme of the discourses found in the Gospel of John. The Lord speaks of his heavenly origin, of his essential character and of his return to glory. He presents himself to the Jews as the Messiah the Son of God, the heavenly manna, the water of life, the true liberator, the light of the world, the good Shepherd, the resurrection and the life, etc. In the Synoptics we find that Jesus only occasionally, and then towards the end of his ministry, speaks of himself. In connection with this we may remark that the self-revelation of Christ both by his words and works differs greatly in the Synoptics and in the fourth Gospel. In the former Jesus begins by speaking of the Kingdom and makes little mention of the King. Only gradually does He reveal his true character and it is not until He is well along in the course of his public ministry that Peter is led up to the confession: "Thou art the Christ, the Son of the living God." Only in the last week of his life does Jesus throw off all reserve and speaks clearly of himself as the Messiah sent from God. In the Gospel of John, however, everything is quite clear from the beginning. John the Baptist points to Christ as "the Lamb of God that taketh away the sin of the world;" to the Samaritan woman Jesus says: "I am He;" and to the Jews attending the unnamed feast he speaks clearly of the unique relation in which He stands to the Father. This is closely connected with another fact. In the synoptic Gospels the humanity of Christ is made very prominent. We behold him there primarily as the Saviour who has taken on our nature, shares in our infirmities, and is tempted even as we are, though without sin. The fourth Gospel, on the other hand, brings the divinity of Christ into strong relief. We notice this at the very beginning of the Gospel: "In the beginning was the Word, and the Word was with God, and the Word was God." It strikes us in the signs which Christ gave to reveal his glory, and in the discourses that speak at length of his essential nature, of his descending out of glory, his being in glory, and his returning to the glory that He possessed from the foundation of the world; and it rings in our ears as we listen to the confession of Thomas: "My Lord and my God."

There are many critics at the present time who magnify these differences into discrepancies, and find in them a ground on which to reject the authorship of John. They maintain that the fourth Gospel is a treatise written with marked theological bias, inspired by the controversy about the person of Christ in the second century. The great stumbling-block for them is the very clear teaching contained in this Gospel respecting the divinity of Christ. This, they hold, could only be the fruit of theological preconceptions. And the great desire on the part of the author to establish this beyond the shadow of a doubt is said to explain a good many of the other special features that characterize this gospel. This explanation contains both a falsehood and a truth.

A careful study of the Gospel of John, a study that takes its true character in consideration, does not bear out the contention that several of the differences between the Gospel of John and the Synoptics amount to discrepancies. Neither does it reveal differences that cannot be accounted for in a perfectly natural way. We desire to point out first of all that there are not only dissimilarities but also correspondences between these Gospels. The incidents that we find mentioned in all the Gospels are the following: The baptism of John, the feeding of the five thousand, the walking on the sea, the anointing at Bethany, the triumphal entry, the last supper, the betrayal, the trial, the crucifixion, the burial and the resurrection. Of course in some cases the details of the narrative vary. Besides these parallel narratives there are many passages in which we find imagery, sayings or words that find their counterpart in the synoptic Gospels. Davidson says that about one-third of the matter in John agrees with that in the Synoptics.

It is evident from the foregoing that the diversity is greater than the similarity, and the great question is: How must we account for the differences? In pointing out the way in which we must look for a solution of this problem we call attention to several particulars.

1. We should not lose sight of the true character of John's writing. Neither it nor the other Gospels are meant to be complete histories of what the Lord did and said during his life in the flesh. If this were its claim, it

would be disappointing in the extreme, since all that John narrates happened in a few days. Like the Synoptics the Gospel of John is a pen-picture of the Lord, is a witness to him from a particular point of view, and represents a phase of the apostolic κήρυγμα. We must allow for the principle of selection and of selective arrangement in the composition of this work. It was John's aim to describe the Lord from a particular point of view. Hence he chose from the great mass of apostolic tradition, whether oral or written, the materials that suited his purpose best, and arranged them in the most effective way, taking in consideration as much as possible the chronological order in which the events occurred. This general truth must be borne in mind continually, if we would understand the differences between the Gospel of John and the Synoptics.

2. The great controlling factor, however, in the construction of this Gospel, was the aim of the writer. Therefore it is necessary that we have some understanding of this. Happily we need not guess at it, because John himself tells us what purpose he had in writing his Gospel. He says in 20:31: "But these things are written that ye might believe that Jesus is the Christ, the Son of God; and that believing ye might have life through His name." According to this statement the apostle had a twofold aim, the one theoretical and the other practical, the one his proximate, the other his ulterior aim. The theoretical aim of the evangelist was twofold: he wanted to show in a convincing manner that the historical Jesus was the Christ sent from God for the salvation of the world; and that this Christ was not a mere man, but the very Son of God, who in his pre-existent state shared in the divine glory, a glory which He radiated even while He dwelt among men in the form of a servant, and that would again shine forth in heavenly splendor after He had finished his task. It was the desire of the writer further, to present this Christ, this Son of God, to his readers in such a manner that they might be led to believe in him, and that they, being united to him the fountain of life by faith, might have life everlasting. With this end in view John, of course, selected those signs and discourses of the Lord that were best adapted to bring out his glory and to lead others to faith in him. He almost seems to tell us this himself, when he concludes his narrative of the first miracle performed by our Lord at Cana with the words: "This beginning of miracles did Jesus in Cana of Galilee, and manifested his glory; and his disciples believed on Him." John views the miracles of which he speaks as σημεῖα that exhibit the divine greatness of Christ. And he limits himself almost exclusively to those of which he can say definitely that they led men

to believe on Christ, or of which Christ himself points out the symbolic significance in His discourses, as:

- The changing of water into wine at Cana ("and his disciples believed on Him.")
- The healing of the ruler's son at Cana (Capernaum) ("and himself believed and his whole house.")
- The healing of the impotent man at the pool Bethesda (Christ the restorer of life).
- The feeding of the five thousand near Bethsaida (Christ the spiritual food, the heavenly manna).
- The restoring of the blind man's sight at Jerusalem (Christ the light of the world).
- The raising of Lazarus at Bethany (Christ the resurrection and the life).

In harmony with his aim too the evangelist records such discourses of the Lord as serve to explain the σημεῖα, to bring, out the unique relation in which Christ stands to the Father, to accentuate Christ's authority, to emphasize the divine character of his mission, etc. Moreover he introduces several individuals to show us how Jesus labored to bring them to the conviction that He was the Christ, the Son of God, as f. i. Nathanael, Nicodemus, the Samaritan woman and Thomas.

Now if we bear these things in mind, many of the differences between this Gospel and the Synoptics are immediately explained. The aim of John being what it is, he naturally speaks of Christ rather than of the Kingdom of God, introduces whatever accentuates the divinity of our Lord, and brings out as much as possible that Christ revealed himself as the Messiah from the very beginning of his public career. But doing this in a historical way, he cannot represent the Galilean peasants but only the leaders of the Jews at Jerusalem as the recipients of this revelation, for it was only to them, who were versed in the Scriptures, that Christ spoke so explicitly from the outset, and it was primarily for them that He expressed his thought in profound discourses rather than in parables. This in turn determines the time of which John speaks in his gospel and also explains how it is that he mentions so many feasts, because it was almost exclusively on these occasions that Jesus visited Jerusalem and came in contact with the Scribes and the Chief Priests. It also sheds light on the difference in the attitude of the

Jews toward Jesus. For a long time the Galileans were attached to Christ and marveled at his words and works; the spirit of opposition was aroused in them especially towards the end of Christ's labors among them and mostly by the machinations of the Pharisees that came from Jerusalem. The leaders of the Jews in Judea, on the other hand, hated Jesus almost from the beginning of his public ministry. Their hatred kept pace with the knowledge they received of Christ.

3. Every attempt at solving the Johannine problem must also make allowance for the fact that John was acquainted with the other Gospels, and avoided as much as was conistent with his aim the repetition of facts that were already generally known. We have no doubt that John had read the other Gospels before he wrote his own. There are certain features in his Gospel that we can understand only on that supposition. According to 21:19 John wrote his Gospel after the death of Peter and therefore comparatively late. Now he certainly would not be such a stranger in his own world of thought as not to know the Gospels that had already been composed. Then we find that in several places the evangelist trusts to the previous knowledge of his readers. He does not describe the institution of the Lord's supper in his Gospel; yet he clearly assumes in 6:51-58 that his readers were acquainted with it. Though he does not give a description of the ascension, he proceeds on the assumption that this fact is well known, 6:62; 20:17. Cf. further 1:40; 3:24; 6:70, etc. In several cases in which the persons introduced in the Gospel misunderstand the Lord, the writer does not deem it necessary to explain for his readers what Jesus really meant, because he knew that they themselves were able to correct the mistake, Cf. 7:35, 36; 3:4; 4:15; 6:52. It is a very weighty consideration in this connection too that John does not deign to answer objections that are brought against the Messiah ship of Christ. Notice f. i. 1:45, 46; 7:41, 42; 7:52. The evangelist does not give a single hint of the solution of the difficulty thus raised repeatedly. We can understand this only on the supposition that he was aware of the fact that his readers knew from the other Gospels how to solve the problem. John evidently read the other Gospels and this explains how he could avoid to such a great extent what they had already brought to the knowledge of the people.

4. Finally we must also bear in mind that the individuality of the author is stamped on his literary production. John was a profound meditative spirit, who drank deeply at the fountain of life. He searched for the mainspring of action in the career of our Saviour; he pondered on the hidden

background of the mysterious, the wonderful life of his Master. He was the best qualified of all the apostles to describe the divine greatness of the Lord. And it was no small achievement of his, that he presented the profoundest truths in the most simple manner. The simplicity of its language is a very striking feature of the fourth Gospel. It is due in part, no doubt, to john's idiosyncracy, and in part to his habit of contemplating Christianity in its most fundamental relations. It need not surprise us that we find the same style in the discourses of Christ, for in these also the style is to a great extent john's. Neither John nor the other evangelists always give us the exact words of Jesus. It is true that he generally employs direct discourse in introducing the words of the Saviour, but this is merely an oriental custom and does not imply that the words were used exactly in that way. But the Spirit of God so guided the writer that he reproduces, though possibly in a slightly different form, the exact truths which Jesus sought to inculcate on his hearers. And this Spirit, which is also the Spirit of Christ, vouching for these words, makes them just as really the words of Christ, as if they had been an exact reproduction of the words Jesus had used in addressing the Jews.

THE INSPIRATION OF THE GOSPELS

During the past century the human origin of the Gospels has been carefully investigated. With a great deal of patience and ingenuity every chapter and verse of these writings has been scrutinized and referred to its supposed ultimate source. The discussion of the divine factor that operated in the composition of these books, however, has been conspicuously absent from these studies. And this neglect is not the result of chance, but of a very deliberate plan. A large number of scholars today do not believe in any special inspiration of these writings; others, who do not wish to deny their divine inspiration, nevertheless maintain that their claim to this prerogative should be waived in the historical investigation of their origin.

In the preceding century many were wont to label the Gospels sneeringly as fictitious narratives, written by a few religious fanatics, who deliberately lied about Jesus. This crude and baseless opinion does not meet with great favor today. People intuitively recoil from that position and feel that they must take a more respectful attitude towards the Gospels. They now regard these as the product of the reverent and in part unconscious invention of the Church; or as the expression of the corporate consciousness and the corporate mood of the first Christian community. Even so, of course, they are simply human productions that contain besides a large quota of truth a great deal of mythical and lengendary matter.

Over against this position we hold that the Gospels were written by men who were inspired by the Holy Spirit, and that they are therefore absolutely trustworthy and authoritative accounts of the life of our Lord. They are inspired records. They constitute one of the most precious fruits of the apostolic inspiration, since they are one and all the literary embodiment of the apostolic κήρυγμα. The substance of what the apostles preached is contained in these writings. Now as well as the prophets in the old dispensation, the apostles in the new were inspired by the Holy Spirit. This is quite evident from the New Testament. Consider the promises which our Lord gave to His disciples: Matt. 10:19, 20," ... for it shall be given you in that same hour what ye shall speak; for it is not ye that speak, but the Spirit of your Father that speaketh in you." John 14:26, "But the Comforter, which is the Holy Ghost, whom the Father will send in my name, He shall teach you all things and bring all things to your remembrance, whatsoever I have said unto you." John 16:13, 14, "Howbeit when the Spirit of truth is come, He will guide you into all truth; for He shall not speak of himself; but whatsoever He shall hear, that shall He speak; and He will show you things to come. He shall glorify me; for He shall receive of mine, and shall show it unto you." Notice too that these promises found their initial fulfilment on the day of Pentecost. We read in Acts 2:4: "And they were all filled with the Holy Ghost, and began to speak with other tongues, as the Spirit gave them utterance." And after this day the apostles were conscious of being guided by the Spirit of God. Paul says in 1 Cor. 2:11-13, "For what man knoweth the things of a man, save the spirit of man which is in him? even so the things of God knoweth no man, but the Spirit of God. Now we have received, not the spirit of the world, but the Spirit which is of God; that we might know the things which are freely given us of God. Which things also we speak, not in the words which man's wisdom teacheth, but which the Holy Ghost teacheth; comparing spiritual things with spiritual." And in 2 Cor. 13:2b, 3, "—and being absent now I write to them which heretofore have sinned, and to all other, that, if I come again, I will not spare; since ye seek a proof of Christ speaking in me, which to you-ward is not weak, but is mighty in you." These few passages, which might easily be multiplied, must suffice for the present.

Some who admit the inspiration of the prophets, do not believe the apostles were also inspired, because in their case they do not hear the familiar formula "thus saith the Lord," nor behold the characteristic phenomena that accompanied the inspiration of the prophets. They do not distinguish between different kinds of inspiration. There are especially three points of difference between the inspiration of the prophets and that of the apostles.

1. Under the Old Covenant the Holy Spirit did not yet dwell in the Church, but operated on believers from without. So it was also in the case of the prophets. The Holy Spirit took possession of them, sometimes suppressed their personality to a certain degree, and then employed their consciousness for his purpose. In the new dispensation, however, He took up his abode in The Church, and first of all in the apostles, who were to be the Church's foundation; and then, identifying himself to a great extent with their conscious life, used them as instruments to produce his revelation.

2. In the case of the prophets it was the entrance of a foreign element, a foreign power into their lives, and something extraordinary in their career that impelled them to prophesy. It was a power that they could not resist, because it became as a fire burning within them. With the apostles, on the other hand, it was the indwelling Spirit in connection with their official task that led them to speak the Word of God. The inspiration of the prophets was intermittent; that of the apostles, continuous in the performance of their regular apostolic duties.

3. The prophets often spoke of unknown and unseen things, while the apostles discoursed on things which they knew and saw. In connection with this the Holy Spirit did not operate through the same faculty in both the prophets and the apostles. In the former it was the imagination, in the latter the understanding, especially memory and reflection, that constituted the medium of divine revelation. Hence the prophets generally spoke in poetic and in symbolic language, while the apostles as a rule clothed their thought in ordinary prose. In the case of the Gospels the inspiration of the apostles has above all the character of a ὑπόμνησις. Cf. John 14:26.

This apostolic inspiration gave birth to the κήρυγμα of the apostles, but does not yet account for the infallible records we have of this in the Gospels. Besides the apostolic we must take into consideration a separate graphical or transcriptive inspiration, if we would fully understand the divine origin of the Gospels. The authors were led by the spirit of God in composing these writings, in giving to the preaching of the apostles a definite written form. They were guided in the selection of their material and its proper arrangement, and in the choice of their words and expressions, so that their records are truly a part of the Word of God for the Church of all ages.

The question naturally arises, whether we have any reasons to think that the Gospels were so inspired. In answer we would say that we have, though we do not flatter ourself with the idea that these reasons would convince anyone who is disinclined to accept the Scriptures as the very Word of God.

1. The contents of the Gospels testify to their divine origin. We find in them a fourfold portraiture of the Saviour. There are many differences in the individual pictures, yet together they form a grand unity. Four writers, each one portraying the life of Christ in his own way, to a great extent without knowing each other's writings or drawing on them, so that their individual portraits blend perfectly into a harmonious whole,—it is marvelous, it can only be understood, if we assume that these four writers were all guided unerringly by the same superintending Spirit. The Gospels are really the work of one author. And the life that is pictured in them is a divine life, unfathomable, mysterious, far surpassing human understanding. And yet that incomparable, that divine life has been so faithfully portrayed, with such a profound insight into its real character and hidden depths, in such a simple, natural, artless manner, that it has been the marvel of ages. Could man, unaided by higher power, describe such a life? No, only they who were inspired by the Holy Spirit, were equal to the task.

2. Taking for granted the inspiration of the Old Testament, which is conclusively proved by the words of Jesus and the apostles, we feel that it calls for an inspired complement. It covers the period of preparation that is prophetic of a future completion, the time in which the Church was in its infancy, that points forward to the maturity of a coming age. It is filled with prophecies that await fulfilment; it contains the shadow that is cast before the coming body, growing more distinct as the ages roll on, until at last it seems as if the body will presently appear, yet it does not—the Old Testament requires a compliment. And in harmony with it this too must be inspired. Of what avail would the inspiration of the Old Testament be, if that in which it culminates is not inspired. The divine surety would be wanting.

3. At least two of our Gospels were written by apostles who, in speaking to their contemporaries, were inpired by the Spirit of God. Now it would be an anomaly that they should be guided by the Holy Spirit in their oral

witnessing to Christ, and be without that divine guidance in perpetuating their testimony for all future ages. It was the will of God that people until the end of the world should believe on him through the word of the apostles, John 17:20; 1 John 1:3. Hence it was of the greatest importance that there should be an infallible record of their testimony.

4. There are some Scripture passages that point to the inspiration of the gospel records. The older Lightfoot, (Works IV p. 113, 114; XII p. 7, and following him Urquhart, The Bible its Structure and Purpose I Ch. 5), find a proof for the inspiration of Luke's Gospel in 1:3, where they would translate the words παρηχολουθηχότι ἄνωθεν by "having had perfect understanding of all things from above." This interpretation is favored by the fact that ἄνωθεν has this meaning in eight of the thirteen times that it occurs in the New Testament, and in three of the remaining instances means again, while it is translated "from the beginning" only here and in Acts 26:4. The expressed purpose of Luke in writing his Gospel also falls in exceedingly well with the rendering from above. It is, he writes to Theophilus, that you may have the certainty of those things in which you have been instructed." Yet the verb παραχολουθέω, meaning, to follow up carefully, and thus, to obtain knowledge, argues decisively against it. What is of greater significance for us, is the fact that the Gospel of Luke is quoted as ἡ γραφή in 1 Tim. 5:18, where we read: "For the Scripture saith, Thou shalt not muzzzle the ox that treadeth out the corn, and, The laborer is worthy of his hire." The only place in the entire Bible where the last words are found, is Luke 10:7. Finally we call attention to 2 Peter 3:15, 16, where the apostle says: "... even as our beloved brother Paul also according to the wisdom given unto him hath written unto you; as also in all his epistles, speaking of these things; in which are some things hard to be understood, which they that are unlearned and unstable wrest, as they do also the other Scriptures, unto their own destruction." Here we find that the writings of Paul are placed on a level with other inspired writings, which Peter calls, "the other Scriptures." There is good reason to believe that this expression refers to the books of the Old Testament, and to those of the New Testament that were already composed, when Peter wrote his second epistle, among which we may also reckon the Gospels of Matthew and Luke.

5. The fact that the early Church from the very beginning accepted these Gospels as canonical, is also a proof of their inspired character, for in it the communal consciousness of the Church expressed itself in regard to these writings; and it is said of believers in their corporate existence that they,

taught by the Holy Ghost, know all things. Dean Alford says: "The apostles being raised up for the special purpose of witnessing to the gospel history,— and these memoirs having been universally received in the early Church as embodying that their testimony, I see no escape left from the inference that they come to us with inspired authority. The Greek Testament, Vol. I, Prolegomena Section VI.

6. Finally the Holy Spirit testifies in the heart of every believer to the divine character of the Gospels, so that they feel assured that these writings contain the very Word of God. Under the influence of the Holy Spirit they realize that these Gospels too minister to the deepest needs of their spiritual life, they realize their infinite value, marvel at their exquisite beauty and find in them ever increasingly the words of everlasting life. Thus they cannot but speak their "Amen" to the contents of these books.

THE CANONICAL SIGNIFICANCE OF THE GOSPELS AS A WHOLE

The Gospels are, of course, closely related to the Old Testament Scriptures. They describe in a vivid manner the initial stage of the fulness of time, showing how all the prophecies that pointed to Christ and to a new and more spiritual dispensation began to be fulfilled. Rather than enlarge on this relation, however, we shall here briefly describe the peculiar function of the Gospels in the New Testament revelation. These writings are related to the rest of the New Testament, as the Pentateuch is to the following books of the Old Testament. Both are of a fundamental character, laying foundations on which an imposing super-structure is raised. In the case of the Gospels this is clearly indicated by the opening words of Luke in the Acts of the Apostles: "The former treatise have I written, O Theophilus, of all that Jesus began both to do and to teach." In this passage the word ἤρξατο is not pleonastic, as was held by some, but emphatic. According to this word the Gospel contained the narrative only of what Jesus began to do and to teach, which would prove to be the solid foundation and the germinating principle of all that He would continue to do on earth (through His apostles) and in heaven. The Gospels mark but an initial stage in New Testament revelation; they lack finality.

The form, the method and the substance of Christ's teaching in the Gospels,—it all bears the stamp of an incipient stage. Everyone that reads the Gospels and compares them with the epistles is struck by the simple manner in which Christ presents his teachings to the multitude. He gave his instruction primarily in the form of parables and proverbial sayings. Now it is the essence of proverbial speech that it detaches itself from particular occasions, and is therefore best adapted to the expression of general fundamental truths. Because parables and proverbs set forth the truth in a lively and concrete way, they were very appropriate in teaching those that were just initiated in the spiritual truths of the new dispensation. Since they generally disclose the truth but partially, they stimulate the spirit of inquiry. A very suitable way of instructing beginners indeed! We notice that the disciples gradually longed for a different form of instruction, and towards the end of his life Christ says to them: "These things have I spoken unto you in proverbs, but the time cometh, when I shall no more speak unto you in proverbs, but I shall show you plainly of the Father." John 16:25.—The method of Jesus' work points to the same general conclusion. His teaching has a fragmentary character. He speaks a word here and a word there, discourses now with this person and then with that one, just as a missionary among the gentiles is apt to do, expressing the deepest truths in a sporadic way. Important doctrines were thus uttered without any attempt to relate them to other truths. All this is in perfect harmony with the initial character of Christ's work.—The contents of Christ's teaching also are primitive and fundamental. Many of the most important truths are indeed taught in the Gospels, but they are not elaborated, nor set forth in all their significance, as f. i. the doctrine of the atonement, of justification by faith, of the forgiveness of sins, of the Kingship of Christ, etc. Other truths were suppressed, because, as the Lord himself says, even the best of his hearers were not yet able to bear them, John 16:12. The works of Christ were also initiatory. His miracles contained within them the promise of still greater works in the future. He says to his disciples: "He that believeth on me, the works that I do shall he do also, and greater works than these shall he do, because I go unto my Father," John 14:12.

Now the writers of the Gospels simply narrated this initial work of Christ, as they remembered it. They do not make mention of the greater works that followed after Christ had gone to heaven, nor do they (except in very rare instances) reflect on or seek to interpret the life and teachings of the Saviour. This remains to be done in later writings.

3

The Gospel of Matthew

CONTENTS[2]

The Gospel of Matthew may be divided into five parts:

I. The Advent of the Messiah, 1:1–4:11. Matthew proves by the legal genealogy that Christ was the Son of David, the child of the promise; that, in harmony with the prophecies, He was born of a virgin at Bethlehem and his way was prepared by John the Baptist; and records his baptism and temptation.

II. The Public proclamation of Messiah's Kingdom, 4:12–16:12. Here we find Jesus, after John is taken captive, choosing his first disciples and beginning his work in Galilee, 4:12–4:25. Then follows a splendid example of Christ's teaching in the Sermon on the Mount, in which the law of the New Kingdom is promulgated, and its righteousness and life are contrasted with those of Pharisees and Scribes, 5–7. This is followed by the description of a series of miracles, interspersed with brief teachings of the Lord and the calling of Matthew, giving clear evidence of the power and mercy of Jesus and establishing his authority to set up the New Kingdom and to proclaim its laws, 8:1–9:38. Next we have a catalogue of the twelve apostles and their commission to announce the coming Kingdom to the house of Israel, 10. It is brought out that the teachings and miracles of Jesus lead to serious questionings on the part of John the Baptist, to open opposition from the side of Pharisees and Scribes, and to the interference of his relatives, 11:1–12:50; that as a result Christ substitutes parabolic for plain teaching, 13:1–53; and that the opposition finally culminates in his rejection by the synagogue of Nazareth, by Herod and by the spiritual leaders of the people, both of Jerusalem and of Galilee, leading in every instance to the withdrawal of his

---

2   In giving the outline of the Gospels I have followed in general Gregory in his *Why Four Gospels?*

gracious works and also to an exposition and condemnation of the hypocracy and wickedness of the leaders of the nation. 13:54–16:12.

III. The Distinct and Public Claim of Messiahship, 16:13–23:39. In this section the evangelist shows, how Christ instructs his disciples regarding the Messiahship. The Lord calls forth their explicit confession of him as Messiah, 16:13–20; and teaches them in a threefold form that He must suffer and die, but will rise again. In connection with these announcements we have the narrative of the transfiguration and the healing of the epileptic demoniac, and instruction regarding the civil and religious relations and duties of the disciples, such as the payment of the temple tribute, the self-denying, humble, loving and forgiving spirit of true discipleship, divorce, the proper attitude toward children, the danger of earthly possessions, the gracious character of the reward in God's Kingdom, and the ministering spirit demanded in his followers, 16:21–20:28. At Jerusalem also He now makes his claim, entering the city as the Son of David and assuming Messianic authority in the temple. He brings out clearly the future rejection of Israel, answers the test questions of his enemies and pronounces a sevenfold woe on Pharisees and Scribes, 20:29–23:39.

IV. The Sacrifice of Messiah the Priest, 24:1–27:66. Matthew demonstrates that Christ, now that He is rejected by the Jews, prepares his disciples for his sacrificial death by unfolding the doctrine of his future coming in glory and by teaching them the true posture of his followers in waiting for the day of his coming, 24:1–25:46. He then describes how Christ brought his sacrifice, after eating the Paschal lamb, being betrayed by Judas, condemned by the Sanhedrin and Pilate, and dying on the cross, 26:1–27:66.

V. The Truimph of Messiah the Saviour and King. The author brings out that Jesus by rising again from the dead fully established his claim to the Messiahship. Abundant evidence of the resurrection is furnished and it is clearly shown that in the end Christ is clothed with Messianic authority.

CHARACTERISTICS

1. As to form we find, in the first place, a characteristically Jewish numerical arrangement of things in this Gospel. The genealogy in ch. 1 consists of three groups of generations of fourteen each. There are seven beatitudes ch. 5; seven petitions in the Lord's prayer ch. 6; a group of seven parables ch. 13; and seven woes on Pharisees and Scribes ch. 23. As to the style of Matthew, in the second place, may be said that it is smoother than that of Mark, though not so vivid. But it is tinged with Hebraisms, less indeed

than the language of Luke, but more than that of Mark. It is rather impersonal, lacking in individuality. Its individualism of language consists mostly in the frequent use of certain words and phrases. The Hebraistic formulae of transition καὶ ἐγένετο and καὶ ἰδού occur repeatedly, and the simple τότε is constantly used, especially with a historical tense. Further the following characteristic expressions are found: ἡ βασιλεία τῶν οὐρανῶν instead of the more common ἡ β. τοῦ θεοῦ; ἵνα πληρωθῇ τὸ ῥηθὲν ὑπό κυρίου διὰ τοῦ προφητοῦ, or an abbreviated form of this expression; and ὅπως instead of ἵνα.

2. The arrangement of the material in this Gospel also differs considerably from that in the other Synoptics. The narrative is not continuous, but is interrupted by five great discourses, such as are not found in the Gospels of Mark and Luke, viz. the Sermon on the Mount, chs. 5-7; the charge to the apostles, ch. 10; the parables of the Kingdom, ch. 13; the discourse on the church, ch. 18; and the final eschatological discourses of Christ on the last judgment, chs. 23-25. After every one of these discourses we find the words: "And it came to pass, when Jesus had ended (made an end of, finished) these sayings, etc.

3. As to contents the following peculiarities deserve our attention: In the first place the Gospel of Matthew has a more Jewish aspect than the other Synoptics. Its predominant subject is, the Messiah and his Kingdom. The discourses of which we spoke all have reference to this Kingdom, and it is clearly brought out that the mission of Christ is to the Jews only and that the establishment of His rule will be a restoration of the fallen throne of David. Cf. the genealogy ch. 1 and also 2:2; 10:5, 6; 15:24; 19:28, etc. Yet we must not think that it positively excludes the idea of salvation for the gentiles; it clearly holds out a hope to them and even announces that the Kingdom will be taken from Israel on account of its unfaithfulness. Cf. 2:1-13; 8:10-12; 15:28; 21:43; 22:1-14. In the second place the first Gospel alludes to the Old Testament more frequently than any other. It emphasizes the fact that the New Testament reveals the fulfilment of Old Testament promises; that Christ was born, revealed himself and labored as the prophets of old had foretold. Matthew contains more than 40 quotations, while Mark has 21 and Luke, 22. The characteristic use of ἵνα (ὅπως) πληρωθῇ in quotations proves that Matthew had an eye for the divine teleology in history.—And in the third place Matthew looks at things in their grand general aspect and pays less attention to the minor details on which Mark so much loves to dwell.

AUTHORSHIP

The superscription ascribes the first Gospel to Matthew. That this embodies the opinion of the early Church is evident from the testimony of Irenaeus, Tertullian, Origen, Eusebius and several others, who all point to Matthew as the author. The Gospel itself shows unmistakably, by its Jewish physiognomy, that its author was a Jew, yea even that he was a Palestinian Jew, for he quotes from the Hebrew and not from the Septuagint. It contains no direct evidence, however to the authorship of Matthew, though there are a couple points of difference between it and the other Synoptics that are best explained on the assumption that Matthew wrote it. When we compare the lists of the twelve apostles in Mt. 10:2-4; Mk. 3:16-19; and Luke 6:14-16, we notice that only in the first Gospel the name Matthew is followed by the less honorable qualification "the publican;" and that it has the order, "Thomas and Matthew" instead of, "Matthew and Thomas."

The apostolic authorship of this gospel is denied by several rationalistic critics, such as Davidson; Jülicher and Baljon. Their reasons for rejecting it are the following:

(1). Legend, misunderstanding and irrelevancy are very prominent in this Gospel, which would not be the case if the writer had been an eye and ear witness of Jesus. The reference is to such narratives as the story of the wise men, the flight into Egypt, and the slaughter of the innocents, ch. 2; the doublet of the miraculous feeding, 14:16-21; 15:32-38; the story of Jesus riding into Jerusalem on two animals, 21:2, 7; the opening of the graves at the resurrection of Christ, 27:52; the setting of a watch at the sepulchre and the bribing of them, etc. (2). The Gospel of Matthew is too closely dependent on Mark, not merely in choice of matter and arrangement but in verbal detail, to be the work of an apostle. (3). The author never indicates by the use of the pronouns I or we that he was an eye witness of the things which he narrates.

In answer to these objections it may be said that one's disbelief in miracles does not prove them false, and that the seeming difficulties to which reference is made easily yield to good exegesis. The dependence of Matthew on Mark (instead of the reverse as the Tübingen school believed) is indeed accepted by a great number of scholars today, but is not absolutely proven. And even if it were, it would be no disparagement for Matthew. The impersonal objective style is the prevailing one in the historical books of the Bible and is irrelevant as an objection to the authorship of the apostle.

Our information regarding Matthew is very scanty. We read of him first in connection with the call to follow Jesus, Mt. 9:9, 10; Mk. 2:14, 15; Lk. 5:27–29. There is no reason to doubt that the Matthew of the first Gospel is the Levi of the second and third. Possibly his name was changed by the Lord after his call to the discipleship, just as those of Peter and Paul. In Mark he is said to be the son of Alphaeus, whom some identify with Alphaeus the father of the apostle James. But this identification does not commend itself to us, since we may assume that, if James and Matthew had indeed been brothers, this would have been stated in their case as well as it is in those of Andrew and Peter and John and James. He belonged to the despised class of publicans and hence cannot have been a very strict Jew. When Jesus called him, he made a great feast for the Lord, to which he also invited many publicans and sinners. Clement of Alexandria describes him as a rigorous ascetic, living "on seeds and herbs and without flesh." It is not impossible that by a very natural reaction his sinful life changed into one of great austerity. A veil of obscurity is cast over the apostolic career of Matthew. Tradition has it that he remained at Jerusalem with the other apostles for about twelve years after the death of the Lord, laboring among his fellow-countrymen. When the work was done, it is said, he preached the Gospel to others, according to the popular opinion in Ethiopia. He probably died a natural death.

COMPOSITION

I. Original Language. A hotly debated question is that regarding the language in which Matthew originally wrote his Gospel. The difficulty of the problem arises from the fact that external testimony and internal evidence seem to disagree. As a result the camp is very much divided, some scholars ardently defending a Hebrew, others with equal zeal a Greek original. The earliest testimony in regard to this matter is that of Papias and runs as follows: "Matthew composed the oracles (λόγια) in the Hebrew dialect, and everyone interpreted them as he was able." It is clear from the original that in these words the emphasis falls on the phrase "in the Hebrew language." But Papias does not stand alone in this assertion; a similar statement is found in Irenaeus: "Matthew among the Hebrews did also publish a Gospel in writing in their own language." Pantaenus is said to have gone to India, where he found "the writing of Matthew in Hebrew letters." Origen quoted by Eusebius also says that "the first Gospel was written by Matthew ... who delivered it to the Jewish believers, composed in the Hebrew language." Eusebius himself makes the following statement: "For Matthew, having first preached to the Hebrews, when he was about to go to other people, delivered to them in their own language the Gospel written by himself." Jerome also states that "Matthew wrote a Gospel of Jesus Christ in Judea in the Hebrew language and letters for the benefit of those of the circumcision who believed. Who afterwards translated it into Greek, is uncertain." To these testimonies might be added those of Athanasius, Cyril of Jerusalem, Epiphanius, Ebedjesu and Chrysostom.

On the other hand it is pointed out that the present Greek Gospel does not impress one as a translation, but has all the appearance of an original work, since: (1.) The hypothesis of a translation fails to account for the identity seen in certain parts of the Synoptic Gospels. (2.) While the author himself indeed quotes from the Hebrew text of the Old Testament, the quotations of our Lord are almost uniformly taken from the Septuagint. Is it conceivable that this would be the case in a Hebrew Gospel? (3.) The Gospel contains translations of Hebrew words, as: "They shall call His name Emmanuel, which being interpreted is, God with us," 1:23; — "A place called Golgotha, that is to say, a place of a skull," 27:33. (4.) There are certain explanations of Palestinian customs and habitual occurrences that would have been altogether superfluous in a Hebrew Gospel, naturally intended only for the natives of Palestine, f. i. in 22:23; 27:8, 15; 28:15.

The conclusion to which this evidence leads is corroborated by the following facts: (1.) In all probability no one has ever seen the Hebrew Gospel of Matthew, and no trace of it can now be found. (2.) All the quotations from Matthew in the early Church fathers are taken from the present Greek Gospel. (3.) The Gospel of Matthew always stood on an equal footing with the other Gospels and is cited just as much as they are.

This evidence both external and internal has given rise to several theories, which we can briefly state in the following manner: (1.) Matthew wrote his Gospel in Hebrew and someone else translated it into Greek. This position was held by the Church in general until the time of the Reformation. Since then several Protestant scholars took another view, because Rome defended the ultimate authority of the Vulgate by pointing out that the Greek Matthew was also merely a translation. The attacks of Rationalism on the so-called second-hand Matthew, and the dubious character of a part of the ancient testimony, also served to bring this theory into discredit. Notwithstanding this, however, some of the ablest scholars have defended it up to the present. The prevailing idea among them is that the Greek Matthew is not so much in all parts a literal translation as a new redaction. According to Westcott it gives in writing the Greek counterpart of the Hebrew Gospel, that had taken shape in oral tradition from the beginning. Zahn regards it as the ripe fruit of the interpretation of the Hebrew original in the congregations to which Papias refers.

(2.) There never was a Hebrew original, but Matthew wrote his Gospel in the Greek language. The present gospel is not a translation, but an original work. They who hold this view are of the opinion that the testimony of Papias and of those following him was a sheer mistake, due partly to ignorance and partly to a confounding of the Gospel of Matthew with the Ebionite Gospel according to the Hebrews.

(3.) Matthew wrote neither a Hebrew nor a Greek Gospel, but, if anything, a work called the λόγια by Papias, which must have been a collection of the sayings or discourses of the Lord. According to some these λόγια are lost, but must probably be identified with one of the supposed sources (Q) of our present Gospels. Others as Godet and Holdsworth believe that the work contained the discourses that we find in the Gospel of Matthew and was therefore incorporated bodily in our present Gospel.

(4.) The evangelist after writing his Gospel in Hebrew with a view to his countrymen, possibly when he had left Palestine to labor elsewhere, translated or rather furnished a new recension of his Gospel in the Greek language with a view to the Jews of the Diaspora. The former was soon lost and altogether replaced by the latter.

In formulating our opinion in regard to this question, we desire to state first of all that we have no sufficient reason to discredit the testimony of the early Church. It is true that Eusebius says of Papias that he was "a credulous, weak-minded, though pious man," but in connection with this we must bear in mind: (1) that Eusebius says this in connection with the chiliastic opinions of Papias that were odious to the historian; (2) that he himself elsewhere testifies that Papias was a man "in the highest degree eloquent and learned and above all skilled in the Scriptures," and (3) that the peculiar views of Papias did not necessarily impair his veracity, nor invalidate his testimony to a historical fact. Let us remember also that it is inconsistent to believe Papias, when he says that Matthew wrote the Gospel, and to discredit his further testimony that the apostle wrote in Hebrew, as some scholars do. It is indeed almost certain that Pantaenus was mistaken, when he thought that he had found the Hebrew Gospel in

India; and that Jerome labored under a delusion, when he imagined that he had translated it at Cesarea. What they saw was probably a corruption of the Hebrew original, known as, "the Gospel according to the Hebrews." But this possible mistake does not invalidate the other independent testimony of Jerome and that of all the early fathers to the effect that Matthew wrote the Gospel in Hebrew.

In the second place we desire to point out that Papias in speaking of the λόγια of Matthew undoubtedly referred to his Gospel. The word λόγια does not mean speeches or sayings, as is now often asserted. It is found four times in the New Testament, viz. in Acts 7:38; Rom. 3:2; Heb. 5:12; 1 peter 4:11, and in every one of these places it has its classical meaning of oracles. It is applied to the divine utterances of God in his Word. In later writers the word is generally employed to indicate inspired writings. There is no reason to think that Papias used the word in the sense of λόγοι. If in addition to this we take in consideration that in all probability the testimony of Irenaeus is based on that of Papias and that he takes the word as referring to the Gospel of Matthew, the presumption is that Papias had the Gospel in mind. The meaning of his testimony is therefore, that the first Gospel was written in Hebrew. The so-called Logia-source is a creature of the imagination.

In the third place the internal evidence of our present Gospel proves conclusively that this is not a mere translation of a Hebrew original. The evidence adduced seems quite sufficient. The Greek Matthew may be and most likely is in substance a translation of the original Hebrew; yet it must be regarded as in many respects a new recension of the Gospel. The loss of the Hebrew original and the general substitution for it of the Greek version is readily explained by the scattering of the Jews after the destruction of Jerusalem, and by the early corruption of the Hebrew Gospel in the circles of the Ebionites and the Nazarenes.

In the fourth place it seems most plausible that Matthew himself, shortly after he had written the Hebrew Gospel, translated it, adjusting it in several respects to the needs of the Jews that were dispersed in different lands. True, early tradition does not speak of this, and Jerome even says that it was not known in his time who translated it into Greek. This favors the idea that it was done very early. Moreover our Greek Gospel was known from the beginning as the Gospel κατά Ματθᾶιον, just as the second and third as the Gospel κατά Μάρκον and κατά Λουκᾶν. As such it is also

universally quoted by those fathers that are accustomed to mention their
authors. The case of Matthew would thus be analogous to that of Josephus.

II. Readers and Purpose. The Gospel of Matthew was undoubtedly destined for the Jews. This is expressly stated by Irenaeus, Origen, Eusebius,
Gregory Nazianzen, e. a. This testimony is corroborated by internal evidence. The genealogy of Jesus goes back only to Abraham, the father of the
Hebrew race; and in harmony with the tenets of the Jews the Messiahship
of Christ is proved from the prophets. The whole Gospel impresses one
as being occasioned by the exigencies of the Jews both in Palestine and
without. In none of the other Gospels is the false position of Pharisees and
Scribes so clearly exposed.

It was Matthew's purpose to convince the Jews that Jesus was the Christ,
the great Davidic King promised by the prophets. He knew that, if this
could be shown clearly, they would be won for the Saviour. This purpose
is very evident from the Gospel. The legal genealogy of Christ is traced
back to Abraham; and it is clearly brought out that prophecy was fulfilled
in the manner of Christ's birth 1:23; the place of his nativity 2:6; his flight
into Egypt 2:15; the murder of the innocents 2:18; his residence at Nazareth
2:23; the ministry of his forerunner 3:3; 11:10, his removal to Capernaum
4:15, 16; his healing the sick 8:17; his meek and retiring disposition 12:18–21;
his teaching by parables 13:34, 35; his entry into Jerusalem 21:4, 5; his rejection by the builders 21:42; his being David's Son and Lord 22:44; his desertion by his disciples 26:31; the price of his betrayal 27:9; the division of his
raiment 27:35; and his cry of agony 27:46. It is Matthew only that records
the sayings of the Lord: "I am not come to destroy, but to fulfill," 5:17; and:
"I was not sent but unto the lost sheep of the house of Israel," 15:24. To him
Jerusalem is "the Holy City," "the Holy Place," and "the City of the great
King." On seven different occasions he calls the Lord "the Son of David."
In harmony with the prophets Christ the King is most prominent in his
Gospel, though of course the prophetic and priestly character of the Lord
are also clearly revealed.

III. Time and Place. Little can be said as to the time, when Matthew
wrote his Gospel; and what few indications we have of the time are rather
uncertain, because we do not know, whether they bear on the origin of
the Hebrew original or of the present Greek Gospel. Tradition generally
points to Matthew's Gospel as being the first. Irenaeus makes a very definite statement, viz.: "Matthew among the Hebrews published a Gospel
in their own language, while Peter and Paul were preaching the Gospel

at Rome and founding a church there." This must have been somewhere between 63-67 A. D.

Something may be gathered in this respect from the contents of the Gospel. We cannot, as some do, infer from 22:7 that it was composed after the destruction of Jerusalem, for then we would have to assume that our Lord could not have predicted this event. Moreover this argument impugns the veracity of the evangelist. A proof for the contrary, viz. that this Gospel was written before the destruction of Jerusalem, is found in 24:15, where we find in a discourse of the Saviour this parenthetic clause of the writer: "let him that readeth understand," in connection with the Lord's admonition to the inhabitants of Judea to flee to the mountains, when they shall see the abomination of desolation standing in the Holy Place. The same inference is drawn by some from the eschatological discourse of Christ in chs. 24-25, where the beginning of sorrows, the destruction of Jerusalem, and the Lord's return in glory are placed alongside of each other, without any distinction of time; and the writer does not by a single word betray any knowledge of the fact that the destruction of Jerusalem would be separated in time from the Lord's return. But this, being an argument from silence, is rather precarious. The dates assigned to this Gospel by rationalistic critics range from about 70 to 125 A. D.

As to the place, where the Gospel was written, Athanasius says that it was published at Jerusalem; Ebedjesu, in Palestine; and Jerome, in Judea for the sake of those in Judea who believed. There is nothing in the Gospel itself that contradicts this. It is very likely, however, that the Greek Gospel was written elsewhere.

IV. Method. The question arises, whether Matthew used sources in the composition of his Gospel. The prevalent opinion at present is that the writer of this Gospel, whoever he may have been, drew in the main on two sources, viz. on the λόγια of Matthew for the discourses of the Lord, and on the Gospel of Mark for the narrative portion of his work. It is found necessary, however, to assume several other minor sources. Thus Weiss, Jülicher, Baljon, Peake, Buckley, Bartlet (in Hastings D. B.) e. a. Against these see Davidson and Salmon. Zahn's opinion is that Mark employed the Hebrew Matthew in the composition of his Gospel, and that the writer of our Greek Matthew in turn used the Gospel of Mark. The great diversity of opinion among New Testament scholars in this respect shows clearly that it is quite impossible to determine with any degree of certainty what sources Matthew employed. All we can say is (1) that in all probability the Hebrew

Matthew depended on oral tradition only; (2) that our Greek Matthew is based on the Hebrew; and (3) that it is not impossible that Matthew had read the Gospel of Mark before he composed the present Greek Gospel.

CANONICAL SIGNIFICANCE

The Gospel of Matthew has been accepted as canonical from the earliest times. There are many traces of its use, especially of the Sermon on the Mount in the Didache. Next we find it clearly quoted in the Epistle of Barnabas, who cites ten passages with the significant formula "it is written." This proves that the Gospel was used and recognized as canonical in the early part of the second century. Further it is abundantly testified to until the beginning of the third century, when all controversy ceases, there being up to that time altogether 21 witnesses, so that this Gospel is one of the best attested books in the New Testament. Among these witnesses are the old Latin and Syriac Versions that contain this Gospel; early church fathers that refer to it as authoritative or quote it; and heretics who, even while attacking the truth, tacitly admit the canonical character of the Gospel.

This book is properly placed at the very beginning of the New Testament. It forms part of the foundation on which the New Testament structure was to be reared. And among the Gospels, which together constitute this foundation, it is rightly put in the first place. It is, as it were, a connecting link between the Old Testament and the New. As the Old Testament had reference to the Jews only, so the Gospel of Matthew is written for the old covenant people. And it is clearly linked to the Old Testament by its continual reference to the prophets. The permanent spiritual value of this Gospel is that it sets forth in clear outline Christ as the One promised of old; and, in harmony with the prophetic literature, especially as the great divine King, before whom the Church of all ages must bow down in adoration.

4

The Gospel of Mark

CONTENTS

We may divide the contents of Mark's Gospel, that treats of Christ as the mighty Worker, into five parts:

I. The Advent of the mighty Worker, 1:1-2:12. Jesus is heralded as the mighty One by John the Baptist, and proclaimed as the Son of God by the Father, 1:1-13. After calling some of his disciples, He taught the Galilean multitudes as one having authority, worked mighty miracles among them, as the casting out of demons, the healing of Peter's mother-in-law, the cleansing of a leper, etc., and showed His authority to forgive sins, 1:14-2:12.

II. The Conflict of the mighty Worker, 2:12-8:26. In connection with the feast of Levi, the fact that the apostles did not fast, and that they plucked ears of corn on the sabbath, Jesus gives the Pharisees instruction regarding the purpose of his coming, and the moral character of the requirements of his Kingdom, 2:13-3:8. The healing of the man with the withered hand leads to the enmity of Pharisees and Herodians, which caused the withdrawal of Jesus. The Lord now chose twelve apostles and continued his mighty works, so that even his friends and relatives sought to restrain him, and his enemies claimed that He did them through the power of the devil, 3:9-35. Next we find him teaching the people regarding the origin, the quiet growth, independent of man's efforts, and the future strength of the Kingdom of God, 4:1-34. His divine power shines forth in his calming the sea, his curing the demoniacs in the land of the Gadarenes and the woman that had the issue of blood, and his raising the daughter of Jairus, 4:36-5:43. He finds no faith at Nazareth, and now sends out the twelve into the cities of Galilee, 6:1-13. Herod, hearing of Christ, stands in awe of him, believing him to be John the Baptist, whom he beheaded, 6:14-29. Withdrawing with the twelve to a desert place, He feeds the five thousand, and after that shows his power over nature by walking on the sea, 6:30-56. The Pharisees accost him, because his disciples eat bread with unclean hands, 7:1–23. He now cures the daughter of the Syro-Phœnician woman and the deaf and dumb man at Decapolis, where He also feeds the four thousand, 7:24–8:9. Once more the Pharisees ask him for a sign. Leaving them, He restores the sight of the blind man at Bethsaida, 8:10–26.

III. The Claim of the mighty Worker, 8:27–13:37. The Lord shows the necessity of his suffering, leads his disciples to confess him as Messiah, and points out what is required of them, 8:27–38. His power and glory are seen in the transfiguration and in the miracle following this, 9:1–29. Then follows a second revelation of his future suffering, followed by teachings regarding humility and offenses, 9:30–50. In Perea Christ, tempted by the Pharisees, gives his opinion on the question of divorce; then He blesses little children and points out the way of life to the young ruler, 10:1–31. For the third time He reveals his future suffering, and prepares his disciples for a life of service, 10:32–45. At Jericho He restores the sight of Bartimeus. Next he enters Jerusalem amid loud hosannas, curses the fig-tree and cleanses the temple, 10:46–11:26. In the temple He reveals his superiority by answering the questions of Pharisees, Sadducees and Herodians, and points to himself as Davids Lord, 11:27–12:44. Then he speaks of his coming in glory, 13.

IV. The Sacrifice of the mighty Worker, 14:1–15:47. Preparation is made for Jesus' death by the Sanhedrin and Judas on the one hand, and by Mary of Bethany on the other, 14:1–11. The passover is eaten and the Lord's supper instituted, 14:12–25: In Gethsemane follows bitter agony and captivity, 14:26–52. Then the Lord is tried and condemned by the Sanhedrin and by Pilate, and finally He is crucified, 14:53–15:47.

V. The mighty Worker as Conqueror of Death, 16:1–20. Women go to the grave on the first day of the week and are directed by the angels to go to Galilee, 16:1–8. The Lord appears several times, gives blessed promises, and at last ascends to heaven, 14:9–20.

CHARACTERISTICS

There are certain characteristics by which the Gospel of Mark is distinguished from the other Gospels:

1. The most striking peculiarity of the second Gospel is its descriptive character. It is Mark's constant aim to picture the scenes of which he speaks in lively colours. There are many minute observations in his work that are not found in the other Synoptics, some of which point to its autoptic

character. He mentions the look of anger that Christ cast on the hypocrites about him, 3:5; relates the miracles, performed immediately after the transfiguration, with greater circumstantiality than the other Gospels, 9:9-29; tells of Jesus taking little children in his arms and blessing them, 9:36; 10:16; remarks that Jesus, looking at the young ruler, loved him, 10:21, etc.

2. This Gospel contains comparatively little of the teaching of Jesus; it rather brings out the greatness of our Lord by pointing to his mighty works, and in doing this does not follow the exact chronological order. Teaching is subordinate to action, though we cannot maintain that it is ignored altogether. Mark, though considerably smaller than Matthew, contains all the miracles narrated by the latter except five, and besides has three that are not found in Matthew. Of the eighteen miracles in Luke, Mark has twelve and four others above this number.

3. In the Gospel of Mark several words of Christ that were directed against the Jews are left out, such as we find in Mt. 3:7-10; 8:5-13; 15:24, etc. On the other hand more Jewish customs and Aramaic words are explained than in the first Gospel, f. i. 2:18; 7:3; 14:12; 15:6, 42; 3:17; 5:41; 7:11, 34; 14:36. The argument from prophecy has not the large place here that it has in Matthew.

4. The style of Mark is more lively than that of Matthew, though not as smooth. He delights in using words like εὐθύς or εὐθέως and πολύς, prefers the use of the present and the imperfect to that of the aorist, and often uses the periphrastic εἶναι with a participle instead of the finite verb. There are several Latinisms found in his Gospel, as κεντυρίων κορδάντης, κράββατος, πραιτώριον, σπεκουλάτωρ and φραγελλοῦν.

AUTHORSHIP

Just as in the case of Matthew we are entirely dependent on external testimony for the name of the author of the second Gospel. And the voice of antiquity is unanimous in ascribing it to Mark. The most ancient testimony to this effect is that of Papias, who says: "Mark, the interpreter of Peter, wrote down carefully all that he recollected, though he did not [record] in order that which was either said or done by Christ. For he neither heard the Lord nor followed him; but subsequently, as I have said, [attached himself to] Peter, who used to frame his teaching to meet the [immediate] wants [of his hearers]; and not as making a connected narrative of the Lord's discourses. So Mark committed no error, as he wrote down some particulars just as he called them to mind. For he took heed to one thing—to omit none of the facts that he heard, and to state nothing falsely in [his narrative] of them." Several other church fathers, such as Irenaeus, Clement of Alexandria, Tertullian, Origen, Jerome, Eusebius, e. a., follow in his wake; there is not a dissentient voice.

We cannot glean a single hint from the Gospel itself as to the identity of the author. It may be that the obscure young man who followed Jesus in the night of his betrayal. 14:51, 52, and who, stripped of his garment fled naked in the darkness of night, was the author himself. The house of Mark's mother was at least in later time a rendezvous for the disciples of the Lord, Acts 12:12; so that it is not improbable that Jesus and his disciples ate the Paschal supper there, and that Mark, hearing them depart, left his bed and stole after them. This would immediately explain the acquaintance of the author with this interesting fact.

Some scholars have expressed doubt as to the identity of Mark, the evangelist, and John Mark, the companion of Barnabas and Paul. The general consensus of opinion, however, favors this. Proceeding on the assumption that this view is correct, we find Mark mentioned first in connection with Peter's deliverance from prison in 44 A. D. After leaving the prison walls the apostle went to "the house of Mary, the mother of John, whose surname was Mark," Acts 12:12. From the way in which Luke introduces his mother we gather that Mark was a well known person, when the Acts were written. The fact that Peter calls him his son, 1 Peter 5:13 naturally leads to the supposition that in his early years he had frequent intercourse with the apostle and was through the instrumentality of Peter led to a saving knowledge of the truth. He was a cousin of Barnabas and hence a Jew, probably even of a priestly family, Acts 4:36. When Barnabas and Paul set out on their first missionary journey, Mark accompanied them until they came to Pamphylia, when for some unknown, but as it seems reprehensible reason, he turned back. At the beginning of the second missionary journey he was minded to accompany the apostles again, but Paul positively refused to accept his services. He now accompanied his uncle to Cyprus. When we next hear of Mark, about ten years later, he is spoken of by Paul as one of those few "fellow-laborers that have been a consolation to him," Col. 4:10; Philem. 24. In his last letter the apostle speaks of Mark once more, and in such a laudatory manner as to prove that Mark has fully regained his confidence, 2 Tim. 4:11. The last we hear of Mark in Scripture is, when Peter sends the greetings of Mark, his son, to the Christians in Asia Minor, 1 Peter 5:13. These four passages lead us to the following construction of his later history: He was with Paul during the apostle's first imprisonment at Rome and then intended to visit the congregation of Colossæ. We have no reason to doubt that he carried out this purpose. After Paul's release Mark was at Rome with Peter, who in writing to the Christians of Asia Minor assumes that they know Mark. Apparently he made another visit to Asia Minor, since Paul requests Timothy, 2 Tim. 4:11 to take Mark with him, when he comes to Rome. After the death of Peter he is said to have visited Alexandria, where he was the first to found Christian churches, and finally died a martyr's death. This tradition, though old, is not without suspicion.

It seems that Mark was "like Peter more a man of action than of deep and abiding principle, a man of fervor and enthusiasm rather than of persevering effort; but he was transfused by the power of the same Christ who transfused Peter into the man of rapid, continued and effective effort in the missionary work of the Church." Gregory, Why Four Gospels, p. 163.

The relation of Mark to Peter deserves special attention. Scripture speaks of this in the two places already mentioned, and tradition abundantly testifies to it. Papias says that "Mark was Peter's interpreter and wrote down carefully all that he recollected." Clement of Alexandria also says that he wrote down the discourses of Peter, as he remembered them. Irenaeus, Tertullian and Jerome all style Mark "the interpreter of Peter." Tertullian even says that "the Gospel published by Mark may be reckoned Peter's, whose interpreter he was." And Origen still stronger: "Mark wrote his Gospel according to the dictates of Peter." Similarly Athanasius. All these testimonies agree in asserting that Mark was dependent on Peter in writing his Gospel; they disagree, however, as to the degree of dependence, some claiming merely that Mark recorded what he remembered of Peter's preaching, and others, that he wrote what Peter dictated. Which representation is the true one?

The title of the Gospel is against the dictation theory, for if Peter had dictated the Gospel, it would in all probability have been called by his name, just as the Epistles dictated by Paul are universally ascribed to him. On the other hand the autoptic touches in the Gospel make it probable that in some parts of his work Mark employed the very words of Peter; they also suggest a possible basis for the later tradition that Peter dictated to Mark. However, it is not impossible that some of the Church fathers accentuated the dependence of Mark on Peter unduly, merely to enhance the authority of his work. The true relation of the evangelist to the apostle is expressed in the words: "Mark was the interpreter (ἑρμηνευτής) of Peter." This does

not mean that he accompanied Peter on his missionary journeys as drago-
man, translating Aramaeic discourses into Greek (Davidson), or Greek into
Latin (Bleek); but that he was Peter's scholar and in his Gospel interprets i.
e. sets forth the doctrine of Peter for those who have not heard the apostle.

The Gospel itself incidentally testifies to the relation in which it stands
to Peter. There are many touches that indicate first-hand knowledge, as in
1:16-20; 1:29; 9:5; 14:54, 72; 16:7. Some things found in the other Synoptics
are unexpectedly omitted by Mark, as Peter's walking on the water, Mt.
14:29; his appearance in the incident of the tribute money, Mt. 17:24-27;
the statement of Christ that He prayed for Peter individually, Lk. 22:32;
the significant word spoken to him as the Rock, Mt. 16:18. In other cases
his name is suppressed, where it is used by Matthew or Luke, as 7:17 cf. Mt.
15:15; 14:13 cf. Lk. 22:8.

The authorship of Mark is quite generally admitted; yet there are some,
such as Beischlag and Davidson e. a. who deny it. They maintain that our
present Gospel does not tally with the description of Papias, where he says
that Mark wrote down the things he heard of Peter "not in order." Wendt
supposes that Papias had in mind a series of narratives that are embodied
in our present Gospel, a sort of Urmarkus. But when Papias said that the
evangelist wrote "not in order," he did not say anything that is not true of
our Mark, for in it we do not find things in the order of their occurrence.
And in ancient literature there is not a single trace of an Urmarkus.

COMPOSITION

1. Readers and Purpose. External testimony enlightens us respecting the
circle for which the Gospel of Mark was intended; it points to Rome and
the Romans. Clement of Alexandria says that many of the converts of
Rome desired of Mark that he should write down the discourses of Peter.
Jerome also speaks of this "request of the brethren at Rome"; and Gregory
Nazianzen says: "Mark wrote his Gospel for the Italians." If we now turn
to the Gospel itself, we find that it was peculiarly adapted to the Romans.
They were a strenuous, a very active people; Mark's Gospel is pre-eminently the Gospel of action, and is written in a brisk lively style. The fact
that the argument from prophecy holds an inferior place in it, and that
so many Jewish customs and Aramæic words are explained, points away
from the Jews; while the Latin words contained in the gospel, the reference to the Roman manner of divorce, 10:12, the reduction of a coin to
the Roman quadrans, 12:42, the knowledge of Pilate presupposed in 15:1

(cf. Mt. 27:1 and Lk. 3:1), and the introduction of Simon of Cyrene as the father of Alexander and Rufus, 15:21 (cf. Rom. 16:13),—all point to Rome.

It stands to reason that the purpose of Mark in writing stood in the closest relation to the circle of readers for whom he intended his Gospel. It is certainly true, as Zahn asserts, that his intention was to record the beginning (ἀρχή) of the Gospel of Jesus Christ, i. e. the beginning of its preaching and of its course; but he has this in common with the other Synoptics; it is nothing distinctive (cf. p. 58 above). The theory of Hilgenfeld and Davidson, following Baur, that the Gospel of Mark was written to conciliate the two opposing parties of the apostolic age, the Petrine and the Pauline, and therefore carefully avoids the exclusivism of Matthew as well as the universalism of Luke can only be sustained by the most forced and artificial interpretations. Neither does the gospel support the view of Weiss, that it was written at a time, when the hope of Christ's second coming was on the decline, and intended to show that the Messianic character of Jesus, mission was sufficiently attested by His earthly life. Mark's aim was simply to record the gospel narrative without any special dogmatic aim, but to do this in such a manner as would be most suitable for the Romans, the busy Romans, the people of action. Hence he places special emphasis on the acts of Christ. For those who loved conquest and admired heroism he desired to picture Christ as the mighty Conqueror that overcame sin and all its consequences, yea even death itself.

2. Time and Place. As to the time when Mark wrote his Gospel the witness of the early Church is not unanimous. Irenaeus says that after the death of Peter and Paul Mark wrote down what he had heard Peter preach. Clement of Alexandria places the composition of the Gospel before the death of Peter, stating that, when Peter heard of it, "he neither obstructed nor encouraged the work." Jerome informs us that Peter "approved and published it in our churches, commanding the reading of it by his own authority." Others say that Peter dictated to Mark. The question to be decided is therefore, whether Mark wrote before or after the death of Peter. It is generally assumed that the testimony of Irenaeus is the most trustworthy. It is possible that some of the later Church fathers insisted on Mark's having written the Gospel during the life of Peter, in order to clothe it with apostolic authority. Zahn would harmonize the testimony of the fathers by assuming that Mark began his work before and finished it after the death of the apostle; and that Peter on hearing of Mark's venture at first said nothing regarding it; then, seeing a part of the work, rejoiced

in it; and still later, when it had almost reached its perfect form, sanctioned it, Einl. II p. 203.

Turning to the Gospel itself, we find that it contains no positive evidence as to the time of its composition. Some inferred from 13:24 as compared with Mt. 24:29 that it was written after the destruction of Jerusalem, the evangelist being conscious of the lapse of a certain period between that catastrophe and the day of Christ's return. But the foundation is too slender for the conclusion. With greater probability others infer from 13:14, "let him that readeth understand," that the destruction of the city was still a matter of expectation. This seems to follow also from Mark's utter silence regarding that calamity. The probable conclusion is therefore that the year 70 A. D. is the terminus ad quem for the composition of this Gospel. From Col. 4:10 we may infer that it was written after 62 A. D., for if Paul had known Mark as an evangelist, he would most likely have introduced him as such. A place of still greater importance is 2 Peter 1:15. "Yea I will give diligence that at every time ye may be able after my decease to call these things to remembrance." Here Peter seems to promise that there will be a record of his preaching after his demise. We would therefore date the Gospel between 67 and 70 A. D. Davidson without good reasons places it in the beginning of the second century, about 125 A. D. Regarding the grounds for his position, (1) that in this Gospel belief in the divinity of Christ is more pronounced than in the first century; and (2) that the word εὐαγγέλιον is used in a sense foreign to the apostolic age, we merely remark that they are both unproved assumptions.

The testimony of the fathers points, almost without a dissenting voice, to Rome as the place, where Mark composed his gospel. Chrysostom, however, testifies that "Mark wrote in Egypt at the request of the believers there. But in another statement he admits that he really knows nothing about it.

3. Method. Augustine called Mark "the abridger of Matthew," assuming that the second Gospel was an abbreviated compilation from the first. This theory has since been defended by several scholars of the Tübingen school, but is now abandoned. The general features of the Gospel do not bear out that view. Zahn finds that Mark based his Gospel both on the oral communications of Peter and on the Hebrew Matthew, Einl. II p. 322. Davidson denies the originality and priority of the Gospel by making it depend to a great extent on Matthew and Luke, Introd. I p. 478. Salmon finds throughout the Gospel many evidences of the priority and independence of Mark,

but believes that in other places he is, with Matthew and Luke, dependent on a common source, Introd. p. 155. The prevalent opinion at present is that Mark's Gospel was prior to the other two, though, at least according to some, he may have employed the λογια of Matthew. But in order to maintain this priority its defenders have resorted to such artificial and unlikely theories that they in part defeated their own purpose. The theory of an Urmarkus has been broached, but found little acceptance. The opinion of Dr. Arthur Wright that we must distinguish between a proto-, a deutero- and a trito Mark, a distinction applied to oral tradition by him, is now by others applied to written documents. Cf. Holdsworth, Gospel Origins p. 108.

Here again the great difference of opinion proves that it is quite impossible to trace in all details the origin of the material found in this Gospel. The great objection to several of the theories propounded is that they seek to account for the origin of Mark in a too mechanical way. We may be certain of two things: (1) that Mark derived the greatest part of his material from the preaching of Peter that had gradually assumed a definite shape in his mind; and (2) that he has recorded partly the ipsissima verba of Peter (except for the occasional change of we into they), and partly merely the substance of the apostles κήρυγμα in a form and with interpretations of his own. For the rest of his material he probably depended on the Hebrew original of Matthew.

INTEGRITY

The integrity of the Gospel of Mark is generally maintained, with the exception, however, of the last twelve verses, regarding which there is a great difference of opinion. The critical camp of the past century is just about equally divided, although at present the tide is somewhat against these verses. The reasons for rejecting them are both external and internal. These verses are wanting in the two oldest and most valuable manuscripts, viz. the Sinaitic and the Vatican. Eusebius and Jerome and a few others state that they were wanting in almost all the Greek copies of the gospels of their time. It is possible, however, that the testimony of Jerome and the rest resolves itself into that of Eusebius. This is all but certain with respect to that of Jerome, as even Davidson admits. They are wanting also in the important MS. k, representing the African text of the old Latin Version, which has another and shorter conclusion, like that in MS. L. They are also absent from some of the best MSS. of the Armenian Version. Then the style of this section is abrupt and sententious, not graphic like that of the rest of the Gospel. It makes the impression of a collection of brief notices, extracted from larger accounts and loosely combined. Its phraseology is also peculiar. Thus πρώτη σαββάτου, verse 9 is used instead of ἡ μία τῶν σαββάτων, as in 16:2. The verb πορεύεσθαι, which occurs three times in this section, is not found in the body of the Gospel. Neither is the word θεᾶσθαι, 16:11, 14. Another unique feature is the use of ὁ κύριος as a designation of Christ, verses 19, 20.

These verses have also found ardent defenders, however, among whom especially Dean Burgon must be named, though he is perhaps a little too positive. In his work on, "The last Twelve Verses of the Gospel according to Mark," he put up an able defense. The authenticity of this section is favored by the following considerations: It is found in most of the uncial MSS. and in all the cursives, though some of these mark it with an asterisk, or indicate that it was absent in older copies. Moreover its absence from Aleph and B looks somewhat suspicious. It is also incorporated in most of the ancient Versions, of which the Itala, the Curatorian and Peshito Syriac, and the Coptic are older than any of our Greek codices. All the existing Greek and Syriac lectionaries, as far as they have now been examined, contain these verses. Irenaeus quotes the 19th verse as a part of the Gospel of Mark. Justin Martyr too in all probability testifies to the authenticity of these verses. And several of the later fathers, such as Epiphanius, Ambrose and Augustine certainly quote from them. And as far as internal evidence is concerned, it seems very unlikely that Mark would end his Gospel with the words ἐφοβοῦντο γάρ, without recording a single appearance of the Lord. Moreover these verses contain too many peculiarities to be a forgery.

We cannot delay to discuss the causes for the variation of the MSS, nor to review the different conclusions to which scholars have come as to the extent of Mark's Gospel. They who wish to study the subject can do so in the work of Burgon, in the Introductions of Guericke and Salmon and in Urquhart's New Biblical Guide VII, where this section is defended; and in the work of Westcott and Hort, "The New Testament in Greek," and in the Introductions of Reuss, Weiss, Davidson and Zahn, who reject it.

It seems to us that the ground offered for the rejection of these verses by external testimony is rather slender and uncertain, while the internal evidence is weighty indeed. In view of it we are inclined to accept one of two possible conclusions: either that Mark himself added these verses some time after he had written his Gospel, possibly culling his material from Matthew and Luke; or that someone else wrote them to complete the work.

The latter is favored by the Armenian Gospel that was written in 986 and was discovered by F. C. Conybeare in 1891, and which has the superscription above this section: "Of the Presbyter Ariston." In either case we see no reason, however, to doubt the canonicity of this part of Mark's Gospel, though some have attempted to make this suspicious especially by pointing to the unlikely (?) miracles of verses 17, 18. Cf. Luke 10:19.

CANONICAL SIGNIFICANCE

Though the external testimony to the canonicity of Mark's Gospel is not so abundant as that for the Gospel of Matthew, yet it is sufficient to establish this beyond a shadow of doubt. It is quoted by at least two of the apostolic fathers, by Justin Martyr and by the three great witnesses of the end of the second century, Irenaeus, Clement of Alexandria and Tertullian, and is referred to as a part of the Word of God by several others. We find no expressions of doubt in the early Church.

The special purpose of this Gospel in the canon is to show us Christ in his divine power, destroying the works of satan, and conquering sin and death. More than other Gospels it places prominently before us the work of Christ in behalf of those that are bound by the shackles of satan and are suffering the consequences of sin. We here see the Lion out of the tribe of Juda, conquering and ever to conquer. Mark is the only one of the evangelists that speaks of the future Kingdom of God as coming with power, 9:1. In that way this Gospel has special significance for the Church of all ages. It gives her the blessed assurance that her future is entrusted to One who has shown himself a mighty Conqueror, and who is abundantly able to save to the uttermost all who believe in Him.

5

The Gospel of Luke

CONTENTS

Like the contents of the previous Gospels we may also divide those of Luke's into five parts:

I. The Advent of the Divine Man, 1-4:13. After stating his aim the evangelist describes the announcement from heaven of the forerunner, John the Baptist, and of Christ himself, and their birth with the attendant circumstances, 1:1-2:20. Then he shows that Christ was made subject to the law in circumcision, in the presentation in the temple, and in his journey to Jerusalem, 2:21-52. He traces the descent of the Son of Man to Adam, and points out that He was prepared for his work by baptism and temptation, 3:1-4:13.

II. The Work of the Divine Man for the Jewish World, 4:14-9:50. In this part we first see Christ preaching in the synagogues of Nazareth, Capernaum and all Galilee; performing many miracles in Capernaum and by the sea of Galilee, such as the curing of Peter's mother-in-law, the wonderful draught of fishes, the cleansing of the leper, and the healing of the palsied man; calling Levi to follow him; and instructing his enemies regarding his authority, his purpose, and the moral character of his demands, as a result of which many were amazed and Pharisees and Scribes were filled with hatred, 4:14-6:11. After a night of prayer the Lord now chooses his twelve disciples and proclaims the constitution of his Kingdom, 6:12-49. He cures the centurion's servant, raises the widow's son, and gives instruction by word and example regarding the nature of his work and the character of the subjects of his Kingdom, 7:1-49. The origin of the Kingdom is now illustrated in the parable of the sower, and the divine power of Christ over both the natural and the spiritual world is shown in the stilling of the storm, in the deliverance of the Gadarene demoniac, in his curing the woman with the issue of blood and raising the daughter of Jairus, 8:1-56.

The twelve are sent out and on their return Christ retires with them to a desert place, where He miraculously feeds the five thousand, after which He once and again announced his future suffering and was transfigured on the Mount, 9:1-50.

III. The Work of the Divine Man for the Gentiles, 9:51-18:30. Jesus in traveling towards Jerusalem sends messengers before him, but these are rejected by the Samaritans; then He sends out the seventy, who return with a good report, teaches that neighborly love is not to be restricted to the Jews (good Samaritan), and gives his disciples instruction regarding prayer, 9:51-11:13. The Pharisees now claim that Christ casts out the devils through Beelzebub, in answer to which He pictures their condition, and when they tempt him in various ways, pronounces his woe upon them and warns his disciples against them, 11:14-12:12. In connection with the parable of the rich fool the Lord warns against covetousness and anxious care, and bids his disciples to be prepared for the day of his coming, 12:13-53. Sitting at meat in the house of a Pharisee, He teaches those present true mercy, true humility, true hospitality, and the fact that they, having refused the supper of the Lord, will be rejected, 14:1-24. Next the necessity of self-denial is impressed on those that would follow Jesus, and in three parables the Pharisees are made acquainted with the real purpose of his coming, 14:25-15:32. The disciples are instructed in the careful use of their earthly possessions, and to the Pharisees the law of retribution is explained, 16:1-31. In various ways the Lord impresses on his followers the necessity of a forgiving spirit, of humility, of faith and gratitude, of constant prayer with a view to the unexpected character of his coming, of trusting in God and of self-denial,—all ending in everlasting salvation, 17:1-18:30.

IV. The Sacrifice of the Divine Man for all Mankind, 18:31-23:49. Jesus announces once more his future suffering and death, at Jericho restores the sight of a blind man and calls Zaccheus, and points out to his followers that his Kingdom would not immediately come, 18:32-19:27. Triumphantly He enters Jerusalem, where He cleanses the temple, answers the questions of the Chief Priests, the Scribes, the Pharisees and the Sadducees, and instructs his followers regarding his future coming, 19:28-21:38. After eating the passover with his disciples He was betrayed, condemned and crucified, 22:1-23:56.

V. The Divine Man Saviour of all Nations, 24. On the morning of the first day Christ arose; women seek him in the grave; He appears to two of his disciples on the way to Emmaus, to the eleven, and finally departs from them with the promise of the Spirit.

CHARACTERISTICS

The following are the most important characteristics of the third Gospel:

1. In point of completeness it surpasses the other Synoptics, beginning, as it does, with a detailed narrative of the birth of John the Baptist and of Christ himself, and ending with a record of the ascension from the Mount of Olives. In distinction from Matthew and Mark this Gospel even contains an allusion to the promise of the Father, 24:29, and thus points beyond the old dispensation to the new that would be ushered in by the coming of the Holy Spirit. The detailed narrative of Christ's going to Jerusalem in 9:51-18:14 is also peculiar to this gospel.

2. Christ is set before us in this Gospel as the perfect Man with wide sympathies. The genealogy of Jesus is trace back through David and Abraham to Adam, our common progenitor, thus presenting him as one of our race. We are told of the truly human development both in body and spirit of Jesus in 2:40-52, and of his dependence on prayer in the most important crises of His life, 3:21; 9:29. Those features of the Lord s miracles of healing are clearly brought out that show his great sympathy. "Peter's mother-in-law suffers from a great fever; and the leper is full of leprosy. The hand restored on the sabbath is the right hand, the centurion's servant is one dear to him, the son of the widow of Nain, is an only son, the daughter of Jairus an only daughter, the epileptic boy at the hill of transfiguration is an only child." Bruce, The Expositor's Greek Testament I p. 47.

3. Another feature of this Gospel is its universality. It comes nearer than other Gospels to the Pauline doctrine of salvation for all the world, and of salvation by faith, without the works of the law. In the synagogue at Nazareth Christ points out that God might again deal with the Jews as He had done in the days of Elijah and Elishah, 4:25-27; He declares that the faith of the centurion was greater than any He had found in Israel, 7:2-10; sends messengers before his face into Samaria, 9:52-56; demands love of Israel even for the Samaritans, 10:30-37; heals the Samaritan leper as well as the others, 17:11-19; and speaks the significant word: "Blessed are they that hear the word of God and keep it, 11:28.

4. More than the other evangelists Luke relates his narrative to contemporaneous history and indicates the time of the occurrences. It was in the days of king Herod that the birth of John the Baptist and Christ was

announced, 1:1, 26; during the reign of Caesar Augustus, that Christ was born, 2:1; while Cyrenius was governor of Syria, that the taxation took place, 2:2; in the fifteenth year of Tiberias, etc., that Christ was baptized and began his public ministry, 3:1, 2. Notice also the following chronological indications: 1:36, 56, 59; 2:42; 3:23; 9:28, 37, 51; 22:1, 7. We should not infer from the foregoing, however, that Luke furnishes us with a chronological record of the Lord's public ministry. Very indefinite expressions of time are found throughout the Gospel, as: "and it came to pass, when he was in a certain city," 5:12; "and it came to pass on a certain day," 5:17; "and it came to pass also on another sabbath," 6:6, etc.

5. Luke writes a purer Greek than any of the other evangelists, but this is evident only, where he does not closely follow his sources. The Greek of the preface is of remarkable purity, but aside from this the first and second chapters are full of Hebraisms. Of the rest of the Gospel some parts approach very closely to classical Greek, while others are tinged with Hebrew expressions. Plummer says: "The author of the Third Gospel and of the Acts is the most versatile of all the New Testament writers. He can be as Hebraistic as the LXX, and as free from Hebraisms as Plutarch." Comm. on Luke in International Crit. Comm. p. XLIX. His style is also very picturesque; he tries to make us see things, just as the eyewitnesses saw them. Moreover his Gospel contains 312 words that are peculiar to him. Several of these are ἅπαξ λεγόμενα. There are also five Latin words, viz. δηνάριον, λεγεών, σουδάριον, ἀσσάριον and μόδιος. Cf. lists in Plummer's Comm. and Davidson's Introd.

AUTHORSHIP

Though the author speaks of himself explicitly in the preface of his Gospel, we are dependent on tradition for his name. And here again the testimony of the fathers is unanimous. Irenaeus asserts that "Luke, the companion of Paul, put down in a book the Gospel preached by him." With this agrees the testimony of Origen, Eusebius, Athanasius, Gregory, Nazianze, Jerome, e. a.

The Gospel itself offers us no direct collateral testimony. Yet there are certain features that strengthen our belief in the authorship of Luke. In the first place the writer evidently looks at things with the eye of a physician. In 1882 Dr. Hobart published a work on, The Medical Language of St. Luke, showing that in many instances the evangelist uses the technical language that was also used by Greek medical writers, as παραλελυμένος, 5:18, 24 (the other Gospels have παραλύτιχος); συνεχομένη πυρετῷ μεγάλῳ, 4:38; ἔστη ἡ ῥύσις τοῦ αἵματος, 8:44 (cf. Mt. 5:29); ἀνεκάθισεν, 7:14, Luke carefully distinguishes demoniacal possession from disease, 4:18; 13:32; states exactly the age of the dying person, 8:42; and the duration of the affliction in 13:11. He only relates the miracle of the healing of Malchus' ear. All these things point to Luke, "the beloved physician."

In the second place there is what has been called the Paulinism of Luke. This has sometimes been emphasized unduly, no doubt, but it certainly is a characteristic feature of the third Gospel, and is just what we would expect in a writing of Paul's companion.

In the third place we find great similarity between this Gospel and the Acts of the Apostles. If Luke wrote the latter, he also composed the former. The general opinion is expressed by Knowling in his introduction to the book of Acts, in the Expositor's Greek Testament II p. 3: "Whoever wrote the Acts wrote also the Gospel which bears the name of Luke." It is true that there are more Hebraisms in the Gospel than in Acts, but this is due to the fact that the writer in composing the former was more dependent on written sources than he was in writing the latter.

The only certain knowledge we have of Luke is derived from the Acts of the Apostles and from a few passages in the Epistles of Paul. From Col. 4:11, 14 it appears that he was not a Jew and that his wordly calling was that of a physician. Eusebius and Jerome state that he was originally from Antioch in Syria, which may be true; but it is also possible that their statement is due to a mistaken derivation of the name Luke from Lucius (cf. Acts 13:1) instead of from Lucanus. The testimony of Origen makes us suspect this. Theophylact and Euthymius had the mistaken opinion that he was one of the Seventy sent out by our Lord. This is refuted by the preface of the Gospel, where Luke clearly distinguishes himself from those that saw and heard the Lord. Apparently the evangelist joined the company of Paul and his co-laborers on the second missionary journey at Troas. This may be inferred from the beginning of the we-sections in Acts 16:10. The first one of these sections ends at 16:17, so that Luke probably remained at Philippi. He stayed there, so it seems, until Paul returned from Greece on his third missionary journey, for in Acts 20:5 we suddenly come upon the plural pronoun of the first person again. Then he evidently accompanied the apostle to Jerusalem, 20:6, 13, 14, 15; 21:1–17. In all probability he was with Paul at Cæsarea, 27:1, from where he accompanied the apostle to Rome, 27:1–28:16. He remained at Rome during the first imprisonment, Col. 4:14; Philem. 24, and was according to these passages a beloved friend and fellow-laborer of the apostle. And when the great missionary of the gentiles was imprisoned for the second time, Luke was the only one with him, 2 Tim. 4:11, and thus gave evidence of his great attachment to Paul. The last part of Luke's life is involved in obscurity. Nothing certain can be gathered from the conflicting testimony of the fathers. Some claim that he gained a martyr's crown; others, that he died a natural death.

The question must be asked, whether Paul was in any way connected with the composition of the third Gospel. The testimony of the early Church is very uncertain on this point. Tertullian says: "Luke's digest is often ascribed to Paul. And indeed it is easy to take that for the master's which is published by the disciples." According to Eusebius, "Luke hath delivered in his Gospel a certain amount of such things as he had been assured of by his intimate acquaintance and familiarity with Paul, and his connection with the other apostles." With this the testimony of Jerome agrees. Athanasius states that the Gospel of Luke was dictated by the apostle Paul. In view of the preface of the gospel we may be sure that the Church fathers exaggerate the influence of Paul in the composition of this Gospel, possibly to give it apostolic authority. Paul's relation to the third Gospel differs from that of Peter to the second; it is not so close. Luke did not simply write what he remembered of the preaching of Paul, much less did he write according to the dictation of the apostle, for he himself says that he traced everything from the beginning and speaks of both oral and written sources that were at his command. Among these oral sources we must, of course, also reckon the preaching of Paul. That the great apostle did influence Luke's representation of "the beginning of the Gospel," is very evident. There are 175 words and expressions in the gospel that are peculiar to Luke and Paul. Cf. Plummer p. LIV. Besides, as we have already seen, some of the leading ideas of Paul are found in the third gospel, such as the universality of the Gospel, the necessity of faith, and the use of the word δικαιόω in a forensic sense, 7:29; 10:29; 16:15; 18:14. A striking resemblance exists also between Luke's account of the institution of the Lord s supper, 22:19-20. and Paul's memoir of this in 1 Cor. 11:23-25, but this may be due to the use of a common source.

The Lukan authorship of the Gospel was generally accepted up to the time, when Rationalism began its attacks on the books of the Bible. The Tübingen school, notably F. C. Baur, maintained that the Gospel of Marcion, who began to teach at Rome in 140 A. D., was the original of our Gospel.

Others followed where Baur led. In later years, however, critical opinion wheeled about completely and the opinion is generally held that Marcion's Gospel is a mutilation of Luke's, though in some parts it may represent another and even an older text. This, of course, made it possible again to maintain the authorship of Luke. But even now there are several German scholars who doubt that Luke wrote the Gospel, and Harnack's protest against their contention seems ineffective. Their objections to the Lukan authorship are based on the Acts of the Apostles rather than on the Gospel, but, as has been intimated, the two stand or fall together. We shall consider these objections, when we treat of Acts.

COMPOSITION

1. Readers and Purpose. The Gospel of Luke was first of all intended for Theophilus, who is addressed as "most excellent Theophilus" in 1:3, and is also mentioned in Acts 1:1. We have no means of determining who this Theophilus was. It has been supposed by some that the name was a general one, applied to every Christian, as a beloved one or a friend of God. But the general opinion now is, and rightly so, that it is the name of an individual, probably a Greek. The fact that he is addressed by Luke in the same manner as Felix, 23:26, 24:3, and Festus, 26:25 are addressed, led to the conclusion that he was a person of high station. Baljon thinks he was undoubtedly a Gentile Christian, while Zahn regards him as a Gentile who had not yet accepted Christ, since Luke would have addressed a brother differently. It is generally agreed, however, that the Gospel was not intended for Theophilus only, but was simply addressed to him as the representative of a large circle of readers. Who were these first readers of the gospel? Origen says that the third gospel was composed "for the sake of the Gentile converts;" Gregory Nazianze, more definitely: "Luke wrote for the Greeks." Now it is quite evident from the gospel itself that the evangelist is not writing for the Jews. He never gives the words of Jesus in the Aramaeic language; instead of ἀμὴν λέγω he has ἀληθώς λέγω, 9:27; 12:44; 21:3; for γραμματεῖς he uses νομικόι, διδάσκαλος, 2:46; 7:30; 10:25; 11:45; and of many places in Palestine he gives a nearer definition. It is very probable that that Gospel of Luke was intended for the Greeks, because Paul labored primarily among them, Theophilus was in all probability a Greek, the preface of the gospel is in many respects like those found in Greek historians, and the whole Gospel is remarkably adjusted to the

needs of the Greeks. Cf. for this last point especially Gregory, Why Four Gospels p. 207 ff.

The purpose of Luke is clearly stated in the preface, viz. that Theophilus and the Gentile readers in general might know the certainty of those things, wherein they had been instructed, 1:4. It is his desire to present clearly the truth of all Gospel facts. In order to do this, he aims at fulness of treatment; traces all things from the beginning; writes an orderly account of all that has happened, recording the sayings of the Lord in their original setting more than the other evangelists do, thus promoting definiteness and strengthening his representation of the reality of things; mentions the names not only of the principal actors in the Gospel history, but also those of others that were in any way connected with it, 2:1, 2; 3:1, 2; 7:40; 8:3; brings the Gospel facts in relation with secular history, 2:1, 2; 3:1, 2; and describes carefully the impression which the teachings of Christ made, 4:15, 22, 36; 5:8, 25; 6:11; 7:29; 8:37; 18:43; 19:37. From the contents of the Gospel we may further gather that it was the author's nearer purpose to present Christ in a very acceptable way to the Greeks, viz. as the perfect man (cf. p. 91 above), as the sympathetic friend of the afflicted and the poor, 1:52; 2:7; 4:18; 6:20; 12:15 ff. 16:19, etc., and as the Saviour of the world, seeking those that are lost, 7:36–50; 15:1–32; 18:9–14; 19:1–10; 23:43.

2. Time and Place. Tradition tells us very little regarding the time, when Luke wrote his Gospel. According to Eusebius Clement of Alexandria received a tradition from presbyters of more ancient times "that the Gospels containing the genealogies were written first." Theophylact says: "Luke wrote fifteen years after Christ's ascension." The testimony of Euthymius is to the same effect, while Eutichius states that Luke wrote his Gospel in the time of Nero. According to these testimonies the evangelist composed his Gospel possibly as early as 54, and certainly not later than 68 A. D.

Internal evidence is even more uncertain. Some infer from 21:24 that Luke realized that a certain time was to elapse between the destruction of Jerusalem and the final judgment, and therefore wrote after the destruction of the Holy City, a very inconclusive argument indeed, since this is a prophetic word of Christ. We might argue in favor of a date after the destruction of Jerusalem from the absence of the warning note that is found in both Matthew and Mark, but being an argument from silence even that does not prove the point. Several scholars, especially of the Tübingen school, date the Gospel near the end of the first or in the beginning of the second century. The main argument for this date is the supposed fact that Luke is in some parts of his Gospel dependent on the Antiquities of Josephus, a rather chimerical idea. Both Zahn and Weiss are of the opinion that Luke wrote after the destruction of Jerusalem, but not later than the year 80 A. D. Zahn settled on this terminus ad quem, because he considers it likely that Luke was a member of the Antiochian congregation as early as the year 40 A. D., and would therefore be very old in the year 80 A. D.; Weiss, since the evangelist evidently expected the second coming of Christ in his time, which was characteristic of the first generation after Christ. The great majority of conservative scholars place the composition of this Gospel somewhere between 58 and 63 A. D. The main arguments for this date are: (1) it is in harmony with ancient tradition; (2) it best explains the total silence of Luke regarding the destruction of Jerusalem; and (3) it is most in harmony with the dating of Acts in 63 A. D., which offers a good explanation of Luke's silence with respect to the death of Paul.

As to the place, where the Gospel of Luke was written tradition points to Achaia and Boeotia. We have no means of controlling this testimony, however, so that it really leaves us in ignorance. Some of the modern guesses are, Rome, Cæsarea, Asia Minor, Ephesus, and Corinth.

3. Method. In view of the preface of Luke's Gospel we have reason to believe that in the composition of it the evangelist depended on both oral tradition and written sources. In present day theories the emphasis is mainly placed on written sources, and the most prevalent hypothesis is that he employed the Gospel of Mark, either in the present form or in an earlier recension; the apostolic source Q or some διήγησις, containing this (from which two sources he derived mainly the matter that he has in common with Matthew and Mark); and a third main source of unknown character and authorship, from which he drew the narrative of the nativity, chs. 1, 2, and the account of the last journey to Jerusalem, contained in 9:51–18:14. Zahn also believes that Luke employed Mark as one of his sources, but does not attempt to give a nearer definition of the other sources used. The opinion that he drew part of his material from Josephus deserves but a passing notice. It seems to us that it is impossible to determine exactly what sources Luke used; all we can say is: (1) Having been an associate of Paul for several years, part of which he spent in Palestine, where he had abundant opportunity to meet other apostles and eyewitnesses of the Lord's works, he must have gathered a large store of knowledge from oral tradition, which he utilized in the composition of his gospel. This accounts for a

great deal of the matter which he has in common with Matthew and Mark. (2) During the time of his research in Palestine he also became acquainted with a goodly number of διηγήσεις, narratives of the Gospel facts, of which we can no more determine the exact nature, and drew on them for a part of his material. One of these probably contained the matter found in chs. 1 and 2, and in 9:51–18:14. (3) It does not seem likely that Luke read either the Gospel of Matthew or that of Mark, and classed them or either one of them with the previous attempts, on which he desired to improve. Oral tradition in connection with the guidance of the Holy Spirit is quite sufficient to explain the resemblance between these Gospels and that of Luke.

CANONICAL SIGNIFICANCE

The canonicity of this Gospel is well attested. Says Alexander in his work on the Canon p. 177: "The same arguments by which the canonical authority of the Gospels of Matthew and Mark was established, apply with their full force to the Gospel of Luke. It was universally received as canonical by the whole primitive Church—has a place in every catalogue of the books of the New Testament, which was ever published—is constantly referred to and cited by the Fathers as a part of sacred Scripture—and was one of the books constantly read in the churches, as a part of the rule of faith and practice for all believers." There are in all 16 witnesses before the end of the second century that testify to its use and general acceptance in the Church.

The gospel of Luke presents to us Christ especially as one of the human race, the Seed of the woman, in his saving work not only for Israel, but also for the Gentiles. Hence it pictures him as the friend of the poor and as seeking sinners, emphasizes the universality of the Gospel blessings, and distinctly bespeaks a friendly relation to the Samaritans. Its permanent spiritual value is that it reminds the Church of all ages that in every nation he that feareth God, and worketh righteousness, is accepted with him; and that we have a great High Priest that was touched with the feeling of our infirmities, and was in all parts tempted like as we are, yet without sin.

— CHAPTER

6

The Gospel of John

CONTENTS

The contents of the Gospel of John is also divided into five parts:

I. The Advent and Incarnation of the Word, 1:1-13. John takes his point of departure in the pre-existence and divine origin of Christ, and points out that He was heralded by John the Baptist, was the light of the world and gave believers the power to become the children of God.

II. The Incarnate Word the only Life of the World, 1:14-6:71. The evangelist records the testimony to the grace and truth of the incarnate Word given by John the Baptist and by Christ himself in word and deed, 1:14-2:11; and the self-revelation of Christ in the cleansing of the temple, 2:12-32; in the conversation with Nicodemus, 3:1-21; followed by the public testimony of John 3:22-36; in the conversation with the Samaritan woman, 4:1-42; and in the healing of the nobleman's son, 4:43-54. More particularly he shows, how Christ reveals himself as the author and sustainer of life in the healing of the impotent man and its vindication, 5:1-47; and in the miracle of the loaves with the following discourse, leading to desertion on the one and to confession on the other hand, 6:1-71.

III. The Incarnate Word, the Life and Light, in Conflict with Spiritual Darkness, 7:1-11:54. On the feast of tabernacles Christ reminds the Jews of the fact that He is the life of the world, and presents himself to them as the water of life, wherefore officers were sent to take him, 7:1-52. The following day He brings out the spiritual darkness of the Jews in connection with the adulterous woman, and declares that He is the light of the world, the only light that can truly enlighten them; and that He only could liberate them from their spiritual bondage; which leads to an attempt to stone him, 8:1-59. On a subsequent occasion He proves himself to be the light of the world by healing the blind man and speaks of himself as the good Shepherd that lays down his life for his sheep; thereby provoking unbelief and rage, 9:1–10:21. At the feast of the dedication He declares that He and the Father are one, which again leads to an attempt to stone him, 10:22–42. In raising Lazarus Jesus presents himself as the resurrection and the life, thus leading some of the people to believe in him, but his enemies to the settled purpose to kill him, 11:1–54.

IV. The Incarnate Word saving the Life of the World through his Sacrificial Death, 11:55–19:42. The enemies plan to kill Jesus, but Mary of Bethany anoints him and the people meet him with glad hosannas; the Greeks seek him at Jerusalem, but the multitude turns from him in unbelief, 11:55–12:50. He sits at the Paschal supper with his disciples, gives them a lesson in humble service, exposes the traitor and announces that the time has now come to leave his disciples, 13:1–38. He discourses on the significance of his departure and on the new life in communion with the Father, 14:1–16:33; and offers the intercessory prayer committing his followers to the Father, 17:1–26. In Gethsemane He is taken captive, and after a preliminary hearing before the high priest is brought before Pilate who, though finding no guilt in Jesus, yet delivers him into the hands of the Jews to be crucified, 18:1–16. After his crucifixion He is buried by Joseph and Nicodemus, 19:17–42.

V. The Incarnate Word, risen from the Dead, the Saviour and Lord of all Believers, 20:1–21:25. Having risen from the dead, Jesus appears to Mary Magdalena and on two successive Lord's days to his disciples, 20:1–31. Later He is seen by some of his disciples at the sea of Tiberias, where He restores Peter and points significantly to the career of John, the writer of the Gospel, 21:1–25.

CHARACTERISTICS

Of the characteristics that mark the fourth Gospel the following especially are to be noted:

1. The gospel of John emphasizes more than any of the others the Divinity of Christ. It has no historical starting-point, like the Synoptics, but recedes back into the depths of eternity, and starts out with the statement sublime in its simplicity: "In the beginning was the Word, and the Word was with God, and the Word was God." Positively, the Logos-doctrine is peculiar to this Gospel; negatively, every indication of Christ's human development and of his gradually awakening self-consciousness is strikingly absent from it. We find no genealogy here, no description of Christ's birth with it's attendant circumstances, and no narrative of his baptism and

temptation. John the Baptist testifies to his Divinity, as soon as He enters on the scene, and He himself publicly claims this prerogative almost from the beginning of his public ministry, cf. 3:13; 5:17 ff; 6:32, 40 ff., etc. The miracles of the Lord, narrated in this Gospel, are of such a character that they give great prominence to his divine power. The nobleman's son was cured from a distance, 4:46 ff.; the man at Bethesda had been infirm thirty-eight years, 5:5; the blind man at Jerusalem had been born blind, 9:1; and Lazarus had already lain in the grave four days, 11:17.

2. The teaching of Christ greatly predominates in john's Gospel, but this is quite different from that contained in the Synoptics. We find no parables here but elaborate discourses, which also contain a couple of allegories. The all-absorbing topic is not the Kingdom of God but the Person of the Messiah. The simple rudimentary teaching regarding the Kingdom is here replaced by a more penetrating (though not developed) instruction in the deeper realities of faith. In connection with his miracles or other historical facts Christ presents himself as the source of life, 4:46–5:47; the spiritual nourishment of the soul, 6:22–65; the water of life, 4:7–16; 7:37, 38; the true liberator, 8:31–58; the light of the world, 9:5, 35–41; and the living principle of the resurrection, 11:25, 26. The farewell discourses of the Saviour, besides containing many profound truths respecting his personal relation to believers, are also significant on account of their clear references to the coming Paraclete.

3. The scene of action in this Gospel is quite different from that in the Synoptics. In the latter the work of Christ in Galilee is narrated at length, while He is seen at Jerusalem only during the last week of His life. In the Gospel of John, on the other hand, the long ministry of Christ in Galilee is presupposed rather than narrated, while his work and teaching in Judea and particularly at Jerusalem is made very prominent. The great feasts afforded the occasion for this work and are therefore distinctly mentioned. John speaks of three, possibly four, Passovers, 2:13; 5:1; 6:4; 13:1; of the feast of Tabernacles, 7:2; and of the feast of the Dedication, 10:22.

4. The Gospel of John is far more definite than the Synoptics in pointing out the time and place of the occurrences that are narrated; it is in a certain sense more chronological than the other Gospels. We are generally informed as to the place of Christ's operation. Definite mention is made of Bethany, 1:28; Cana, 2:1; Capernaum, 2:12; Jerusalem, 2:13; Sychar, 4:5; Bethesda, 5:2, etc. The designations of time are equally distinct, sometimes the hour of the day being given. The chronological framework of the gospel

is found in its reference to the great feasts. John the Baptist sees Christ coming to him the day after he had met the delegation from Jerusalem, 1:29; and again on the following day, 1:35. A day later Christ called Philip and Nathanael, 1:43-51; on the third day there was a marriage in Cana, 2:1; it was at the sixth hour that Christ sat down at the well, 4:6; at the seventh, that the nobleman's son was cured, 4:52; in the midst of the feast that Jesus went into the temple, 7:14; and again on the last great day, 7:37; and about the sixth hour that Christ was delivered unto the Jews by Pilate, 19:14.

5. The style of the fourth Gospel is not like that of the other three. It is peculiar in that "it contains, on the one hand, except in the prologue and χαρᾷ χαίρει in 3:29, hardly any downright Hebraisms," Simcox, The Writers of the New Testament p. 73, while, on the other hand, it approaches the style of Old Testament writers more than the style of any other New Testament writing does. John evidently commanded a fairly good Greek vocabulary, but does not attempt any elaborate sentences. Rather than do this, he will repeat part of a previous statement and then add a new element to it. His sentences are generally connected in the most simple way by καί, δέ or οὖν, and his descriptions are often elaborate and repetitious. He exhibits a special fondness for contrasts and for the use of the parallelismus membrorum. A very characteristic expression of his is ζωὴ αἰώνος, which occurs 17 times in the Gospel. For other phrases and expressions see Simcox. He also employs several Aramaean words, as ῥαββί, ῥαββουνὶ, κηφᾶς, μεσσίας, Γαββαθά, Γολγοθά ἀμὴν ἀνήν.

AUTHORSHIP

The voice of antiquity is all but unanimous in ascribing the fourth Gospel to John. The Monarchian sect, called by Epiphanius, "the Alogi," forms the only exception. Little is known of this sect, except that it rejected the doctrine of the Logos. Salmon says: "In fact I now believe that "the Alogi" consisted of Caius and, as far as I can learn, of nobody else." Introd. p. 229. The internal evidence for the authorship of the Gospel is now generally arranged under the following heads:

1. The author was a Jew. He evidently had an intimate acquaintance with the Old Testament, had, as it were, imbibed the spirit of the prophetical writings. He knew them not only in the translation of the LXX, but in their original language, as is evident from several Old Testament quotations. Moreover the style of the author clearly reveals his Jewish nationality. He wrote Greek, it is true, but his construction, his circumstantiality and his

use of parallelism, are all Hebraic. "There is a Hebrew soul living in the language of the evangelist." Luthardt, St. John the Author of the Fourth Gospel, p. 166. Ewald comes to the conclusion, "that the Greek language of the author bears in itself still the clearest and strongest mark of a genuine Hebrew, who born among the Jews in the Holy Land, and grown up in this society without speaking Greek, carries in himself the whole spirit and breath of his mother-tongue even in the midst of the Greek raiment that he afterwards learnt to cast about him, and has no hesitation to let himself be led by that spirit." Quoted by Luthardt, p. 167.

2. The author was a Palestinian Jew. He clearly shows that he is well at home in the Jewish world. He is intimately acquainted with Jewish customs and religious observances and with the requirements of the law, and moves about with ease in the Jewish world of thought. He knows that, according to the strict Jewish conception, it was unlawful to heal on the sabbath, 5:1 ff.; 9:14 ff.; and also that circumcision was allowed, 7:22 ff. He is aware of the Jewish expectation of Elijah, 1:21; and of the ill-feeling between the Jews and the Samaritans, 4:9. He understood that the Jews regarded a misfortune as the result of some particular sin, 9:2; and that they considered one unclean who had entered the house of a Gentile, 18:28. He is thoroughly acquainted with Jerusalem, 5:2; with the valley of Sichem and mount Gerezim, 4:5 ff.; with the temple, 8:20; and with Capernaum and other places around the sea of Galilee, 7.

3. The writer was an eyewitness of the events he relates. He claims this explicitly, if not already in 1:14, "we beheld his glory" (Cf. 1 John 1:1–3), certainly in 19:35. "And he that saw it bare record, and his record is true; and he knoweth that he saith true that ye might believe." This claim is corroborated by the lively and yet simple manner in which he pictures the events; by the many definite chronological data and naming of localities, to which we have already referred; and by the great prominence given to certain individuals with whom Jesus came in contact.

4. The author was the apostle John. He often makes mention in his Gospel of a disciple whom he never names, but to whom he constantly refers as "the (an) other disciple," or as "the disciple whom Jesus loved." Cf. 13:23; 18:15; 19:26; 20:2, 3, 4, 8; 21:7. At the close of his Gospel he says of him: "This is the disciple which testifieth these things; and we know that his testimony is true," 21:24. Who was this disciple? The evangelist names only seven of the disciples of the Lord, the five that are not named being John and his brother James, Matthew, Simon the Canaanite and James the

son of Alpheus. Now it is evident from 1:35-41 that said disciple was one of the first ones called by the Lord, and these according to Mark 1:16-19 were Peter, Andrew, John and James. The first two are explicitly named in John 1:41-43, so that the one whose name is suppressed must have been either John or James. But we cannot think of James as the author of this Gospel, since he died a martyr's death as early as A. D. 44. Therefore John must have been the writer.

According to Mt. 27:56 and Mk. 1:20; 15:40, John was the son of Zebedee and Salome who probably belonged to the middle class of society. His mother was among the faithful followers of the Saviour, Mt. 27:56; Mk. 16:1. He was one of the very first followers of Jesus and soon appears as one of the innermost circle of the disciples, one of the three that always accompany the Saviour. With the Lord he enters the dwelling of Jairus, ascends the mount of transfiguration and penetrates into the dark recesses of Gethsemane. As he stands by the cross, the mother of Jesus is entrusted to his care. On the morning of the resurrection he is one of the first to visit the grave of the Saviour. In the first part of the Acts of the Apostles he appears as one of the faithful witnesses of the resurrection of the Lord. After that we lose sight of John in Scripture, but tradition tells us that he spent the last part of his life in Asia Minor, especially at Ephesus, where he died in venerable age.

There is an apparent contradiction between the synoptical data regarding the character of John and the conception of it derived from his own writings, but this is easily explained. The very first indication of his character we glean from the statement in Mk. 3:17, that the Lord named him and his brother James "Boanerges, which is, the sons of thunder." This conveys the idea of an ardent temper, of great strength and vehemence of character. And on two occasions we find that they reveal just such traits, viz. when they peremptorily forbade one who was casting out devils in the name of Jesus to continue this, Mk. 9:38; Lk. 9:49; and when they desired permission to command fire to come down from heaven to devour the Samaritans, Lk. 9:54. In both cases the Lord reproves their show of temper. Another trait of their character is revealed in their request to sit in the places of honor in the future Kingdom of Jesus, Mt. 20:20-24; Mk. 10:35-41. Their ambition was such as to offend the other disciples and to call forth a severe rebuke from the Lord. John was, no doubt, zealous for the Lord, but his zeal was mistaken; he had a passionate desire to be near his Master, but he showed this in a manner that was not free from selfishness and pride.

The Lord directed his zeal and ambition into other channels by pointing out their unspiritual character and by teaching him that one can be great in the Kingdom of God only by being the servant of one's brethren. This undoubtedly made a profound impression on the sensitive John and begot within him the habit of introspection, of self-examination. He became more quiet, more reserved with an inclination to ponder on the mysteries that he encountered in his daily association with the Lord, and penetrated farther than the other disciples into the hidden depths of the mysterious life of Christ. As a result John, as he reveals himself in his writings, is quite different from the John of the Synoptics. From his Gospel and Epistles we learn to know him as a man of deep religious feeling, beloved of Christ; a man that lived in close communion with his Lord, a communion more spiritual, however, than he desired in his youthful years. His exclusivism has made place for a love that would embrace all; his zeal is still operative, but it has been sanctified and led into proper channels; his strength has become a tower of defense for spiritual truth.

Not until the last part of the eighteenth century was the authorship of John attacked on critical grounds, and even then the attacks were of small significance. Bretschneider in 1820 was the first to assail it in a systematic way. But he was soon followed by others, such as Baur, Strauss, Schwegler, Zeller, Scholten, Davidson, Wrede e. a. It has been their persistent endeavor to show that the Gospel of John is a product of the second century. Some would ascribe it to that shadowy person, the presbyter John, whose existence Eusebius infers from a rather ambiguous passage of Papias, but who, in all probability, is to be identified with John the apostle. Others positively reject this theory. Wrede, after arguing that the authorship of John cannot be established, says: "Far less can the recent hypothesis be regarded as proven which purports to find the author of the Gospel in John the presbyter." The Origin of the New Testament p. 89.

The most important considerations that led many rationalistic critics to the conclusion that the fourth Gospel was written in the second century, are the following: (1) The theology of the Gospel, especially its representation of Christ, is developed to such a degree that it points beyond the first and reflects the consciousness of the Church of the second century. (2) The Gospel was evidently written under the influence of the philosophic and religious tendencies that were prevalent in the second century, such as Montanism, Docetism and Gnosticism. (3) The great difference between the fourth Gospel and the Synoptics appears to be the result of second century cavilling respecting the nature of Christ, and of the Paschal controversy.

But the idea that the Gospel of John is a second century product goes counter to both the internal evidence to which we already referred, and to the external testimony, which is exceptionally strong and which can be traced back to the very beginning of the second century. Some of the Epistles of Ignatius show the influence of John's Christology, and the writings of both Papias and Polycarp contain allusions to the first Epistle of John, which was evidently written at the same time as the Gospel. The latter was in existence, therefore, in the beginning of the second century. The theology of the Gospel of John is no more developed than that of Paul's Epistles to the Ephesians and the Colossians, that were written between A. D. 61 and 63. Critics generally ceased to place any reliance on the so-called Montanistic features of the Gospel, and although they still maintain that some passages contain traces of a Docetic Gnosticism, these are purely imaginary and readily vanish, when the light of exegesis is turned on. The connection of the Gospel with the Paschal controversy is now admitted to be very dubious. And the difference between it and the Synoptics can be satisfactorily explained without regarding it as a work of the second century. Cf. above p. 19 ff.

Critics of the Tübingen school, who accepted the Johannine authorship of the Apocalypse, were wont to deny that John had written the Gospel, because it differed in so many respects from the former work. At present this argument is not insisted on, because scholars are not so sure as they once were, that John wrote the book of Revelation. Reuss, who still argues in that fashion, says: "It must be admitted that even in the most recent times the decision of the question as to the apostolic genuineness of the Apocalypse has by both sides been made to depend upon a previously formed judgment as to the fourth Gospel." History of the N. T., I p. 161.

COMPOSITION

1. Readers and Purpose. The Gospel of John was in all probability written primarily for the Christians of Asia Minor, among whom especially the heresy of Cerinthus had arisen. Early tradition has it that John wrote it at the request of the bishops of Asia to combat that heresy. Internal evidence certainly favors the hypothesis that it was composed for Greek readers. The author carefully interprets Hebrew and Aramaeic words, as in 1:38, 41, 42; 9:7; 11:16; 19:13, 17; 20:16. He makes it a point to explain Jewish

customs and geographical designations, 1:28; 2:1; 4:4, 5; 11:54, ... 7:37; 19:31, 40, 42. Moreover, notwithstanding his characteristically Hebrew style, he usually quotes from the Septuagint.

It was not John's purpose to furnish a supplement to the Synoptics, though his Gospel certainly contains a good deal of supplemental matter; neither did he mean to produce a direct polemic against the Cerinthian heresy, even if this did to a certain degree determine his special way of stating the truth. He did not aim at conciliating the discordant parties of the second century by leading them up to a higher unity, as the Tübingen school asserted; nor at refuting "Jewish objections and invectives," and at providing "his fellow-Christians with weapons ready to hand;" a hypothesis of which Wrede asserts: "This view is on the whole a recent one, but it is making victorious progress among scholars." The Origin of the New Testament, p. 84.

The apostle himself gives expression to his purpose, when he says: "These things are written that ye might believe that Jesus is the Christ, the Son of God; and that believing, ye might have life in his name," 20:31. His aim is twofold, therefore, theoretical and practical. He desires to prove that Jesus is the Christ, the Son of God, and to lead believers to a life of blessed communion with him. The means he employs to that end are: (1) The miracles of the Lord, on which special emphasis is placed, cf. 20:30; 21:25; and which are contemplated as σημεῖα, as signs of the divine glory of Christ. (2) The long discourses of the Saviour, which serve to interpret his signs and to describe the unique relation in which He stands to the Father. And (3) the narratives touching Jesus' dealing with individuals, such as Nathanael, Nicodemus, the Samaritan woman, Philip, Mary Magdalena and Thomas, showing, how He led them to faith, a faith culminating in the confession of Thomas: "My Lord and my God."

2. Time and Place. Since John was undoubtedly the writer of the fourth Gospel, we have a terminus ad quem in A. D. 98, for Irenaeus says that John lived to the time of Trajan, who began his reign in that year. The testimony of Jerome is to the same effect: "The apostle John lived in Asia to the time of Trajan, and dying at a great age in the sixty-eighth year of our Lord's passion, was buried near the city of Ephesus." The same writer places the death of John in A. D. 100. In all probability, however, John wrote his Gospel several years before his death, since its style is, as Alford remarks, "that of a matured, but not of an aged writer." Prolegomena to the Gospels Ch. V., Sec. VI, 10. It is not an easy matter to find a terminus a quo. We may be

sure that the apostle did not compose the Gospel until after the death of Paul in A. D. 68. The congregations of Asia Minor were the special charge of the great apostle of the Gentiles, and he never makes any mention in his Epistles of john's being in their midst, nor does he send him a single salutation; and when he parted from the Ephesian elders, he evidently did not anticipate the coming of an apostle among them. Moreover we infer from 21:19 that John knew of the manner in which Peter died, and presupposes this knowledge in his readers. Therefore it is unlikely that the Gospel was written before A. D. 70. Bengel in his Gnomon infers from the use of the present tense in 5:2 that Jerusalem was still intact. But this argument is not conclusive, since the city was not completely demolished by the Romans, and because we can with equal propriety conclude from 11:18 that both Jerusalem and Bethany had been swept off the face of the earth. John's utter silence regarding the destruction of the city favors the idea that he wrote the Gospel several years after that calamity. Zahn would date the Gospel after A. D. 80, his terminus ad quem for the composition of Luke's Gospel, since tradition teaches that John wrote later than the Synoptics. Among rationalistic critics the most divergent dates are suggested. Baur held that the Gospel was composed between A. D. 160 and 170. At present the tendency is to revert to some date nearer the limits indicated above. Thus Pfleiderer dates it A. D. 140; Hilgenfeld believes that it originated between A. D. 130 and 140. Harnack and Jülicher are not inclined to place it later than A. D. 110, and the former even admits that it may have been written as early as A. D. 80.

Tradition points to Ephesus as the place of composition. Origen testifies "that John, having lived long in Asia, was buried at Ephesus." This is confirmed by Polycrates, a bishop of Ephesus. Jerome says: "John wrote a Gospel at the desire of the bishops of Asia." And Cosmas of Alexandria informs us definitely that John composed his Gospel, while dwelling at Ephesus. There is no reason to doubt this testimony.

3. Method. John's Gospel is evidently of an autoptic character. He may have read the Synoptics before he composed his work, but he did not use them as sources from which he drew a part of his material. In several places the author indicates that he related what he had seen and heard, cf. 1:14; 13:23; 18:15; 19:26, 35; 20:2. Compare what he says in his first Epistle 1:1–3. While the Synoptic Gospels were in all probability based to a great extent on oral tradition and written sources, neither of these played an appreciable part in the composition of the fourth Gospel. John, who had

carefully stored in memory the profound discourses of the Lord regarding his own Person, discourses that made a deep and lasting impression on the beloved disciple, drew on that fountain of knowledge and, guided by the Holy Spirit in all the truth, supplied us with an exact record of the signs and words of the Saviour.

It has often been remarked that there is a great difference between the style of Christ's discourses in the Synoptics and that of those contained in the fourth Gospel; and that in this gospel there is so much similarity between the narrative of the evangelist and the discourses of the Saviour that it seems as if John clothed these in his own language. But the Synoptics and John have so little such matter in common that we cannot safely build a conclusion on it, and in the discourses of Christ which they do have in common no great difference of style in observable. And as far as the second point is concerned, it may be, as Alford thinks probable, that the Lord influenced John so profoundly that the latter's style became very similar to that of the Master. But even if John did reproduce the discourses of the Saviour in his own style and language, we may rest assured that he gives us the exact teaching of the Lord.

CANONICAL SIGNIFICANCE

The Gospel of John was accepted as canonical in all parts of the Church from the earliest time, the only exceptions being the Alogi and Marcion. It is true, the apostolic fathers do not quote it, but the writings of three of them show traces either of it or of the first Epistle. Among the Church fathers Irenaeus, Clement of Alexandria, Tertullian, Origen, Justin Martyr, Jerome e. a. either freely quote it, or refer to it as an integral part of the Word of God. Moreover it is included in Tatian's Diatessaron, the Muratori canon, and the Syriac and old Latin Versions. In all at least nineteen witnesses testify to the use and recognition of the Gospel before the end of the second century.

The great significance of this Gospel in Holy Writ is that it places prominently before us the Son of Man as the Son of God, as the eternal Word that became flesh. According to this Gospel Christ is the Son of God, who descended from the Father, stood in a unique relation to the Father, had come to do the Father's will on earth, and would return to the glory that He had eternally possessed with the Father, that He might send the Holy Spirit from the Father to abide with his Church throughout all ages. In that Spirit He himself returns to his followers to dwell in them forever. He is the highest revelation of God, and our relation to him, either of faith or of unbelief, determines our eternal destiny. Before this Christ the Church bows down in adoration with Thomas and calls out: "My Lord and my God."

7

The Acts of the Apostles

The contents of this book is naturally divided into two parts; in each of which the main topic is the establishment of the Church from a certain center:

I. The establishment of the Church from Jerusalem, 1:1-12:25. In this part we first have the last discourse of Christ to his disciples, the ascension, the choice of an apostle in the place of Judas, the fulfilment of the promise in the outpouring of the Holy Spirit and the conversion of three thousand, 1:1-2:47. Then follows the healing of the lame man by Peter and John; their faithful witnessing for Christ in the temple, for which they were taken captive by the priests, the captain of the temple and the Sadducees; their release, since the enemies feared the people; and their thanksgiving for deliverance, 3:1-4:31. Next the condition of the Church is described: they had all things in common, and severe punishment was meted out to Ananias and Sapphira for their deception, 4:32-5:11. On account of their words and works the apostles were again imprisoned, but delivered by the angel of the Lord; they were brought before the council of the Jews and dismissed after a warning, 5:12-42. The murmuring of the Grecians leads to the appointment of seven deacons, one of which, viz. Stephen, wrought miracles among the people, and after witnessing for Christ before the council, became the first Christian martyr, 6:1-7:60. This is followed by a description of the persecution of the Church and the resulting scattering of believers, of the work of Philip in Samaria, of Saul's conversion, and of Peter's healing of Eneas and raising of Tabitha, 8:1-9:43. Then we have Peter's vision of the descending vessel, his consequent preaching to the household of Cornelius, and the defense of his course before the brethren in Judea, 10:1-11:18. The narrative of the establishment of the Church at Antioch, of James' martyrdom, and of the imprisonment and miraculous deliverance of Peter concludes this section, 11:19-12:25.

II. The Establishment of the Church from Antioch, 13:1-28:31. From Antioch Barnabas and Saul set out on the first missionary journey, including visits to Cyprus, Pisidian Antioch, Iconium, Lystra and Derbe, from where they returned to Antioch, 13:1-14:28. Then an account is given of the council of Jerusalem and its decisions affecting the Gentiles, 15:1-34. After his contention with Barnabas, Paul starts out on the second missionary journey with Silas, passing through the Cilician gates to Derbe, Lystra, Iconium and Troas, whence he was directed by a vision to pass into Europe, where he visited Philippi, Thessalonica, Berea, Athens and Corinth, preaching the gospel and establishing churches. From Corinth he again returned to Jerusalem and Antioch, 15:35-18:22. Shortly after Paul began his third missionary journey, going through Asia Minor, staying at Ephesus for over two years, and passing into Corinth, from where he again returned to Jerusalem by way of Troas, Ephesus and Cesarea, 18:23-21:16. At Jerusalem the Jews sought to kill him, his defense both on the steps of the castle and before the Sanhedrin merely inciting greater rage and leading to a positive determination to kill him, 21:17-23:14. A conspiracy leads to Paul's deportation to Cesarea, where he defends his course before Felix, Festus and Agrippa, and on account of the unfair treatment received at the hands of these governors, appeals to Cæsar, 23:15-26:32. From Cesarea he is sent to Rome, suffers shipwreck on the way, performs miracles of healing on the island Melita, and on reaching his destination preaches the gospel to the Jews and remains a prisoner at Rome for two years, 27:1-28:31.

CHARACTERISTICS

1. The great outstanding feature of this book is that it acquaints us with the establishment of Christian churches, and indicates their primary organization. According to it churches are founded at Jerusalem, 2:41-47; Judea, Galilee and Samaria, 9:31; Antioch, 11:26; Asia Minor, 14:23; 16:5; Philippi, 16:40; Thessalonica, 17:10; Berea, 17:14; Corinth, 18:18, and Ephesus, 20:17-38. From the sixth chapter we learn of the institution of the deacon's office, and from 14:23 and 20:17-38 it is clear that elders, also called bishops, were already appointed.

2. The narrative which it contains centers about two persons, viz. Peter and Paul, the first establishing the Jewish, the second the Gentile churches. Consequently it contains several discourses of these apostles, as Peter's sermon on the day of Pentecost, 2:14-36; and in the temple, 3:12-26; his defenses before the Jewish council, 4:8-12; 5:29-32; his sermon in the house

of Cornelius, 10:34-43; and his defense before the brethren in Judea, 11:4-18. And of Paul the book contains the sermons preached at Antioch, 13:16-41; at Lystra, 14:15-18; and at Athens, 17:22-31; his address to the Ephesian elders, 20:18-35; and his defenses before the Jews on the stairs of the castle, 22:1-21; before the Sanhedrin 23:1-6; and before Felix and Agrippa, 24:10-21; 26:2-29.

3. The many miracles recorded in this writing constitute one of its characteristic features. Besides the miracles that are not described and of which there were many "signs and wonders" by the apostles, 2:43; 5:12, 15, 16; by Stephen, 6:8; by Philip, 8:7; by Paul and Barnabas, 14:3; and also by Paul alone, 19:11, 12; 28:1-9;—the following miracles are specifically described: the gift of tongues, 2:1-11; the lame man cured, 3:1-11; the shaking of the prayer hall, 4:31; the death of Ananias and Sapphira, 5:1-11; the apostles delivered from prison, 5:19; the translation of Philip, 8:39, 40; Eneas made whole, 9:34; Dorcas restored to life, 9:36-42; Paul's sight restored, 9:17; the deliverance of Peter from prison, 12:6-10; the death of Herod, 12:20-23; Elymas, the sorcerer, struck blind, 13:6-11; the lame man at Lystra cured, 14:8-11; the damsel at Philippi delivered, 16:16-18; the jail at Philippi shaken, 16:25, 26; Eutychus restored to life, 20:9-12; Paul unhurt by the bite of a poisonous viper, 28:1-6; the father of Publius and many others healed, 28:8, 9.

4. The style of this book is very similar to that of the third Gospel, though it contains less Hebraisms. Simcox says that "the Acts is of all the books included in the New Testament the nearest to contemporary, if not to classical literary usage,—the only one, except perhaps the Epistle to the Hebrews, where conformity to a standard of classical correctness is consciously aimed at." The Writers of the New Testament, p. 16. The tone is most Hebraic in the first part of the book, especially in the sermons in chs. 2 and 13 and in the defense of Stephen ch. 7, in all of which the Old Testament element is very large;—and it is most Hellenic in the last part of the book, as in the epistle of the church at Jerusalem, the letter of Lysias, the speech of Tertullus, and the defense of Paul before Agrippa. This is undoubtedly due to the fact that the first part of the book deals primarily with Jewish, and last part especially with Gentile Christianity.

TITLE

The Greek title of the book is πράξεις ἀποστόλων, Acts of Apostles. There is no entire uniformity in the MSS. in this respect. The Sinaiticus has simply πράξεις, although it has the regular title at the close of the book. Codex D is peculiar in having πράξις ἀποστόλων, Way of acting of the Apostles. We do not regard the title as proceeding from the author, but from one of the transcribers; nor do we consider it a very happy choice. On the one hand the title, if translated, as is done in both the Authorized and the Revised Version, by "The Acts of the Apostles," is too comprehensive, since there are but two apostles whose acts are recorded in this book, viz. Peter and Paul. On the other hand it is too restricted, because the book contains not only several acts, but also many words of these apostles; and also, since it records besides these acts and words of other persons, such as Stephen, Philip and Barnabas.

AUTHORSHIP

The voice of the ancient Church is unanimous in ascribing this book to Luke, the author of the third Gospel. Irenaeus in quoting passages from it repeatedly uses the following formula: "Luke the disciple and follower of Paul says thus." Clement of Alexandria, quoting Paul's speech at Athens, introduces it by, "So Luke in the Acts of the Apostles relates." Eusebius says: "Luke has left us two inspired volumes, the Gospel and the Acts." The external testimony for the Lukan authorship is as strong as we could wish for.

Now the question arises, whether the internal evidence agrees with this. The book does not directly claim to have been written by Luke. Our Scriptural evidence for the authorship is of an inferential character. It seems to us that the Lukan authorship is supported by the following considerations:

1. The we-sections. These are the following sections, 16:10-17; 20:5-15; and 27:1-28:16, in which the pronoun of the first person plural is found, implying that the author was a companion of Paul in part of the apostle's travels. Since Paul had several associates, different names have been suggested for the author of this book, as Timothy, Silas, Titus and Luke, who according to Col. 4:14; Philemon 24; and 2 Tim. 4:11, was also one of the apostle's companions and best friends. The first two persons named are excluded, however, by the way in which they are spoken of in 16:19 and 20:4, 5. And so little can be said in favor of Titus that it is now quite generally agreed that Luke was the author of the we-sections. But if this is true, he is also the author of the book, for the style of the book is similar throughout; there are cross-references from the we-sections to the other parts of the book, as f. i. in 21:8, where Philip is introduced as one of the seven, while we know only from ch. 6 who the seven were, and from 8:40,

how Philip came to be in Cesarea; and it is inconceivable that a later writer should have incorporated the we-sections in his work in such a skillful manner that the lines of demarcation cannot be discovered, and should at the same time leave the tell-tale pronoun of the first person undisturbed.

2. The medical language. Dr. Hobart has clearly pointed out this feature in both the Gospel of Luke and the Acts of the Apostles. Some make light of this argument, but Zahn says: "W. K. Hobart hat für Jeden, dem Überhaupt etwas zu beweisen ist, bewiesen, dass der Verfasser des lucanischen Werks em mit der Kunstsprache der griechischen Medicin vertrauter Mann, ein griechischer Arzt gewesen ist." Einl. II p. 429. We find instances of this medical language in ἀχλύς, 13:11; παραλελυμένος, 8:7; 9:33; πυρετοῖς κὰι δυσεντερία συνερχόμενον, 25:8.

3. Assuming that Luke wrote the third Gospel, a comparison of Acts with that work also decidedly favors the Lukan authorship, for: (1) The style of these two books is similar, the only difference being that the second book is less Hebraistic than the first,—a difference that finds a ready explanation in the sources used and in the author's method of composition. (2) Both books are addressed to the same person, viz. Theophilus, who was, so it seems, a special friend of the author. (3) In the opening verse of Acts the author refers to a first book that he had written. Taking the points just mentioned in consideration, this can be no other than our third Gospel, though Baljon, following Scholten, denies this. Geschiedenis v/d Boeken des N. V. p. 421.

4. The book contains clear evidence of having been written by a companion of Paul. This follows not only from the we-sections, but also from the fact that, as even unfriendly critics admit, the author shows himself well acquainted with the Pauline diction. We have reasons to think that he did not derive this acquaintance from a study of Paul's Epistles; and if this is true, the most rational explanation is that he was an associate of Paul and heard the great apostle speak on several occasions. Moreover the author's characterization of Paul is so detailed and individualized as to vouch for personal acquaintance.

The authorship of Luke has not found general acceptance among New Testament scholars. The main objections to it appear to be the following: (1) The book is said to show traces of dependence on the Antiquities of Josephus, a work that was written about A. D. 93 or 94. The reference to Theudas and Judas in 5:36, 37 is supposed to rest on a mistaken reading of Josephus, Ant. XX, V, 1, 2. (2) The standpoint of the author is claimed to be that of a second century writer, whose Christianity is marked by universality, and who aims at reconciling the opposing tendencies of his time. (3) The work is held by some to be historically so inaccurate, and to reveal such a wholesale acceptance of the miraculous, that it cannot have been written by a contemporary. There is supposedly a great conflict especially between Acts 15 and Galatians 2.

We cannot enter on a detailed examination of these objections; a few remarks anent them must suffice. It is by no means proven that the author read Josephus, nor that he wrote his work after the Jewish historian composed his Antiquities. Gamaliel, who makes 'the statement regarding Theudas and Judas, may very well have derived his knowledge from a different source; and his supposed mistake (which may not be a mistake after all) does not affect the authorship, nor the trustworthiness of the book. That the standpoint of the author is more advanced than that of the Pauline Epistles (Baljon) is purely imaginary; it is in perfect harmony with the other New Testament writings. And the idea of a struggle between the Petrine and Pauline factions is now generally discarded. Historical inaccuracy does not necessarily imply that a book was written a considerable time after the events. Moreover in the book of Acts there is no such inaccuracy. On the contrary, Ramsay in his, St. Paul the Traveler and the Roman Citizen has conclusively proved that this book is absolutely reliable and is a historical work of the highest order. It may be that some difficulties have not yet found an altogether satisfactory solution, but this does not militate against the authorship of Luke.

COMPOSITION

1. Readers and Purpose. It is not necessary to speak at length about the readers for whom this book was first of all intended, because like the Gospel of Luke it is addressed to Theophilus, and like it too it was undoubtedly destined for the same wider circle of readers, i. e. the Greeks.

But what was the purpose of the author in writing this book? This is a very much debated question. The book of Acts is really a continuation of the third gospel and was therefore, in all probability, also written to give Theophilus the certainty of the things narrated. We notice that in this second book, just as in the first, the author names many even of the less important actors in the events, and brings out on several occasions the relation of these events to secular history. Cf. 12:1; 18:2; 23:26; 25:1. Of what did Luke want to give Theophilus certainty? From the fact that he himself says that he wrote the first book to give his friend the certainty of the things that Jesus began to do and to teach, we infer that in the second book he intended to give him positive instruction regarding the things that Jesus continued to do and to teach through his apostles. It seems that he found his program in the words of the Saviour, 1:8: "But ye shall receive power, after that the Holy Ghost is come upon you, and ye shall be my witnesses both in Jerusalem and in all Judea, and in Samaria, and unto the uttermost parts of the earth." In harmony with this program he describes the march of Christianity from Jerusalem, the center of the Jewish Theocracy, to Rome, the center of the world. With Paul in Rome, therefore, the author's task is finished.

Opposed to this view are those that regard the book as a tendency writing, in which history has been falsified with a definite purpose. As such we have:

(1) The theory of the Tübingen school, that the book was written to conciliate the Petrine and Pauline factions in the early Church, and therefore represents Peter as more liberal, and Paul as more Judaistic than is in harmony with their own writings. The supposed parallelism between Peter and Paul, according to some, ministers to the same purpose. This theory in the bald form in which it was broached by Baur, is now generally abandoned, and has been modified in various ways.

(2) The view defended by some later scholars, such as Overbeck and Straatman, that the book of Acts is really an apology for Christianity over against the Gentiles, especially the Romans. Hence the author gives the Romans due honor, and clearly brings out the advantages which Paul derived from his Roman citizenship. He desires to convey the impression that the doctrine taught by Paul, who was protected by the mighty arm of Rome, who was acquitted of false charges by Roman governors, and who with a good conscience appealed to Cæsar himself, could not be regarded as dangerous to the state. Wrede considers this a subordinate purpose of the author.

The abiding merit of these theories is that they contemplate the book of Acts as an artistic whole. For the rest. however, they do not commend themselves to our serious consideration. The basis on which they rest is too uncertain; they are not borne out by the facts; they are inimical to the well established historicity of the book; and they come to us with the unreasonable demand, born of unbelief and aversion to the miraculous, to consider the author as a falsifier of history.

2. Time and Place. As to the time, when the book was composed little can be said with certainty. It must have been written after A. D. 63, since the author knows that Paul staid in Rome two years. But how long after that date was it written? Among conservative scholars, such as Alford, Salmon, Barde e. a. the opinion is generally held that Luke wrote his second book before the death of Paul and the destruction of Jerusalem, because no mention whatever is made of either one of these important facts. Zahn and Weiss naturally date it about A. D. 80, since they regard this date as the terminus ad quem for the composition of the third gospel. Many of the later rationalistic critics too are of the opinion that the book was written after the destruction of Jerusalem, some even placing it as late as A. D. 110 (Baljon) and 120 (Davidson). Their reasons for doing this are: (1) the supposed dependence of Luke on Josephus; (2) the assumption, based on Lk. 21:20; Acts 8:26 ff. that Jerusalem was already destroyed; and (3) the supposed fact that the state of affairs in the book points to a time, when the state had begun to persecute Christians on political grounds. None of these reasons are conclusive, and we see no reasons to place the book later than A. D. 63.

The place of composition was in all probability Rome.

3. Method. The problem of the sources used by Luke in the composition of this book has given rise to several theories, that we cannot discuss here. And it is not necessary that we should do this, because, as Zahn maintains, none of these repeated attempts has attained any measure of probability; and Headlam says: "The statement of them is really a sufficient condemnation." Hastings D. B. Art. Acts of the Apostles. For a good discussion of the various theories of Van Manen, Sorof, Spitta and Clemen cf. Knowling's Introduction to Acts in the Expositor's Greek Testament. With Blass we believe that, if Luke is the author, the question of sources for the greater part of the book need not be raised. The writer may have learnt the early history of the Jerusalem church from Barnabas at Antioch and from several others who found refuge in that city after the persecution; from Philip, whose guest he was for several days, 21:8-15, and with whom he must have had frequent intercourse during Paul's later stay at Cesarea; and from Mnason, an old disciple, 21:16. And regarding the missionary journeys of Paul he, in all probability, received full information from the apostle himself, and could partly draw on his own memory or memorandum. It is quite possible that the author had written records of

the speeches of Peter and Paul, but he certainly did not reproduce them literally but colored them in part with his own style.

INSPIRATION

The book of Acts is a part of the inspired Word of God. We have in it the fruit of apostolic inspiration, in so far as we find here speeches of some of the apostles and of Stephen, who was filled with the Holy Ghost, when he defended his course before the Jewish council, 6:5, 10. And in the composition of his book Luke was guided by the Holy Spirit, so that the whole work must be regarded as a product of graphical inspiration. This follows from the fact that this book is a necessary complement of the Gospels, which are, as we have seen, inspired records. It is a continuation of the Gospel of Luke, that is quoted as Scripture in 1 Tim. 5:18 (cf. Luke 10:7). If the Gospel is inspired, then, assuredly, the work that continues its narrative is also written by inspiration. Moreover we find that the Church fathers from the earliest time appeal to this book as of divine authority,— as an inspired work.

CANONICAL SIGNIFICANCE

The place of Acts in the canon of Holy Scripture has never been disputed by the early Church, except by such heretical sects as the Marcionites, the Ebionites and the Manichaeans, and then only on dogmatical grounds. Traces of acquaintance with it are found in the apostolic fathers, as also in Justin and Tatian. Irenaeus, Clement of Alexandria and Tertullian frequently quote from this book. It is named in the Muratorian canon, and is also contained in the Syriac and old Latin Versions. These testimonies are quite sufficient to show that it was generally accepted.

As an integral part of Scripture it is inseparably connected with the Gospels, and reveals to us, how the Gospel was embodied in the life and institution of the Church. We here see that the sowing of the precious seed that was entrusted to the apostles resulted in the planting and extension of the Church from three great racial centers of the world, from Jerusalem, the center of the Jewish Theocracy, from Antioch, the center of Greek culture, and from Rome, the capital of the world. The Gospels contain a revelation of what Jesus began to do and to teach; the book of Acts shows us what he continued to do and to teach through the ministry of men. There is an evident advance in the teaching of the apostles; they have learnt to understand much that was once a mystery to them. In the Gospels we find that they are forbidden to tell anyone that Jesus is the Messiah; here we read repeatedly that they preach Christ and the resurrection. They now exhibit Christ in his true character as the Prince of Life and as the King of Glory. And the effect of their teaching was such as to bear striking evidence to the regenerating power of Him, who by the resurrection from the dead was powerfully declared to be the Son of God.

8

The Epistles in General

THE EPISTOLARY FORM IN BIBLICAL LITERATURE

The revelation of God comes to us in many forms, in diverse manners. It is not only embodied in facts, but also in words; it is borne not only by the prophets, but also by the sweet singers and by the wise men of Israel; it finds expression not only in the Gospels, but also in the Epistles. About one-third of the New Testament is cast in the epistolary form.

This form of teaching was not something absolutely new in the time of the apostles, although we find but few traces of it in the Old Testament. Mention is made there of some letters written by kings and prophets, f. i. in 1 Kings 21:8, 9; 2 Kings 5:5-7; 19:14; 20:12; Jer. 29:1; but these are quite different from our New Testament Epistles. The letter as a particular type of self-expression took its rise, so it seems, among the Greeks and the Egyptians. In later time it was also found among the Romans and in Hellenistic Judaism, as we notice from the epistle of Aristion, that treats of the origin of the Septuagint. According to Deissmann the Egyptian papyri especially offer a great amount of material for comparison.

In all probability, however, it was Paul who first introduced the epistle as a distinct type of literary form for the conveyance of divine truth. Aside from the Gospels his Epistles form the most prominent part of the New Testament. In this connection it is well to bear in mind the important distinction made by Deissmann between a letter and an epistle, of which the former is non-literary, or, as J. V. Bartlet says, "pre-literary," and the latter is a literary artistic form of communication. It is Deissmann's conviction that the writings of Paul have been very much misunderstood. "They have been regarded as treatises, as pamphlets in letter form, or at any rate as literary productions, as the theological works of the primitive Christian dogmatist." He insists that they are letters, serving the purpose of communication between Paul and the congregations, letters that were not intended by Paul for publication, but only for the private use of the addressees, arising from some historical exigency, unsystematic and pulsating with the life of the writer. Deissmann, St. Paul p. 7 ff. This writer certainly rendered us good service by calling attention to the fact, often lost sight of, that the Epistles of Paul are the living spontaneous expression of a great mind, continually meditating and reflecting on the truth of God; that they are letters, often clearly revealing the changing moods of the apostle. They are marked as letters by their occasional character, by their being calculated for a single community and situation, and by their addresses, praescripts and salutations.

With respect to the fitness of this form for the communication of the divine thoughts the remarks of Bernard are very valuable. He finds that it is in perfect harmony "with that open and equal participation of revealed truth, which is the prerogative of the later above the former dispensation; indicating too that the teacher and the taught are placed on one common level in the fellowship of the truth. The prophets delivered oracles to the People, but the apostles wrote letters to the brethren, letters characterized by all that fulness of unreserved explanation, and that play of various feeling, which are proper to that form of intercourse. It is in its nature a more familiar communication, as between those who are or should be equals." ... "The form adopted in the New Testament combines the advantages of the treatise and the conversation. The letter may treat important subjects with accuracy and fulness, but it will do so in immediate connection with actual life. It is written to meet any occasion. It is addressed to peculiar states of mind. It breathes of the heart of the writer. It takes its aim from the exigencies, and its tone from the feelings of the moment." Bernard, The Progress of Doctrine in the N. T. pp. 156, 157.

THE INSPIRATION OF THE EPISTLES

The Scriptural Epistles are as well as the Gospels and Acts divinely inspired. Even as in their preaching, so also in writing their letters the apostles were guided by the Holy Spirit. Here again we must distinguish between the apostolic and the graphical inspiration, although in this case the two are very closely connected. For a general description of the apostolic inspiration we refer to p. 30 ff. above. It is necessary to remark, however, that in the case of the Epistles, as distinguished from that of the Gospels, it did not almost exclusively assume the character of a ὑπόμνησις, but was also to a great extent a διδασκαλία. Both of those elements are indicated in the promise of the Holy Spirit given by Christ before his departure: "But the Comforter, even the Holy Ghost, whom the Father will send in my name, He shall teach you all things, and bring to your remembrance all that I said unto you." John 14:26. Cf. also 16:12, 13. In the Gospels we have the totality of the apostolic κήρυγμα; hence their production naturally depended in great measure on a faithful memory. The Epistles, on the other hand, contain the fruit of the apostles reflection on this κήρυγμα, their interpretation of it. Therefore it was not sufficient that the writers in composing them should faithfully remember former things; they needed more light on them, a better understanding of their real meaning and profound significance. For that reason the Holy Spirit became their διδάσκαλος.

The apostles were evidently conscious of being inspired by the Holy Ghost in the composition of their Epistles. This follows from the authority with which they address the congregations. They feel sure that their word is binding on the conscience; they condemn in unqualified terms those who teach any other doctrine as coming from God; they commend and praise all that diligently follow their directions; but they also reprimand and censure those that dare to follow another course. If this is not due to the fact that they were conscious of divine inspiration, it bespeaks an overweening arrogance; which, however cannot be harmonized with their life of service and their many expressions of deep humility.

Moreover there are several explicit statements in the Epistles testifying to the fact that the apostles were aware of being the instruments of God's Spirit. Thus Paul claims that the Spirit revealed to him the hidden things of God, which he also spoke, not in words which man's wisdom taught, but in words which the Spirit taught, 1 Cor. 2:10, 13. He is willing to subject his words to the judgment of the prophets, 1 Cor. 14:37; and to give a proof of Christ speaking in him, 2 Cor. 13:3. He thanks God that the Thessalonians received the word of his message, not as the word of man, "but as it is in truth, the word of God," 1 Thess. 2:13; and admonishes them to hold the traditions which they were taught by his word or by his Epistle. Peter places the word of the prophets and that of the apostles on a level as the Word of God, in 1 Pet. 1:10-12; and elsewhere he arranges his Epistle alongside of those of Paul, which he calls Scripture by implication, and thus clearly shows that he also regards his own writing as a product of the Spirit of God, 2 Pet. 3:15, 16. John writes: "We are of God; he that knoweth God knoweth us; he that is not of God knoweth us not. By this we know the spirit of truth and the spirit of error." 1 John 4:6. This language is intelligible only on the supposition that John spoke the words of God.

Now we must bear in mind that the apostles speak thus regarding their written words, so that they were evidently conscious of the guidance of the Holy Spirit in writing their Epistles. To that extent they too shared in a separate transcriptive inspiration. Their Epistles are a part of the Word of God, and have been accepted as such by the Church. It is true that for a time five of them, viz., the Epistles of James and Jude, II Peter and II and III John, were classed as antilegomena, but this only means that their canonicity was subject to doubt and dispute for a while, not that they were ever numbered among the spurious books. They have been recognized by the majority of ecclesiastical writers from the very beginning, and were generally accepted by the Church after the council of Laodicea in A. D. 363.

THE CANONICAL SIGNIFICANCE OF
THE EPISTLES IN GENERAL

The Old and the New Testament revelations run on parallel lines. In the Old Testament we have the fundamental revelation of the Law in the Pentateuch; in the New Testament, the fundamental revelation of the Gospel in the fourfold witness of the evangelists. This is followed in the Old Testament by the historical books, revealing the institutions to which the Law gave rise; and in the New Testament, by a historical book, showing how the Gospel of Jesus Christ found embodiment in the Church. After this we find in the New Testament the Epistles that reveal the operation of the truth in the churches, and contain, in connection with the life of the churches, the interpretation of the Gospel; thus corresponding in part to the Old Testament books of experience, such as Job, Psalms, Proverbs, etc., and in part to the prophets as interpreters of the Law. The Gospels show us, how Christ was preached to the world; the Epistles, how he was taught to the Church. The former contain the facts of the manifestation of Christ; the latter the effects of it in the spiritual experience of the churches.

In the Epistles we get a glimpse of the inner life of the congregations; we see, how they receive the truth and to what degree they are guided by it in their actions. We behold Christian life in operation, working on the great principles that have been received. We find that some heartily embrace the truth and endeavor to apply it consistently to life in its manifold forms; that others grasp it but imperfectly and, as a result, misapply it in practical life;

and that still others resist the truth and pervert it to their own condemnation. And in connection with these conditions the truth is now set forth and interpreted and applied to the multifarious relations of life.

This teaching is given in the epistolary form, of which we have already spoken. Cf. p. 129 above. And the method employed by the writers in presenting the truth is, as Bernard says, "one of companionship rather than of dictation." They do not announce a series of revelations that come to them from without, but they speak out of the fulness of their own Christian knowledge and experience. Neither do they approach their readers with the authoritative prophetic formula, "Thus saith the Lord," which in the Old Testament was the end of all contradiction; but they appeal to the judgment and conscience of those whom they address. They state their propositions and then substantiate them by giving the grounds on which they rest. They argue with their readers from the Old Testament, from generally admitted truths and from experience, often employing the argumentum ad hominem to give point to their teachings; and they intercept the objections of their readers and refute them. This method of teaching, as compared with that of the prophets, is more truly human, the divine factor being less prominent; and as compared with that of Christ in the Gospels, is far more argumentative, calculated to train the minds of men to that thoughtfulness that leads to a thorough assimilation of the truth.

In their contents as well as in their form the Epistles are a distinct advance on the Gospels. After the latter have presented to us the manifestation of Christ in the world, the former treat of the life in Christ, in which the acceptance of his manifestation issues. After the Spirit of God has been poured out, Christ, who had formerly dwelt among men, makes his abode in the very hearts of believers. Hence it is especially of that new life of believers in union with Christ, that the Epistles speak. They constantly emphasize the fact that the individual believers and that the churches are "in Christ," and that therefore their conversation too must be "in Christ." They clearly interpret the significance of Christ's work for believers out of every nation and tribe. and point out that his experiences are paralleled in the life of every believer. All those that are united with Christ by faith suffer with Christ, are crucified with Christ, die with Christ, and live with Christ in newness of life. And their future life is hid with Christ in God. The origin of that new life, its conditions, its nature, its progressive and communal character, and its final perfection and glory,—are all clearly described in the Epistles. As the foundation on which all these blessings rest we are pointed to the redemptive, the justifying, the sanctifying, and the intercessory work of Jesus Christ. He is the beginning and the end. The Epistles contain clear evidence that believers are gathered from every nation and tribe to Christ who is the Head of the Church, and in whom they are builded together for a habitation of God in the Spirit, that God may be all in all.

CLASSIFICATION

The New Testament contains in all twenty-one Epistles, which may be divided into two classes, viz., 1. The Pauline Epistles; and, 2. The General Epistles.

1. The Pauline Epistles. Thirteen of the New Testament Epistles bear the name of the great apostle to the gentiles. Hence they are generally known as the Pauline Epistles. By some the Epistle to the Hebrews is added to this number, though it nowhere claims to have been written by Paul. The Church has always been divided on the question of its authorship, the Eastern church affirming and the Western denying that Paul wrote it. Clement of Alexandria states that the apostle composed it in the Hebrew language, and that Luke translated it into Greek. From a statement of his we may probably infer that his teacher, Pantaenus, also affirmed the Pauline authorship of this Epistle, which would carry the testimony back another generation. Origen admits that a very old tradition points to Paul as the author, but he comes to the conclusion that only God knows who wrote the book. Irenaeus does not attribute the Epistle to Paul; nor does Tertullian, who regards Barnabas as the author. Eusebius says: "Of Paul the fourteen Epistles commonly received are at once manifest and clear. It is not, however, right to ignore the fact that some have rejected the Epistle to the Hebrews, asserting that it is gainsaid by the church of Rome as not being Paul's." He was inclined to believe that the apostle wrote it in Hebrew and that Luke, or more likely, Clement of Rome translated it. The catalogue of the council of Laodicea also speaks of fourteen Epistles of Paul. We shall leave the question of the authorship of this Epistle in suspense for the present, and classify the fourteen Epistles of which we have now spoken, as follows:

I.   Pauline Epistles:

    1.   Those written during the period of Paul's missionary activity:

        a.   The two Epistles to the Thessalonians;

        b.   The Epistle to the Galatians;

        c.   The two Epistles to the Corinthians;

        d.   The Epistle to the Romans.

2.   Those written during Paul's imprisonment:

        a.   The Epistle to the Ephesians;

        b.   The Epistle to the Colossians;

        c.   The Epistle to Philemon;

        d.   The Epistle to the Philippians.

3.   Those written after Paul's release from the Roman prison:

        a.   The two Epistles to Timothy;

        b.   The Epistle to Titus.

II.   Of uncertain Authorship:

The Epistle to the Hebrews.

It may well be supposed that Paul who always remained in touch with the churches he founded wrote many more letters than we now possess of him. This is evident also from the Epistles themselves. 1 Cor. 5:9 refers to a letter now lost, and it is possible that 2 Cor. 7:8 does also, although this may refer to first Corinthians. Col. 4:16 speaks of a letter out of (ἐκ) Laodicea, of which we have no further knowledge. Although these letters were undoubtedly inspired as well as the ones we still possess, we may rest assured that no Epistle intended by God for the canon of Holy Scriptures was ever lost.

We may further remark that Paul evidently wrote very little with his own hand; he generally employed an amanuensis in the composition of his Epistles and merely added with his own hand the salutation to his friends and the authenticating signature, cf. 2 Thess. 3:17; Philem. 19; and Gal. 6:11, which is, however, of uncertain interpretation. Only in one letter do we find a definite designation of the amanuensis, viz., in Rom. 16:22.

2. The General Epistles. This is a group of seven Epistles which in the old manuscripts usually follows immediately after the Acts of the Apostles and therefore precedes the Pauline Epistles, perhaps because they are the works of the older apostles and in general represent the Jewish type of Christianity. Their representation of the truth naturally differs from that of the Pauline Epistles, but is in perfect harmony with it. Among these general Epistles there are:

1.   Those written to a community of Christians:

        a.   The Epistle of James;

        b.   The two Epistles of Peter;

c. The first Epistle of John;

d. The Epistle of Jude.

2. Those written to a certain individual:

a. The second Epistle of John; (?)

b. The third Epistle of John.

Of these seven Epistles the first one of Peter and the first one of John were generally accepted as canonical from the beginning, while the other five were at first subject to doubt and only gradually found acceptance throughout the Church. Yet they were never regarded as spurious.

Why these Epistles should be called general or catholic, is more or less of an enigma. Various interpretations of the name have been given, but none of them is entirely satisfactory. Some hold that they were so called, because they contain the one catholic doctrine which was delivered to the churches by the apostles; but this is not a characteristic mark of these Epistles, since those of Paul contain the same doctrine. Others maintain that the adjective catholic was used by some of the church fathers in the sense of canonical, and was by them applied first to the first Epistle of Peter and the first of John to indicate their general acceptance, and afterwards to the entire group. But this explanation is unlikely, because (1) there is scant proof that the term catholic was ever equivalent to canonical; and (2) it is hard to see, if this really was the case, why the term should not have been applied to the Pauline Epistles as well, that were all accepted from the beginning. Still others think that they received this appellation, because they were not addressed to one person or church like the Epistles of Paul, but to large sections of the Church. We consider this to be the best explanation of the name, since it is most in harmony with the usual meaning of the term, and accounts best for the way in which it is used in patristic literature. Even so, however the name cannot be regarded as entirely correct, because on the one hand the second (?) and third Epistles of John are written to individuals, and on the other, the Epistle to the Ephesians is also an encyclical letter. These two Epistles of John were probably included in this group, because of their smallness and close relation to the first Epistle of John.

9

The Epistles of Paul

PAUL

There is no apostle of whose life we have such full information as we have regarding that of Paul. He was born of Hebrew parents in the intellectual atmosphere of Tarsus in Cilicia, where besides receiving the regular Jewish education, he may have visited one of the many Greek schools found there. Being exceptionally bright, he was sent to Jerusalem to complete the study of the law and to be introduced into rabbinic lore. In that center of Jewish learning he received instruction at the feet of the greatest Jewish teacher of his age, Gamaliel I, and a bright future was opening up before him, since he was zealous for the law.

We first meet him in Scripture as a youth in connection with the violent death of Stephen, and soon find in him the most active persecuter of the Church of Christ. After he has finished his destructive work at Jerusalem, he repairs to Damascus with authority from the high priest to persecute the Church in that city. On the way thither his course is checked by the Lord of the Church, he becomes a penitent, and turns into a zealous advocate of the principles that were formerly obnoxious to him. Leaving Damascus, he spent three years in Arabia, where he received further instruction from God himself, and he learnt to adjust himself to the new conditions of life; after which he again returned to Damascus. Being threatened with death at the hands of the Jews, he fled from Damascus to Jerusalem, and from Jerusalem to his native city in Cilicia. After laboring there for some years, he accompanied Barnabas to Antioch in Syria, where he aided in establishing the youthful church in that city. He ministered to the needs of that congregation for a whole year, during which time he and Barnabas also went to Jerusalem to bring the contributions for the poor. Soon after they were directed by the Holy Spirit to preach the Gospel among the Gentiles. On this first journey they labored on the island of Cyprus and in Pisidian

Antioch, Iconium, Lystra and Derbe, preaching the Gospel and working miracles. Notwithstanding fierce opposition from the Jews, they succeeded in founding several churches. Having finished their work, they returned to Antioch in Syria, and during their stay there were delegated to the council of Jerusalem to consult the mother church regarding the debated question, whether circumcision was binding on the Gentiles. Next Paul sets out on his second missionary journey with Silas, revisiting the churches founded on the first tour and by the direction of the Holy Spirit crossing over to Europe, where he labored with varying success at Philippi, Thessalonica, Berea, Athens and Corinth, founding churches in most of these places. From Corinth he returned to Antioch, after first visiting Jerusalem. His third missionary journey followed shortly. Passing through Asia Minor, he finds a fruitful field of labor in Ephesus, where he remains three years, bringing all Asia to the knowledge of the truth and contending with idolatry and superstition. From there he again passes through Macedonia to Corinth, spending the winter in that city, and then returning by way of Troas, Ephesus and Cesarea to Jerusalem. Here he takes the necessary precautions to avoid all possible provocation of the Jews, but notwithstanding this they seek to kill him. Having been rescued by the chief captain, he defends his course before the Jews. This only increases their rage, however; wherefore he is taken into the castle and is brought before the Sanhedrin on the following day, where his defense leads to dissension between the Pharisees and the Sadducees. In the following night he receives encouragement from the Lord and is told that he must also bear witness in Rome. On account of a plot laid by the Jews he is transferred to Cesarea, where he again defends his course before Felix, Festus and Agrippa. The wavering attitude of the governors, who are convinced of his innocence and yet desire to favor the Jews, induces him to appeal to Ceasar. As a result he is taken to Rome, arriving there after suffering shipwreck, and remaining a prisoner in his own dwelling for two years. From the pastoral epistles and tradition we may infer that his first trial ended in acquittal. His movements after this are uncertain, though there are hints of visits to Philippi, Colossae, Ephesus, Crete, Nicopolis and even Spain. After being imprisoned again he was condemned and died as a martyr in A. D. 68.

Little can be said regarding the personal appearance of the great apostle. In the Acts of Paul and Thecla he is represented as "short, bald, bow-legged, with meeting eyebrows, hooked nose, full of grace." John of Antioch preserves a similar tradition, which adds, however, that he was "round-shouldered and had a mixture of pale and red in his complexion and an ample beard." His opponents at Corinth said of him: "His letters are weighty and powerful, but his bodily presence is weak and his speech contemptible," 2 Cor. 10:10 ff. He himself refers once and again to his physical weaknesses. In all probability he was not a man of magnificent physique.

His personal life was full of contrasts, as Deissmann correctly observes. He was encumbered with an ailing body, and yet was a man of great endurance and of almost unlimited capacity for work in the Kingdom of God. The secret of his strength lay in his God, who spoke to him: "My grace is sufficient for thee, and my strength is made perfect in weakness." He was a man of great humility, but was at the same time capable of uttering words of the greatest self-confidence, "before God a worm, before men an eagle" (Deissmann). It is Paul that says: "I am the least of the apostles," 1 Cor. 15:9; "I am less than the least of all the saints," Eph. 3:8; and: "of whom (sinners) I am chief," 1 Tim. 1:16. But it is the same Paul that speaks: "I labored more abundantly than they all," 1 Cor. 15:10; and: "For I suppose I was not a whit behind the very chiefest apostles," 2 Cor. 11:5. But he realizes that all that is commendable in him and that is praiseworthy in his work, is fruit of the grace of God. Hence he follows up the statement in 1 Cor. 15:10 by saying: "yet not I, but the grace of God which was with me." Paul was a tenderhearted man, and was yet on certain occasions very severe. He was capable of the most affectionate feeling, always solicitous for the welfare of the churches; but just on that account inexorable over against all those that were enemies to the truth. Compare in this respect the epistle to the Philippians with that to the Galatians. He placed himself entirely at God's disposal, following where He led, and was willing to be the unworthy instrument in the hand of his Lord in spreading the glad tidings of salvation. Hence he was great in the Kingdom of God.

The chronology of the life of Paul is a subject of great difficulty. Aside from the date of the first Pentecost there is but a single date in the Acts of the Apostles of which we are sure, viz., that of the death of Herod in A. D. 44, and this has little value in determining the chronological order of the events in Paul's life. A question of great importance is, in what year Felix was succeeded by Festus. We cannot enter into the dispute about this date, but assume that Schürer is correct, when he fixes it at A. D. 60. Geschichte des Jüdischen Volkes I p. 577. In the same year Paul was sent to Rome, arriving there in the spring of the following year, A. D. 61. He remained a prisoner at Rome for two years, i. e., until A. D. 63, when he was probably released; and lived until the fall of A. D. 67 (Eusebius), or until the spring of A. D. 68 (Jerome), when he was martyred at Rome.

Figuring back from the same date, we find that Paul was imprisoned at Caesarea in A. D. 58, Acts 24:27. Since he had spent the previous winter in Corinth and the fall in Macedonia, Acts 20:2, 3, and had labored in Ephesus for a period of three years, Acts 20:31, he must have begun his third missionary journey in the spring of A. D. 54. His second missionary tour was concluded shortly before, probably in the fall of A. D. 53, Acts 16:23. This journey undoubtedly lasted about two years and a half, since the apostle would naturally set out in the spring of the year and his stay of a year and a half at Corinth together with all the work done in other places makes it impossible that he started on his journey in A. D. 52, cf. Acts 15:36-17:34. Hence the second journey began in A. D. 51. This second journey was preceded by the council of Jerusalem that most likely convened in A. D. 50, Acts 15. The first missionary journey must be placed somewhere between the date just named and the year of Herod's death, A. D. 44.

Now it is probable that we must identify the visit of Paul to Jerusalem mentioned in Gal. 2:1 with that of Acts 15. What is the apostles point of departure there, when he says: "Then fourteen years after, etc."? Exegetically it may be the visit spoken of in Gal. 1:18; more likely, however, it is the time of his conversion, cf. Ellicott on Gal., so that the year 37 was probably the year in which that momentous change was wrought in his life. Then he spent the years 37-40 in Arabia, at the end of which period he again visited Jerusalem, Acts 9:26; Gal. 1:18. In the same year he went to Tarsus, where he labored until about the year of Herod's death, Acts 11:25-12:1.

Thus we obtain the following result:

Paul's Conversion	A. D. 37
First Visit to Jerusalem	A. D. 40
Beginning of His Work at Antioch	A. D. 44
First Missionary Journey	A. D. 45-48
Delegated to the Council of Jerusalem	A. D. 50
Second Missionary Journey	A. D. 51-53
Third Missionary Journey	A. D. 54-58
Captivity at Jerusalem and Caesarea	A. D. 58-60
Arrives at Rome	A. D. 61
First Captivity at Rome	A. D. 61-63

Period between First and Second Captivity	A. D. 63–67
Second Captivity and Death	A. D. 67 or 68

10

The Epistle to the Romans

CONTENTS

This Epistle consists of two clearly marked but very unequal parts, viz. the doctrinal (1:1-11:36) and the practical part (12:1-16:27).

I. The Doctrinal Part, 1:1-11:36. In this part we have first the introduction, containing the address, the customary thanksgiving and prayer, and an expression of the apostle's desire to preach the gospel also at Rome, 1:1-15. In the following two verses the apostle states his theme: "The gospel is the power of God unto salvation to every one that believeth. For therein is the righteousness of God revealed from faith to faith," 1:16, 17. After announcing this he describes the sinful state of the Gentiles, points out that the Jews are likewise guilty, and declares that their prerogatives do not exempt them from punishment but rather increase their guilt, 1:18-3:20. He then defines the righteousness which God has provided without the works of the law, and proves that this is revealed in the Old Testament, is the basis of a Christian experience that is rich in spiritual fruits, and proceeds on the same principle of moral government on which God dealt with Adam, 3:21-5:21. Next he replies to the objections that on his doctrine men may continue in sin and yet be saved; that his teaching releases men from moral obligation; and that it makes the law of God an evil thing, 6:1-7:25. In the following chapter he shows that on the basis of man's justification by faith his complete sanctification and final glorification is assured, 8:1-39. Having stated the way of salvation through faith, he now points out that this does not conflict with the promises given to Israel by showing that these pertained only to the elect among them; that the rejection of Israel is due to their refusal of the way of salvation; that it is not a complete rejection; and that in the end the Jews will be converted and will turn to God, 9:1-11:36.

II. The Practical Part, 12:1-16:27. The apostle admonishes the Christians at Rome that they be devoted to God and love one another, 12:1-21. He desires that they willingly subject themselves to the civil authorities and meet all their obligations, 13:1–14. He enjoins upon them due regard for the weakness of others in matters of indifference, and the proper use of their Christian liberty, 14:1–23. Then he holds up to them Christ as their great example, and speaks of his purpose to visit Rome, 15:1–33. Finally he sends a long list of greetings to Rome and closes his epistle with a doxology, 16:1–27.

CHARACTERISTICS

1. The characteristic feature of this Epistle is found in the fact that it is the most systematic writing of the apostle, an elaborate treatment of a single theme with appropriate practical exhortations. It contains a careful and rather full statement of what Paul himself calls, "my Gospel," 2:16; 16:25. His Gospel is that man is justified by faith and not by the works of the law. In harmony with this theme the contents of the Epistle are Soteriological rather than Christological. The apostle points out that both Gentiles and Jews need this justification; that it is the way of salvation provided by God himself; that it yields the most blessed spiritual fruits; that it does not issue in the moral degradation of man, but in a life sanctified by the Spirit and culminating in everlasting glory; and that, though the Gentiles will have precedence over the Jews, who rejected the Gospel, these too will at last accept it and be saved. Godet calls this Epistle, "The Cathedral of Christian Faith." Because of its methodical character some have mistakenly regarded it as a treatise rather than as a letter. If it were a treatise, it might have been sent to one church as well as another, and it may be regarded as accidental that it was sent to Rome. But this is not the case. We cannot understand this, the greatest of Paul's literary productions, unless we study it historically in its relation to the church of Rome.

2. The style of the Epistle is described by Sanday and Headlam in the following words: "This Epistle, like all the others of the group (I and II Cor. and Gal.), is characterized by a remarkable energy and vivacity. It is calm in the sense that it is not aggressive and that the rush of words is always well under control. Still there is a rush of words rising repeatedly to passages of splendid eloquence; but the eloquence is spontaneous, the outcome of strongly moved feeling; there is nothing about it of labored oratory. The language is rapid, terse, incisive; the argument is conducted by a quick cut and thrust of dialectic; it reminds us of a fencer with his eye always on his antagonist." Intern. Crit. Comm., Romans p. LV.

AUTHORSHIP

Both external and internal evidence clearly point to Paul as the author. We find the first direct evidence for his authorship in the Apostolicon of Marcion. The letter is further ascribed to Paul by the Muratori canon, and is quoted as his by Irenaeus, Clement of Alexandria, Tertullian and a host of others. The Epistle itself claims to have been written by Paul, and this claim is borne out by the contents, so that even Davidson says: "The internal character of the epistle and its historical allusions coincide with the external evidence in proving it an authentic production of the apostle." Introd. I p. 119.

The authenticity of this great letter, along with that of the Epistles to the Corinthians and to the Galatians has been well-nigh universally admitted. The first one to attack it was Evanson in 1792, followed by Bruno Bauer in 1852. Their rather reckless criticism has made little impression on German critical opinion. In more recent times the Pauline authorship has been denied by the Dutch scholars Loman (1882), Pierson and Naber (1886) and Van Manen (1892), and by the Swiss scholar Steck (1888); but their arguments, of which an epitomy may be found in Sanday-Headlam, Romans p. LXXXVI; Baljon, Gesch. v/d Boeken des N. V. p. 97 ff.; and Godet, Introd. to the N. T. I St. Paul's Epistles p. 393,—failed to carry conviction among New Testament critics.

THE CHURCH AT ROME

Regarding the church to which this letter is addressed there are especially two questions that call for discussion, viz. 1. Its Origin; and 2. Its Composition.

1. Its Origin. There are three theories respecting the origin of the church at Rome.

a. According to a tradition dating from the fourth, and probably from the third century, that found general acceptance in the Roman Catholic church, the congregation at Rome was founded by Peter in A. D. 42 (Jerome and Eusebius) or in A. D. 44 (Acts 12:17). This view is now generally given up and is even rejected by some Catholic scholars. It finds no support in Scripture, but is rather contradicted by its plain statements. From Acts 16:9, 10 we get the impression that Paul was the first missionary to pass into Europe (A. D. 52), and this is just what we would expect, since he, in distinction from the other apostles, was sent to the Gentiles. Moreover we still find Peter in the East, when in A. D. 50 the council of Jerusalem is held, which does not agree with the tradition that he was at Rome 25 years. And neither in this Epistle, nor in those written from Rome do we find the slightest trace of Peter's presence there; yet Paul would certainly have mentioned him, had he been the bishop of the Roman church. It is also impossible to reconcile Paul's plan to visit Rome with the principle he himself lays down in 15:20, if the local church had been founded by Peter. And finally tradition tells us that Linus was the first bishop of Rome, and Clement, the second.

b. Protestants often ascribed the origin of this church to the Roman Jews that were in Jerusalem at the feast of Pentecost, Acts 2:10, and witnessed the extraordinary phenomena that accompanied the descent of the Holy Spirit. On that theory the church really originated among the Jews. In proof of this the report which Suetonius gives of the decree of expulsion issued by the emperor Claudius against the Jews of Rome, is adduced: "Judaeos impulsore Chresto assidue tumultuantes Roma expulit." It is said that this Chresto must be Christ, whose religion spread in the Jewish synagogue and caused violent dissensions that were dangerous to the public peace; but this may well be, and indeed is, questioned by many scholars. Moreover it is rather doubtful, whether the Jews converted at the time of Pentecost were in a position to evangelize others and to establish a Christian church. And finally this explanation does not square with the fact that the church at Rome, as we know it from the Epistle, does not bear a Judaeo- but a Gentile-Christian complexion.

c. It seems more likely, therefore, that the church at Rome originated somewhat later, and in a different fashion. We know that before A. D. 44 the gospel had been brought to Antioch in Syria and spread rapidly among the Gentiles of that region, Acts 11:20. Soon a flourishing church was established in that beautiful city on the Orontes, a church endowed with great spiritual gifts, having in its midst an abundance of men that were well qualified for the work of evangelization, Acts 13:1. Now there was at that time a lively intercommunication between Syria and Rome, and it is certainly not improbable that some Gentile Christians, filled with the spirit of evangelization, set out from here for the capital of the world. Or if not from here, some such persons may have gone forth from the other centers of Christianity, established by Paul on his missionary journeys. This would explain, how the great apostle acquired so many acquaintances at Rome as he names in chapter 16, mostly Gentiles, some of whom he calls his fellow-laborers (cf. 3, 9, 12), while he characterizes others with some word of endearment (cf. 5-8, 10, 11, 13). Some such friends they must have been who went out to meet Paul on the Appian way, Acts 28:25, while the Jews at Rome were evidently quite ignorant as to the teachings of Christianity, Acts 28:17-29. On this theory the Gentile character of the church at Rome causes no surprise.

2. Its Composition. Quite a controversy has been waged about the question, whether the church at Rome was predominantly Jewish- or Gentile-Christian. The traditional idea was that it consisted primarily of Christians from the Gentiles; but the view that it was composed mainly of Jewish Christians gained currency through Baur and was widely accepted for some time. In support of this theory scholars appealed: (1) To the passages in the epistle, in which Paul seems to include himself and his readers in the first person plural, as 3:9 and 5:1. But notice the same feature in 1. Cor. 10:1, though the Corinthians were certainly Gentiles. (2) To those passages that speak of the relation of the readers, or of Paul and his readers alike to the law, as 7:1-6. This argument is stronger than the preceding one; yet we find that the apostle employs similar language with reference to the Galatians, Gal. 3:13-4:9, while most of these were certainly outside the pale of Jewry. (3) To the character of Paul's argumentation and the dialectical form in which he presents his Gospel to the Romans. But even this does not necessarily imply that he was writing primarily to Jewish Christians, since he argues in similar fashion in the Epistle to the Galatians, and because this finds a ready explanation partly in the Jewish training of the apostle and partly in the fact that Paul was fully conscious of the objections which legalistic adversaries were wont to bring against his doctrine. Besides, he knew that there were Jewish converts in the church at Rome too, who might make similar strictures. (4) To the chapters 9-11, regarded by Baur as the kernel of the epistle, which relate particularly to the Jews. Yet in these very chapters Paul addresses, in the most unambiguous manner, the Gentiles, and refers to Israel as distinct from his readers, cf. 9:3, 24; 10:1-3; 11:13, 17-20, 24, 25, 30, 31.

When in 1876 Weizsäcker again took up the defense of the older view, he produced a decisive reaction in its favor. And, no doubt, it deserves the preference, for: (1) In 1:5, 6 Paul writes: "By whom we have received grace and apostleship, for obedience to the faith among the Gentiles (τοῖς ἔθνεσιν) for his Name; among whom ye are also the called of Jesus Christ." (2) In verse 13 he says that he had often purposed to come to Rome "that I might have some fruit among you also, even as among other Gentiles." (3)

When the apostle says in 11:13: "For I speak to you Gentiles, inasmuch as I am the apostle of the Gentiles, I magnify mine office," it is best to assume with Meyer and Godet that he is addressing the whole congregation in its chief constituent clement. (4) According to 15:15 ff. the writer has spoken the more boldly to the Romans, because of the grace that was given him "that he should be the minister of Jesus Christ to the Gentiles, ministering the Gospel of God, that the offering up of the Gentiles might be acceptable, being sanctified by the Holy Ghost." On the strength of these passages we conclude that, though there was a Jewish constituency in the church at Rome, it consisted primarily of Gentile Christians, so that in ministering to it also Paul was the apostle of the Gentiles. It seems almost certain, however, that a legalistic tendency had sprung up in the congregation, but this tendency may have been characteristically Roman rather than specifically Judaistic. For further details of this controversy cf. Holtzmann, Einleitung p. 232 ff.; Sanday-Headlam, Comm. p. XXXI ff.; The Expositor's Greek Test. II p. 561 ff.; and Zahn, Einleitung I p. 299 ff. etc.

COMPOSITION

1. Occasion and Purpose. It is impossible to speak with absolute certainly respecting the occasion of Paul's writing this Epistle, although scholars are quite well agreed that the apostle found it in the fact that he had finished his work in the East and now intended to visit the imperial city, on which he had long since cast his eye. Probably an imminent journey of Phebe to the capital offered him, on the eve of his departure for Jerusalem, the desired opportunity to send his communication to Rome.

But if the question is asked, why the apostle wrote this letter to the Romans, why he gave it the particular character that it has, we find that there is a great variety of opinions. Some regard the Epistle as historical and occasional; others, as dogmatic and absolute. There are those who hold that the particular form of the letter was determined by the condition of the readers; and those that would make it dependent on the state of Paul's mind. Some believe that the apostle in writing it had in mind his Gentile readers, while others hold that he had special reference to the Jewish constituents of the church at Rome. The different theories respecting the purpose of the letter may be reduced to three.

a. According to some the purpose of the letter is dogmatic, the Epistle containing a systematic exposition of the doctrine of salvation. But if Paul meant to give in it nothing but an objective statement of the truth, the question may be asked, why he should send it to Rome, and not to some other church.

b. Others affirm that the aim of the Epistle is controversial, Paul giving an exposition of the truth with special reference to the opposition of Judaeism to his gospel. Now we need not doubt that there is a polemic element in this Epistle, but the question may well be raised, whether the apostle did not combat legalism in general rather than Judaeism.

c. Still others believe that the purpose of the letter is conciliatory, aiming at the unity of Jew and Gentile in the church at Rome. This theory also contains an element of truth, for Paul certainly was very solicitous about that unity, when he wrote this Epistle; but it is a mistake to regard the promotion of it as his sole purpose in writing.

It seems to us that, with Holtzmann, Sanday-Headlam and Denney (in Exp. Gk. Test.), we should combine these various elements in stating the purpose of the Epistle. Paul had long cherished a desire to visit the city on the Tiber. Through his friends and associates he had received some intelligence regarding the church that had been founded there. And now that he is about to depart for Jerusalem, he has evil forebodings; he may never see Rome; and yet he deems it desirable that the Roman church, which had not been founded by an apostle, should not only be notified of his intended visit, but receive a full and clear statement of his Gospel. Hence he prepares for the Romans a careful exposition of the Gospel truth. And knowing, as he did, the legalistic tendency of the human heart, accented, as it often was in his time, by Judaeism,—a tendency that probably found a fruitful soil among the moralistic Romans, he clearly exhibits its antagonism to the doctrine of salvation, at the same time carefully guarding and assiduously cultivating the unity of the believers at Rome, of the weak and the strong, of Jews and Gentiles.

2. Time and Place. As to the time, when Paul wrote this Epistle, we can infer from 1:13 that he had not yet been in Rome, and from 15:25 that he was still a free man. Therefore he must have written it before Pentecost of A. D. 58, for then he was taken captive at Jerusalem. On the other hand it is clear from 15:19-21 that the apostle has finished his task in the East and is now about to transfer his ministry to the West. Hence it follows that he composed this letter at the end of his third missionary journey, i. e. in the fall of A. D. 57, or in the spring of A. D. 58. This also agrees with the fact that the apostle in the Epistles to the Corinthians (1 16:1-4; 2 8, 9) is still

occupied with the collection for the saints at Jerusalem, while this work is finished, when he writes to the Romans, 15:25.

If this date is correct, then the Epistle must have been written at Corinth. And there are some data that corroborate this conclusion. The bearer of the letter is a member of the church at Cenchrea, one of the ports of Corinth, 16:1; and Gajus, the host of Paul, is most likely the person mentioned in 1 Cor. 1:14. Moreover the salutations of Timothy and Sopater or Sosipater in 16:21 is in perfect agreement with what is said in Acts 20:4 regarding the presence of these men at Corinth, when Paul started for Jerusalem.

INTEGRITY

Touching the integrity of the Epistle to the Romans two questions have arisen: 1. Is the doxology, 16:25-27, in the right place, or does it belong between 14:23 and 15:1, or is it spurious? And 2. Are the chapters 15 and 16 genuine or spurious?

1. The place of the doxology at the end of chapter 16 was doubted as early as the days of Origen. External testimony favors it, since it is found there in most of the MSS, while some have it at the end of chapter 14, and a few, in both places. Zahn is of the opinion, however, that internal evidence decidedly favors placing it at the end of chapter 14, because: (1) Paul's letters are often interspersed with doxologies, but never end with them. (2) It seems unlikely that Paul should add a doxology, closely connected with the body of the letter, after a list of personal greetings not so connected with it. (3) The doxology is closely related to the subject-matter of 14:23 and 15:1. (4) It is far harder to explain its transfer from the 16th chapter to the 14th than the reverse. Einl. I p. 268 ff.

Some, as f. i. Davidson and Baljon, doubt the genuineness of the doxology, but: (1) It is found in all the MSS. (2) The thought expressed in it is too rich and varied to be an interpolation. (3) No possible motive can be found for forging such a doxology.

2. The 15th chapter is regarded by some as spurious, (1) because it is not found in the canon of Marcion; and (2) since the appellative applied to Christ in verse 8 is considered very strange as coming from Paul; the expression in verse 19 is not characterized by the usual Pauline modesty; and the verses 24, 28, 29 are held to be in conflict with 1:10-15, because they imply that Paul merely desired to pay a short visit to Rome, when he was on his way to Spain. But the first argument has little weight, since Marcion omits many other parts of the New Testament, and several that

are generally admitted to be genuine; and the difficulties mentioned under (2) easily yield to exegesis.

A far greater number of scholars reject chapter 16, (1) because Marcion's canon does not contain it; (2) since it is contrary to the apostle's custom to end his letters with so many greetings; and (3) because Paul was not in a position to know so many persons at Rome. To the first argument we need not reply again (cf. above); and as far as the greetings are concerned, it may be that Paul intentionally greeted so many persons at Rome to bring out clearly that, though he had not founded the church there, he was not a stranger to it, and to cultivate a certain familiarity. It deserves our attention that the only other Epistle in which we find a list of greetings is that to the Colossian church, which was like the church of Rome, in that it was not founded by the apostle. And taking in consideration the extensive travels of Paul in the East, and the constant movement of people in all parts of the empire to and from Rome, it causes no surprise that so many of the apostle's acquaintances were in the capital.

Some who doubt the destination rather than the genuineness of this chapter surmise that it or a part of it originally constituted an epistle, or a fragment of one, that was addressed to the Ephesians. They point out that Phebe would be more likely to journey to Ephesus than to Rome; that, in view of what is said in Acts 18:19; 1 Cor. 16:19; 2 Tim. 4:19, there is a greater probability that Aquila and Priscilla were at Ephesus than in the imperial city; and that Epenetus is called "the first-fruits of Achaia unto Christ, 16:5. But none of these proofs are conclusive. Moreover Dr. Gifford points out in the Speaker's Commentary that of the twenty-two persons named in verses 6–15, not one can be shown to have been at Ephesus; while (1) Urbanus, Rufus, Ampliatus, Julia and Junia are specifically Roman names; and (2) besides the first four of these names, "ten others, Stachys, Apelles, Tryphaena, Tryphosa, Hermes, Hermas, Patrobas (or (Patrobius), Philologus, Julia, Nereus are found in the sepulchral inscriptions on the Appian way as the names of persons connected with 'Cæsar's household' (Phil. 4:22), and contemporary with St. Paul."

CANONICAL SIGNIFICANCE

The Epistle to the Romans is one of the best attested writings of the New Testament. Its canonicity was never doubted by the Church, and it has been remarkably free from the attacks of Rationalism up to the present time. Before the beginning of the third century there are nineteen witnesses to the canonicity of the letter, including some of the apostolic fathers, the Testament of the Twelve Patriarchs, Justin Martyr, the Muratori Canon, Marcion, Irenaeus, Clement of Alexandria and Tertullian. Both friends and foes of Christianity accepted it as authoritative.

It is the most systematic of all the writings of Paul, containing a profound and comprehensive statement of the way of salvation, a statement made with special reference to the legalistically inclined Romans. That salvation can be had through faith only, and not by the works of the law, not by one's works of morality, on which the man of the Roman type was inclined to place his reliance, is at once the great central doctrine of this epistle and its permanent lesson for all ages.

11

The First Epistle to the Corinthians

CONTENTS

The contents of this Epistle may be divided into five parts:

I. Condemnation of the Factions in the Church, 1:1-4:21. After a brief introduction in 1:1-9 Paul states that he had heard of the divisions among the Corinthians, 1:11-12. In arguing against these he points out that his conduct was free from party spirit, since this is opposed by the gospel and forbidden by the character of Christ, 1:13-31. Moreover he reminds the Corinthians that his preaching had been free from all partisanship which glories in the wisdom of man, because the gospel is the message of divine wisdom, is revealed by the Spirit and is understood only through the Spirit; white party spirit misapprehends the nature of the ministry, 2:1-3:23. He concludes this argument by pointing to his own example, 4:1-21.

II. The Necessity of Church Discipline urged, 5:1-6:20. The Corinthians are exhorted to cast out the incestuous person, 5:1-13; to desist from law-suits before the unrighteous, 6:1-11; and to flee from fornication, 6:12-20.

III. Answer to Inquiries sent from the Church, 7:1-14:39. Here we find a discussion of the lawfulness of marriage and its duties; directions about mixed marriages and an apostolic advice to the unmarried, 7:1-40. Then follows a discussion of Christian liberty in the participation of food offered to the idols, in which love must rule, and one must beware of any participation in idolatrous practices. The apostle illustrates this principle at length by pointing to his own example, 8:1-11:1. Next the place of woman in the assemblies of the church, and the proper observance of the Lord's supper is considered, 11:2-34. And finally the spiritual gifts manifest in the congregation come in for consideration. Their source and diversity, their functions, the superiority of love over the extraordinary gifts, and of prophecy over the speaking of tongues, and the right service of God,— all receive due treatment, 12:1-14:40.

IV. A Discussion of the Resurrection, 15:1-58. The apostle shows that the resurrection of Christ is an essential article of the apostolic testimony, and is the pledge of our resurrection; and answers various objections, describing the nature of the resurrection body and the final victory over death.

V. Conclusion, 16:1-24. In this chapter the apostle commends to the Corinthians the collection for the saints at Jerusalem, bespeaks a good reception for Timothy, and ends his epistle with friendly admonitions and salutations.

CHARACTERISTICS

1. This Epistle is the most comprehensive of all the writings of Paul. It is just about as long as the letter to the Romans, and contains the same number of chapters; but, while the Epistle to the Romans systematically treats a single theme, this letter discusses a great variety of subjects, such as party spirit, church discipline, marriage and celibacy, Christian liberty, the place of woman in the church, the significance and use of the charismata, and the resurrection of the dead. And the apostle treats of these matters in a very orderly way, first taking up the accusations contained in the report of those from the household of Chloe, and then answering the questions that were put to him in the letter sent by the Corinthians.

2. Closely connected with the first is a second characteristic, viz. that this Epistle is the most practical of all the Pauline letters. It reveals to us, as no other New Testament writing does, the snares and pitfalls, the difficulties and temptations to which a church just emerging from heathendom and situated in a wicked city, is exposed. Many of the problems that arose in the Corinthian church constantly recur in city congregations. As important as the Epistle to the Romans is for instruction in Christian doctrine, the first Epistle to the Corinthians is for the study of social relations.

3. Little need be said regarding the language of Paul in this Epistle; it is the Greek of a Hellenistic Jew. We cannot call it Hebraistic; neither is it literary Greek. It is rather the Greek of Paul's own period, containing, aside from a few Hebrew loanwords, such as πάσχα, very few words that are found exclusively in the Septuagint. Findlay says: "Paul has become in this epistle more than elsewhere τοῖς Ἕλλησιν ὡς Ἕλλην." Exp. Gk. Test. II p. 748. The argumentative form too in which the apostle's thought is cast here, as elsewhere, is far more Greek than Hebrew, more Western than Oriental.

AUTHORSHIP

This epistle also claims to have been written by Paul, 1:1, 2, and bears upon the face of it the earmarks of the great apostle. The language, the style, the doctrine, and the spirit which it breathes,—are all his; and the historical allusions in chapters 9 and 16 fit in exactly with what we know of his life and acquaintances from other sources. Besides this there is an imposing body of external evidence from Clement of Rome down to the authenticity of the letter. Hence it, like that written to the Romans, has been remarkably free from hostile attacks. Robertson and Plummer truly say in the Introduction to their Commentary on this Epistle p. XVI: "Both the external and the internal evidence for the Pauline authorship are so strong that those who attempt to show that the apostle was not the writer succeed chiefly in proving their own incompetence as critics."

The free-lance Bruno Bauer was the first, and for a long time the only one, to attack the genuineness of I Corinthians. But in the last two decennia of the preceding century the Dutch critics Loman, Pierson, Naber and Van Manen, and the Swiss professor Steck chimed in with a most irresponsible kind of criticism, founded on supposed inconsistencies and evidences of composite authorship found in the Epistle, and on imaginary conflicts between it and the Acts of the Apostles. No critic of name takes their argument serious; according to the general estimate they are scarcely worth the paper on which they are written.

THE CHURCH AT CORINTH

1. Its Origin. After Paul left Athens on his second missionary journey, he came to the capital of Achaia,—to Corinth, a city situated on the isthmus of the Peloponnese between the Ionian and the Aegean sea. It was not the old Corinth, since this had been destroyed by Mummius in 146 B. C., but Corinth redivivus, Corinth rebuilt by Ceasar just a hundred years later, that had rapidly risen in fame, and now had a population of between six and seven hundred thousand, consisting of Romans, Greeks, Jews and people of such other nationalities as were attracted by the commercial advantages of Corinth. The East and the West met there, and it soon became the mart of the world, where unparalleled riches were found alongside of the deepest poverty. And with the increase of riches and luxury came a life of ease and licentiousness. Worldly wisdom and great moral degradation went hand in hand. On the Acropolis shone the temple of Venus, where a thousand maidens devoted themselves to the

sensual service of the goddess. Corinthian immorality became a byword; and the expression to live like a Corinthian (κορινθιάζειν) was indicative of the greatest licentiousness. Farrar says: "Corinth was the Vanity Fair of the Roman Empire, at once the London and the Paris of the first century after Christ." St. Paul I p. 556.

To that worldly-wise profligate Corinth Paul wended his way with a sad heart in A. D. 52. Depressed in spirit because of past experiences, he began his labors in the synagogue, preaching to the Jews; but when they opposed him, he turned to the Gentiles and taught them in the house of a certain Justus. Crispus, the ruler of the synagogue, became one of his first converts, and many others believed and were baptized, Acts 18:1–8. Encouraged by a vision, he now began a ministry of a year and a half in that city. The Jews, filled with hatred, brought him before Gallio, the proconsul of Achaia, but did not succeed in making out a case against him. Even after this incident he labored a long time in Corinth and the adjacent country and undoubtedly established the Corinthian church on this occasion, Acts 18:18; 1 Cor. 1:1.

2. Its Composition and Character. We may be sure that the church consisted primarily of Christians from the Gentiles. This impression is conveyed by the account of Paul's work in Corinth, preserved for us in Acts 18, and is strengthened by a careful study of the epistle. The apostle says of the congregation, describing it according to its main constituent element: "Ye know that ye were Gentiles, carried away unto these dumb idols, even as ye were led," 12:1. Yet the church also comprised many Jews, as we may infer from Acts 18:8; 1 Cor. 1:12; 7:18; 12:13. The majority of the converts were of the poorer classes, 1:26; but there were also Crispus, the ruler of the synagogue, Acts 18:8; 1 Cor. 1:14, Erastus, the chamberlain of the city and Gajus, Paul's host, Rom. 16:23, and several others that were in more favorable circumstances, as we may infer from 1 Cor. 11:21, 22.

As far as the complexion of the church is concerned we find that it bore the impress of its surroundings. There was a shallow intellectualism, coupled with a factiousness that was "the inveterate curse of Greece." Lax morals and unseemly conduct disgraced its life. Christian liberty was abused and idolatrous practices were tolerated. Even the gifts of the Holy Spirit gave rise to vainglory; and a false spiritualism led, on the one hand, to a disregard of bodily sin, and, on the other, to a denial of the bodily resurrection. But these faults should not blind us to the fact that there was a great deal in the church of Corinth that was praise worthy. The social relations among the Corinthians had already undergone to a certain degree the elevating and sanctifying influence of the Holy Spirit; the church was rich in spiritual gifts, and was willing to impart of its substance to the poor saints at Jerusalem.

The divisions at Corinth deserve more than a passing notice, since they are made so prominent in the Epistle. The question is, whether we can determine the character of the existing parties. In attempting this we desire to point out first of all that they were no parties in the strict sense of the word, each with an organization of its own, but merely dissensions in the church, representing a difference of opinion. They had not led to an absolute split in the ranks of believers, for Paul distinctly recognizes a certain feeling of unity in the church of Corinth, since he mentions meetings of the whole church repeatedly, 11:18; 14:23. Yet there were four divisions of which each one had his own slogan.

a. Some said: "I am of Paul!" This party is mentioned first, not necessarily because it comes first in chronological order. Since the church had been founded by Paul, it would seem that a separate party, using the apostle's name as their shibboleth, could only arise in opposition to another. It consisted most likely of those serious-minded believers who had regard to the contents of the gospel preaching rather than to its form; and who heartily accepted the simple doctrine of the cross, as Paul preached it, who had come to them without wisdom of words that the cross of Christ might not be made of non-effect.

b. Others said: "I am of Apollos!" We do not believe that the preaching of Apollos differed essentially from that of Paul, nor that he was to blame for the dissension that arose as a result of his work. Paul himself bears witness to his perfect unity of spirit with Apollos, where he says that Apollos watered what he had planted, and that he that planteth and he that watereth are one, 3:6–8; and that he had greatly desired to send Apollos with Timothy and the other brethren to Corinth, 15:12. And is it not likely that Apollos refused to go, just because he feared that it might foster the party spirit? The Apollos Christians were in all probability those cultured Greeks who, while they were in accord with the doctrine of free grace, greatly preferred a speculative and oratorical presentation of it to the simple preaching of Paul.

c. Still others said: "I am of Cephas!" While the two former parties undoubtedly constituted the bulk of the congregation, there were also some who had scruples regarding the doctrine of free grace. They were conservative Jewish believers that adhered to the decisions of the council of Jerusalem and persisted in certain legal observances. Naturally they in spirit rallied around Peter, the apostle of circumcision. It may be that the tradition preserved by Dionysius of Corinth is true that Peter has at one time visited Corinth. If it is, this helps to explain their watchword.

d. Finally there were also those who said: "I am of Christ!" This party has always been the most difficult to characterize, and, as a result, a great number of theories have been broached. After F. C. Baur many interpreted this "of Christ" in the light of 2 Cor. 10:7, where the opponents of whom Paul speaks are ultra-Judaeists. On that theory the Christ-party would be even more strictly Jewish than the party of Peter. Others, such as Hilgenfeld and Hausrath maintain that it consisted of those that had been in personal relation with the Lord, and probably belonged to the five hundred of 1 Cor. 15:5. Godet suggests that they were such as were embued with the spirit of Cerinthus, and believed in Christ in distinction from the human Jesus. He identifies them with those who would call Jesus accursed, 1 Cor. 12:3. We prefer to think with Meyer, Ellicott, Alford, Findley (Exp. Gk. Test.) and Biesterveld that it consisted of the ultra-pious ones who, despising all human leadership, arrogated the common watchword as their own private property, and by so doing made it a party slogan. They regarded themselves as the ideal party, were filled with spiritual pride, and thus became a great stumblingblock for the apostle. The key to this interpretation is found in 3:22, 23, where the apostle offers a corrective for the party spirit, when he says: "Whether Paul, or Apollos, or Cephas, or the world, or life, or death, or things present, or things to come; all are yours; and ye are Christ's and Christ is God's." Findlay correctly remarks that "the catholic ὑμεῖς Χριστοῦ swallows up the self-assertive and sectarian Ἐγὼ δὲ Χριστοῦ.

3. Paul's Communications with it. There are two questions that call for consideration under this heading: a. How often did Paul visit Corinth? and b. Did he write more letters to the Corinthian church than we now possess?

a. We know that Paul visited Corinth in A. D. 52, Acts 18:1, and again in 57, Acts 20:2. Are there traces of any other visits? The allusions in 2 Cor. 2:1; 12:14; 13:1 seem to imply that he had been in Corinth twice before he wrote II Corinthians, and hence prior to the visit of A. D. 57. In all probability we must assume a visit not recorded in the Acts of the Apostles. The question is, however, whether we must place it before the writing of I Corinthians, or between this and the composition of II Corinthians. This cannot be decided absolutely with the data at hand, but we consider it preferable to place it before the first Epistle: (1) because the time intervening between the two letters is so short that a trip to Corinth in that time is exceedingly improbable; (2) Since, Timothy and Titus having been in Corinth a part of that time, we cannot understand, what could make it imperative for Paul to make such a hasty visit; and (3) II Corinthians constantly refers to things written in the first Epistle in a way that would not have been necessary if Paul had already been in Corinth himself. In favor of placing it after the writing of the first Epistle, it is urged that I Corinthians does not refer to a visit that shortly preceded it.

b. It seems to us that Paul unquestionably wrote more epistles to the Corinthians than those which we now possess. In 1 Cor. 5:9 the author clearly refers to an earlier letter, forbidding intercourse with immoral persons. That letter had been misunderstood, and therefore the impression it made is now corrected by the apostle. Very likely it also spoke of the collection for the saints at Jerusalem, 16:1, and conveyed the apostle's intention to visit Corinth both before and after his visit to Macedonia, to which 2 Cor. 1:15, 16 refers, and which he changed before writing I Corinthians (cf. 16:5), thereby unwittingly exposing himself to the calumny of his enemies, 2 Cor. 1:15–18. From 2 Cor. 7:6–8 some infer that another letter, far more censorious than I Corinthians intervened between the two canonical letters, and caused the apostles uneasiness; but the evidence is not strong enough to warrant the conclusion.

COMPOSITION

1. Occasion and Purpose. This letter was occasioned by reports which Paul received from Corinth and by a series of questions that were put to him by the Corinthians. Those who were of the house of Chloe told him of the divisions in their home church, 1:11, and common report had it that fornication and even incest was permitted in the congregation, 5:1. Moreover the church sent a letter, probably by the hand of Stephanas, Fortunatus and Achaicus, 16:17, asking the apostles opinion in several matters, as marriage, 7:1; the eating of meat offered to the idols, 8:1; the proper conduct in the church, 11:2; the right use of the spiritual gifts, 12:1; and in all probability also respecting the doctrine of the resurrection, 15.

In harmony with this occasion the purpose of the Epistle is especially twofold: In the first place the apostle desires to quench the party spirit that was rife among the Corinthians that he might lead them all to the unity of faith that is in Jesus Christ; and to correct the other evils that were found in the church, such as the case of incest and the irregularities that disgraced their Agapae, which culminated in the Lord's Supper. And in the second place it was his aim to give the young church, struggling with temptations and baffled by many difficult questions, further instruction along the lines indicated by them in their letter. With great diligence and care and solicitude for the welfare of the congregation the apostle applies himself to this task. In answer to the question, whether he also intended to defend his apostleship over against his enemies we would say that, though this was not altogether absent from his mind (cf. chs. 4 and 9), he does not aim at this directly like he does in writing II Corinthians, when the hostility of the false teachers has become far more pronounced.

2. Time and Place. The place, where this Epistle was written, is clearly indicated in 16:8, and therefore does not call for further discussion. This also aids us in determining the time of writing. The only stay of Paul at Ephesus of any duration is described in Acts 19. If our chronological calculations are correct, he came there in A. D. 54 and, after a stay of three years, left there again in 57. According to 1 Cor. 16:8 he wrote the epistle toward the end of his Ephesian ministry, before Pentecost of A. D. 57, and therefore probably in the early part of that year. We cannot conclude from 1 Cor. 5:7 that it was when the feast of unleavened bread was celebrated, although it is very well possible that the nearness of that feast gave rise to the line of thought developed in that chapter.

CANONICAL SIGNIFICANCE

The canonicity of the Epistle is abundantly attested by early Christian literature. It is the first one of the New Testament writings that is cited by name by one of the apostolic fathers. Clement of Rome says in his first Epistle to the Corinthians: "Take the Epistle of the blessed Paul the apostle into your hands etc." The writings of the other apostolic fathers, viz. Barnabas, Hermas, Ignatius and Polycarp show clear traces of the use of this Epistle. From Irenaeus on it is quoted as Holy Scripture. The Gnostics regarded it with special favor. It was found in Marcion's canon, in the Muratorian Fragment etc. The testimony to it is very full and clear.

In the Epistle to the Romans we have a statement of the way of salvation with special reference to the legalistic Romans; in this Epistle we find an exposition of it particularly with a view to the philosophically inclined Greeks. It clearly reveals that the way of wordly wisdom is not the way of life, a valuable lesson for the Church of all ages. But there is still another phase that gives the Epistle permanent value; it contains the doctrine of the cross in its social application. In it we see the church of God in the world with all its glitter and show, its temptations and dangers, its errors and crimes, and are taught to apply the principles of the Christian religion to the diversified relations of life, as we meet them in the bustle of a great and wicked city.

12

The Second Epistle to the Corinthians

CONTENTS

The contents of this Epistle are naturally divided into three parts:

I. Review of Paul's Relations with the Corinthians, 1:1-7:16. After the usual epistolary introduction, 1:1-11, the apostle vindicates himself with respect to the change in his intended visit, and with reference to what he had written respecting the offender, 1:12-2:13. Having done this, he takes up the discussion of the apostleship. In the first place he considers the office of an apostle, comparing the ministry of the Law with that of the Gospel, 3:6-18, and vindicating his own position as an apostle of the New Covenant, 2:14-3:5; 4:1-6. Then he treats of the sufferings of an apostle which are inseparably connected with his work, but are alleviated by the hope of future glory, 4:7-5:10. Next the life of an apostle passes the review, which finds its constraining motive in the love of Christ, has its spiritual basis in the life of the Redeemer, and is marked by sufferings, dishonor and poverty, on the one hand; but also by longsuffering and kindness, by knowledge and righteousness, on the other, 5:11-6:10. This is followed up by an appeal of the apostle to the Corinthians that they should give him place in their hearts, and should not be unequally yoked together with unbelievers, 6:11-7:4. Finally the apostle tells the Corinthians that he had been comforted greatly by the coming of Titus, by whom his fears that the former letter might have estranged them, were allayed and made place for rejoicing, 7:5-16.

II. The Collection for the Judaean Christians, 8:1-9:15. The apostle points the Corinthians to the example of the Macedonians who gave abundantly for the poor at Jerusalem, 8:1-7; and to the example of Christ who became poor that the Corinthians might be enriched, 8:8-15. He commends to them Titus and the two brethren that are sent with him to gather the collection, 8:16-24; and exhorts them to give abundantly for this worthy cause, 9:1-18.

III. Paul's Vindication of his Apostleship, 10:1-13:14. In this part Paul deals directly with his opponents. First of all he points out that the ministry entrusted to him also extended to the Corinthians, 9:1-15. Then he replies to his opponents that he had been perfectly loyal to the cause of Christ, 11:1-6; that he had not dealt deceitfully with the Corinthians, when he refused support from them, 11:7-15; that he had far greater things in which to glory than they could boast of, 11:16-12:10; and that it had never been and was not now his aim to make a gain of the Corinthians, 12:11-18. Finally he gives them warnings in view of his coming visit, and closes his epistle with final salutations and benediction, 12:19-13:13.

CHARACTERISTICS

1. II Corinthians is one of the most personal and the least doctrinal of all the letters of Paul, except the one written to Philemon. The doctrinal element is not altogether wanting; the great truths of salvation find expression in it, as well as in the other letters of the apostle; but, though they enter into its composition, they have a subordinate place and are, as it were, eclipsed by its large personal element, in which we see the very heart of the apostle, with all its varying moods of courage and anxiety, of love and aversion, of hope and disappointment. Alford says: "Consolation and rebuke, gentleness and severity, earnestness and irony succeed one another at very short intervals and without notice."

2. The second characteristic of this Epistle is closely connected with the preceding one; it is the most unsystematic of all the letters of Paul. How greatly it differs in this respect from the Epistle to the Romans and from First Corinthians, becomes perfectly evident, when one attempts to give an outline of the contents. This irregularity is due to the fact that in this letter we do not find a calm discussion of doctrinal subjects or of certain phases of Christian life, but above all an impassioned self-defense against unjust charges and calumnies and insinuations. However humble the apostle may be, and though he may regard himself as the least of all the saints, yet in this letter he finds himself constrained to boast of his sufferings and of his work.

3. The language of this Epistle has been judged variously, some criticizing it severely and others praising its excellencies. We cannot deny that it is more rugged and harsh, more obscure and difficult of interpretation than we are accustomed to in Paul's other writings. "Parentheses and digressions often intersect the narrative and disturb its sequence." (Davidson) Meyer

says beautifully: "The excitement and varied play of emotion with which Paul wrote this letter, probably also in haste, certainly make the expression not seldom obscure and the sentences less flexible, but only heighten our admiration of the great delicacy, skill and power with which this outpouring of Paul's spirit and heart, possessing as a defense of himself a high and peculiar interest, flows and gushes on, till finally, in the last part, wave on wave overwhelms the hostile resistance." Comm. p. 412.

AUTHORSHIP

The external testimony to the authorship of Paul is inferior to that of I Corinthians; yet it is so strong that it leaves no room for honest doubt. Irenaeus, Clement of Alexandria, Tertullian and many others, from all parts of the early Church, quote it by name.

But even if this were not so strong, internal evidence would be quite sufficient to settle the question of authenticity. In the first place the Epistle claims to be a product of the great apostle. In the second place it is written in a style that is in many respects characteristically Pauline, notwithstanding its unique features; it contains the doctrine of salvation, as we are wont to hear it proclaimed by the apostle of the Gentiles; and it reveals his character, as no other Epistle does. And in the third place the thought of this Epistle is closely interwoven with that of I Corinthians. In 1 Cor. 16:5 Paul speaks of his plan of travel, and in 2 Cor. 1:15-24 he comments on it; in 1 Cor. 5 he urges that discipline be applied to the incestuous person, and in 2 Cor. 2:5-11 he says, with reference to this case, that they have inflicted sufficient punishment, and restrains their evident severity; respecting the collection for the Judaean Christians which he enjoins on the Corinthians in 1 Cor. 16:1-4, he gives further directions in 2 Cor. 8 and 9; to the Judaeizers who cast doubt on his apostleship he refers in 1 Cor. 4 and 9, and speaks of them more at length in 2 Cor. 10-13.

The authenticity of the Epistle too was attacked by Bruno Bauer and by the Dutch critics that we mentioned in connection with the first Epistle. But their work failed to convince anyone but themselves. Godet truly says: "—the scholars who cannot discern, across these pages, the living personality of St. Paul, must have lost in the work of the study, the sense for realities." Introd. to the N. T. I p. 337.

COMPOSITION

1. Occasion and Purpose. In order to understand the occasion that induced Paul to write this Epistle to the Corinthians, we must bring it

in connection with the first letter, which was in all probability borne to Corinth by Titus, Paul's spiritual son. After it had gone forth, the apostle pondered on what he had written in that letter, and it caused him some uneasiness of mind, 2 Cor. 7:8. He reflected that he had written in a rather severe strain regarding the divisions at Corinth and the incestuous person, and feared for a time that his words might be misconstrued, that his letter might create a false impression, and that his severity might provoke resentment and thus injure the cause of the gospel that lay so near to his heart.

We are aware that some scholars, as f. i. Hausrath, Schmiedel, Kennedy, Baljon, Findlay, Robertson (in Hastings D. B.) and Davidson hold that 2 Cor. 2:4, 9; 7:8 refer to a second lost epistle of Paul, the so-called Painful Letter; but with Zahn, Holtzmann and Bernard (in Expositor's Gk. Test.) we believe it to be a rather gratuitous assumption that such an epistle ever existed.

Shortly after Paul had sent I Corinthians, he left Ephesus for Troas, where a splendid opportunity for work offered. Yet he was keenly disappointed, for he had expected to find Titus there with tidings from Corinth; and when he did not find him, his very anxiety caused him to sail for Macedonia that he might meet his beloved brother and co-laborer the sooner and be reassured by him, 2 Cor. 2:12, 13. The mere change of the field of labor brought him no relief, for he says: "When we were come into Macedonia, our flesh had no rest, but we were troubled on every side; without were fightings, within were fears." 7:5. Soon, however, he was comforted by the coming of Titus, 7:6; the painful uncertainty now made place for calm assurance, yea even for joy and thanksgiving. But his happiness was not unalloyed, since the report of Titus was not altogether favorable. The Corinthian congregation as a whole had taken kindly to the warnings and directions of the previous letter. The words of reproof had made a deep impression on them, had saddened their hearts, had filled them with sorrow,—but it was a godly sorrow that worked repentance. Hence the apostle had occasion to rejoice and did rejoice, 7:7-16. The enemies of Paul, however, had been embittered by the former Epistle and had increased their sinister work, attempting to undermine the apostolic authority of Paul by charging that he was fickle and vacillating, 1:15-24; that he was controlled by fleshly motives, 10:2; that he was bold at a distance, but cowardly, when present, 10:10; that he was dealing deceitfully with the Corinthians even in taking no support from them, 11:7-12; and that he had not shown himself an apostle by his works, 12:11-13.

The question may be asked to which one of the four parties mentioned in I Corinthians the enemies belong with which the apostle deals in 2 Cor. 10–13. It is quite clear, and scholars are generally agreed, that they were in the main, if not exclusively, ultra-Judaeists. But there is no such unanimity in classifying them with one of the divisions of which the first Epistle speaks. Following F. C. Baur many, such as Baljon, Davidson, Weiss, identify them with those whose watchword was: "I am of Christ!" Others, however, as Meyer and Zahn regard them as belonging to the party that professed special allegiance to Peter. To this view we give preference; however, with the proviso's that in this letter Paul does not deal with the whole party, but rather with its leaders, who had probably come from Judaea with letters of commendation, 3:1, and whom Paul qualifies as "false apostles, deceitful workers, transforming themselves in apostles of Christ," 11:13;—and that it is quite possible that some of his words refer to those who, ignoring and dispising all human authority, claimed to be of Christ, and did not uphold the honor and faithfulness of the apostle against the false teachers. Cf. 10:7.

This being the situation at Corinth, when the apostle wrote his second letter, he was naturally led to write with a twofold purpose. In the first place it was his desire to express his gratitude for the way in which the Corinthians had received his former letter, and to inform them of the joy he experienced, when they had manifested their willingness to mend their ways and had been filled with godly sorrow. And in the second place he considered it incumbent on him to defend his apostleship against the calumnies and the malignant attacks of the Judaeistic adversaries.

2. Time and Place. In view of the account we have given of the course of events that followed the writing of I Corinthians, it is not very difficult to establbish approximately both the time and the place of writing. We may assume that, in accordance with the plan expressed in 1 Cor. 15:8, the apostle remained at Ephesus until Pentecost of A. D. 57. On leaving Ephesus he went to Troas, from where he crossed over to Macedonia. There he soon met Titus, presumably in the summer of that same year, and therefore some time before he was ready to visit Corinth, and received information from him regarding the condition of the Corinthian church. Overjoyed by what he heard, but at the same time apprehending the danger that lurked in the agitation of the Judaeizers, he immediately wrote II Corinthians, and sent it to Corinth by the hand of Titus, who was accompanied on his journey by two of the brethren, whose names are not recorded, 8:18, 22. The letter was written, therefore, in the summer of A. D. 57, somewhere in Macedonia.

INTEGRITY

The integrity of the letter has been attacked especially on two points. It is claimed by some that the verses 6:14-7:1 do not belong, where they stand, but form an awkward interruption in the course of thought. A few scholars regard them as a part of the lost letter to which 1 Cor. 5:9 refers. Now it is true that at first sight these verses seem out of place, where they stand, but at the same time it is very well possible to give a plausible explanation for their insertion at this point. Cf. Meyer, Alford, Expositor's Greek, Testament.

Several critics opine that the chapters 10-13 did not originally form a part of this letter. Hausrath and Schmiedel advocated the theory that they constituted a part of the so-called Painful letter that intervened between I and II Corinthians. The reasons why they would separate this section from the other nine chapters, are the following: (1) The 10th chapter begins with the words Αὐτός δὲ ἐγὼ Παῦλος, which δὲ marks these words as an antithesis to something that is not found in the preceding. (2) The tone of the apostle in these last chapters is strikingly different from that in the other nine; from a calm and joyful tone it has changed to one of stern rebuke and of sharp invective. (3) Certain passages found in the first part point back to statements that are found in the last chapters, and thus prove that these are part of a previous letter. Thus 2:3 refers to 13:10; 1:23 to 13:2; and 2:9 to 10:6.

But to these arguments we may reply, in the first place, that δὲ often does no more than mark the transition to a new subject (cf. 1 Cor. 15:1; 2 Cor. 8:1); in the second place, that the change of tone need not surprise us, if we take in consideration the possibility that Paul did not write the whole Epistle at a single sitting and therefore in the same mood; and the fact that in the last chapters he deals more particularly with the false teachers among the Corinthians; and in the third place, that the passages referred to do not necessitate the construction put on them by the above named critics. Moreover, if we adopt the theory that another letter intervened between our two canonical Epistles, we are led to a very complicated scheme of Paul's transactions with Corinth, a scheme so complicated that it is its own condemnation.

CANONICAL SIGNIFICANCE

The ancient Church was unanimous in accepting the Epistle as a part of the Word of God. Of the apostolic fathers Polycarp plainly quotes it. Marcion included it in his canon, and it is also named in the Muratorian

Fragment. The Syriac and old Latin Versions contain it, and the three great witnesses of the end of the second century quote it by name.

This Epistle too has permanent value for the Church of God. It is inseparably connected with I Corinthians, and as such also brings out that it is not the wisdom of the world but the foolishness of the cross that saves; and sheds further light on the application of Christian principles to social relations. More than any other Epistle it reveals to us the apostle's personality, and is therefore a great psychological aid in the interpretation of his writings. It also has considerable doctrinal interest in that it exhibits a part of the apostle's eschatology, 4:16–5:8; brings out the contrast between the letter and the spirit, 3:6–18; describes the beneficent influence of the glory of Christ, 3:18–4:6; and contains an explicit statement of the reconciliation and renovation wrought by Christ, 5:17–21.

13

The Epistle to the Galatians

CONTENTS

The Epistle to the Galatians may be divided into three parts:

I. Paul's Defense of his Apostleship, 1:1-2:21. After the usual introduction the apostle states the occasion of his writing, 1:1-10. In defense of his apostle'ship he points out that he has been called by God himself and received his Gospel by direct revelation, and had no occasion to learn it from the other apostle's, 1:11-24; that the apostle's showed their agreement with him by not demanding the circumcision of Titus and by admitting his mission to the gentiles, 2:1-10; and that he had even rebuked Peter, when this "pillar of the church" was not true to the doctrine of free grace, 2:11-21.

II. His Defense of the Doctrine of Justification, 3:1-4:31. Here the apostle clearly brings out that the Galatians received the gift of the Spirit by faith, 3:1-5; that Abraham was justified by faith, 3:6-9; that delivery from the curse of the law is possible only through faith, 3:10-14; and that the law has merely a parenthetic character, coming, as it does, between the promise and its fulfillment, 3:15-29. He compares Judæism to a son who is minor, and Christianity to a son that has attained his majority, 4:1-7; admonishes the Galatians that, realizing their privilege, they should not return to the beggarly elements of knowledge, 4:8-20; and says that the Jew is like the child of Hagar, while the Christian resembles the child of Sara, 4:21-31.

III. Practical Exhortations, 5:1-6:18. The Galatians are exhorted to stand in their Christian liberty, 5:1-12, a liberty that is not license but obedience, 5:13-18. The works of the flesh and the fruits of the Spirit are described that the Galatians may avoid the former and yield the latter, 5:19-26. The right way of treating the erring and weak is pointed out, and also the relation of what one sows to what one reaps, 5:1-10. With a brief summary and benediction Paul ends his letter, 6:11-18.

CHARACTERISTICS

1. The Epistle to the Galatians has a great deal in common with that written to the Romans. They both treat the same general theme, viz. that by the works of the law no man will be justified before God. The same Old Testament passage is quoted in Rom. 4:3 and Gal. 3:6; and the same general argument is built on it, that the promise belongs to those who have faith like that which Abraham had even before he was circumcized. In both Epistles Paul aims at reconciling his admission that the Mosaic law came from God with his contention that it was not binding on Christians. Besides these similarities there are also several verbal agreements and parallel passages in these letters. Of the latter we may mention Rom. 8:14-17 and Gal. 4:5-7; Rom. 6:6-8 and Gal. 2:20; Rom. 13:13, 14 and Gal. 5:16, 17.

2. But however similar these Epistles may be, there are also striking differences. In the Epistle to the Romans Paul does not directly encounter such as are hostile to the truth or personal adversaries; hence it is written in a calm spirit and is at most indirectly polemical. This is quite different in the Epistle to the Galatians. There were those in the churches of Galatia who perverted the doctrine of the cross and called the apostolic authority of Paul in question. As a result this is one of the most controversial writings of the apostle; it is an outburst of indignant feeling, written in a fiery tone.

3. This Epistle abounds in striking contrasts. Grace is contrasted with the Law in its Jewish application, and especially on its ritual side; faith is placed in antithetic relation to the works of man; the fruits of the Spirit are set over against the works of the flesh; circumcision is opposed to the new creation; and the enmity of the world to the cross of Christ is brought out in strong relief.

4. The style of this letter is rather unique in that it unites the two extreme affections of Paul's admirable character: severity and tenderness. At times he speaks in a cold severe tone, as if he would scarcely recognize the Galatians as brethren; then again his whole heart seems to yearn for them. It is hard to imagine anything more solemnly severe than the opening verses of the epistle and 3:1-5; but it is equally difficult to conceive of something more tenderly affectionate than appeals such as we find in 4:12-16, 18-20. We find in this letter a beautiful blending of sharp invective and tender pleading.

AUTHORSHIP

The authorship of the Epistle need not be subject to doubt, since both the external and the internal evidence are very strong. The letter is found in Marcion's canon, is named in the Muratorian Fragment, and from the time of Irenaeus is regularly quoted by name. But even if the external testimony were not so strong, internal evidence would be quite sufficient to establish the Pauline authorship. The letter is self-attested, 1:1, and clearly reveals the character of the great apostle; it does this all the better, since it is so intensely personal. And though there are some harmonistic difficulties, when we compare 1:18 and Acts 9:23;—1:18, 19 and Acts 9:26;—1:18; 2:1 and Acts 9:26; 11:30; 12:25; 15:2,—yet these are not insuperable, and, on the whole, the historical allusions found in the epistle fit in well with the narrative in Acts.

For a long time Bruno Bauer was the only one to question the authenticity of this letter, but since 1882 the Dutch school of Loman and Van Manen joined him, followed by Friedrich in Germany. The principal reason for doubting it is the supposed impossibility of so rapid a development of the contrast between Jewish and Pauline Christianity as this letter presupposes. But the facts do not permit us to doubt that the conflict did occur then, while in the second century it had died out.

THE CHURCHES OF GALATIA

Among the Epistles of Paul this is the only one that is expressly addressed, not to an individual nor to a single church, but a group of churches, ταῖς ἐκκλησίαις τῆς Γαλατίας, 1:2. When did the apostle found these Galatian churches? The answer to that question will necessarily depend on our interpretation of the term Galatia, as it is used by the apostle. There is a twofold use of this appellative, viz. the geographical and the political. Geographically the term Galatia denotes one of the Northern districts of Asia Minor, a district that was bounded on the North by Bithynia and Paplagonia, on the East by the last named province and Pontus, on the West by Phrygia, and on the South by Lycaonia and Capadocia. The same name is employed in an official, political sense, however, to designate the Roman province which included Galatia proper, a part of Phrygia, Pisidia and Lycaonia. This twofold significance of the name Galatia has led to two theories respecting the location of the Galatian churches, viz. the North and the South Galatian theory. The former still represents the prevailing view; but the latter is accepted by an ever increasing number of scholars.

According to the North Galatian theory the churches of Galatia were situated in the geographical district indicated by that name. Since about 280 B. C. this territory was inhabited by a Celtic people, consisting of three separate tribes, that had migrated thither from Western Europe, and who constituted shortly before Christ the kingdom of Galatia. They were given to the worship of Cybele "with its wild ceremonial and hideous mutilations;" and were characterized by fickleness and great instability of character. "Inconstant and quarrelsome," says Lightfoot, Com. p. 14, "treacherous in their dealings, incapable of sustained effort, easily disheartened by failures, such they appear, when viewed on their darker side." The adherents of this theory are generally agreed that Paul, in all probability, founded the Galatian churches in the most important cities of this district, i. e. in the capital Ancyra, in Pessinus, the principal seat of the hideous service of Cybele, and at Tavium, at once a strong fortress and a great commercial center. The South Galatian theory, on the other hand, identifies the Galatian churches with those founded by Paul on his first missionary journey at Pisidian Antioch, Iconium, Lystra and Derbe, not excluding any other churches that may have been founded in the province.

The North Galatian theory is supported by the following considerations: (1) It is unlikely that Paul would address the inhabitants of Phrygia, Pisidia and Lycaonia as Galatians. That name could properly be given only to the Celts, the Gauls that lived in Galatia proper. (2) It is improbable that Paul would have referred to the churches founded by him and Barnabas jointly, as if they had been established by him alone. (3) The character of the Galatians, as it is reflected in this letter, is in remarkable agreement with that of the Celts whose changeableness was a subject of common comment. (4) Since in the Acts of the Apostles Mysia, Phrygia and Pisidia are all geographical terms, without any political significance, the inference seems perfectly warranted that the name Galatia, when it is found alongside of these, is employed in a similar sense. (5) "The expression used in the Acts of Paul's visit to these parts, 'the Phrygian and Galatian country,' shows that the district intended was not Lycaonia and Pisidia, but some region which might be said to belong either to Phrygia or Galatia, or the parts of each contiguous to the other." (Lightfoot).

Now we are not inclined to underrate the value of these arguments, but yet it seems to us that they are not altogether conclusive. The first one impresses us as a rather gratuitous assumption. Taking in consideration that the Roman province of Galatia was organized as early as 25 B. C. (Cf.

Ramsay, Historical Comm. on the Galatians, p. 103 ff. and J. Weiss, Real-Enc. Art. Kleinasien), and had therefore existed at least 75 years, when Paul wrote this letter, it is hard to see, why he could not address its inhabitants as Galatians. This is true especially in view of the fact that the apostle shows a decided preference for the imperial nomenclature, probably since it was the most honorable. Moreover in writing to the congregations in South Galatia he could not very well use any other name, if he did not wish to address them in a very cumbrous way.—In connection with the second argument we must bear in mind that this Epistle was written after the rupture between Barnabas and Paul, when, so it seems; the labor was divided so that Paul received charge of the South Galatian churches. It was but natural therefore that he should feel the sole responsibility for them.—On the third argument Salmon, who also advocates the North Galatian theory, would wisely place little reliance, because "it may be doubted whether Celts formed the predominating element in the churches of Galatia," and since "men of different nationalities show a common nature." Introd. p. 412.—We do not feel the cogency of the fourth argument for, granted that Luke does use the term Galatia in its geographical sense, this does not prove anything as to Paul's usage. In fact the presumption is that the apostle did not so use it.—And the last argument is of rather dubious value, since it rests on an uncertain interpretation of the expressions τὴν Φρυγίαν καὶ Γαλατικὴν Χώραν, Acts 16:, and τὴν Γαλατικὴν Χώραν κὰι Φρυγίαν, Acts 18:23. The expression in 16:6 can probably also be translated "the Phrygo-Galatic region," referring to that part of the province Galatia that included Antioch and Iconium, and that originally belonged to Phrygia. In 18:23, however, where the names are reversed, we must translate, "the Galatic territory and Phrygia," the last name then, according to Ramsay, referring to either Phrygia Galatica or Phrygia Magna. In any event it seems peculiar that Paul, if in these places he has reference to Galatia proper, should speak of the Galatian territory rather than of Galatia.

The North Galatian theory is defended by Weiss, Davidson, Jülicher, Godet and especially by Lightfoot. But the South Galatian theory also has able defenders, such as Renan, Hausrath, Zahn, Baljon and above all Ramsay, whose extended travels and research in Asia Minor, combined with great learning, enable him to speak with authority on questions pertaining to that district. This theory assumes that Paul used the name Galatia in its official political sense, and that the Galatian churches were those of Antioch, Iconium, Lystra and Derbe, e. a. Although we do not feel inclined to speak dogmatically on the subject, it seems to us that this theory deserves preference for the following reasons: (1) It was evidently Paul's uniform custom to denote the location of the churches which he founded, not by the popular but by the official nomenclature. Thus he speaks of the churches of Asia, 1 Cor. 16:19; the churches of Macedonia, 2 Cor. 8:1; and the churches of Achaia, 2 Cor. 1:1. And that this was not something peculiar to Paul, is proved by the fact that Peter does the same in 1 Peter 1:1, where the term Galatia is obviously used in its political sense, since all the other names refer to Roman provinces. Even Lightfoot admits that this is probably the case. (2) That Paul founded churches in the Roman province of Galatia is a well attested fact, of which we have a detailed narrative in Acts 13 and 14; on the other hand, we have no record whatever of his establishing churches in the district of that name. It is certainly not very obvious that Luke in Acts 16:6 wants to convey the idea that the apostle established churches in North Galatia. The most that can be said, is that Acts 18:23 implies such previous activity on the part of Paul; but even this depends on the correct interpretation of the phrase, "the country of Galatia and Phrygia." Lightfoot himself regards it as "strange that, while we have more or less acquaintance with all the other important churches of St. Paul's founding, not a single name of a person or place, scarcely a single incident of any kind, connected with the apostle's preaching in Galatia, should be preserved either in the history or in the epistle." Comm. p. 20. (3) The Epistle refers to the collection for the Judaean saints, 2:10 and in 1 Cor. 16:1 Paul says that he commanded the churches in Galatia to take part in this. What is the meaning of the term Galatia here? From the Epistles of Paul we gather that the churches of Galatia, 1 Cor. 16:1, Macedonia, 2 Cor. 8:1; 9:2; and Achaia, Rom. 15:26, contributed for this cause; while from Acts 20:4 we learn that representatives from Asia also accompanied Paul to Jerusalem, according to the principle laid down in 1 Cor. 16:3, 4. Now if we take the name Galatia in its official sense here, then all the churches founded by Paul are seen to participate in this work of charity; while if we interpret it as referring to North Galatia, the churches of Antioch, Iconium, Lystra and Derbe are not mentioned, and the impression is created that they did not take part. But this is exceedingly improbable, and the improbability is heightened by the fact that among the representatives accompanying Paul we also find Secundus and Gajus of Derbe and Timotheus of Lystra, while there are none to represent North Galatia. (4) From Gal. 4:13 we learn that Paul first preached the gospel to the Galatians through infirmity of the flesh. This may mean that Paul, traveling through Galatia, was detained there by sickness, or that he repaired to this district, in order to recuperate from some disease. But the road through North Galatia did not lead to any place, where Paul was likely to go, and its climate was very undesirable for an invalid. On the other hand the supposition is altogether natural that the apostle contracted some disease in the marshy lowlands of Pamphylia, and therefore sought restoration in the bracing atmosphere of Pisidian Antioch. (5) In this Epistle Paul repeatedly mentions Barnabas as a person well known to the Galatians, 2:1, 9, 13. Now he was Paul's co-laborer in establishing the South Galatian churches, but did not accompany the apostle on his second missionary journey, when the churches of North Galatia are supposed to have been founded. It is true that this argument is somewhat neutralized by the fact that Barnabas is mentioned also in 1 Cor. 9:6; yet this is not altogether the case, since the references in Galatians are more specific. In 2:9, where Paul seeks to establish his apostle'ship, he also seems to consider it desirable to vindicate the legitimacy of Barnabas' mission; while in 2:13 he presupposes that his readers have knowledge of the stand taken by Barnabas with reference to the doctrine of free grace. We conclude, therefore, that the Galatian churches were in all probability those founded by Paul on his first missionary journey in South Galatia. Cf. especially Ramsay, The Church in the Roman Empire pp. 3–112; St. Paul the Traveler and the Roman Citizen pp. 89–151; and Zahn's Einleitung II pp. 124–139.

The Galatian churches were mainly composed of Gentile-Christians, but also contained an important Jewish element. This can be inferred from the narrative in Acts 13 and 14. The Gentiles were eager to receive the truth, 13:42, 46–48; 14:1, while the Jews were very much divided, some believingly accepting the word of the apostle's, 13:43; 14:1, and others rejecting it with scorn and mal-treating the messengers of the cross, 13:45, 50; 14:2, 5, 19. The impression received from the narrative is corroborated by the Epistle, which in the main addresses itself to the Greeks who had not yet accepted circumcision, but had of late been urged to submit to this rite, if not to all the Jewish ceremonies, that they might share in the covenant blessings of Abraham. The apostle describes the whole congregation according to the majojrity of its members, when he says in 4:8, "Howbeit then, when ye knew not God, ye did service unto them which by nature are no gods." Yet it is evident from 3:23–25, 28 that he also bears the Jewish element in mind. We need not doubt, however, that the majority of the Greeks that constituted the Galatian churches had already for some time attended the synagogue of the Jews before they were converted to Christianity, and therefore belonged to the proselytes, the so-called devout persons of whom Acts repeatedly speaks. This may be inferred from Acts 13:43; 14:1, and from the fact that the apostle presupposes a certain familiarity in his readers with the patriarchal history, the Law, the Psalms and the Prophets.

COMPOSITION

1. Occasion and Purpose. After Paul had preached the gospel to the Galatians and had seen them well started on the royal road to salvation, Judaeizing teachers entered the field, jealous of their Jewish prerogatives. Probably they were emissaries from Jerusalem that abused a commission entrusted to them, or assumed an authority which they in no way possessed. They did not combat Christianity as such, but desired that it should be led in Judaeistic channels. Every convert to Christianity should submit to circumcision, if not to the whole ceremonial law. Their teaching was quite the opposite of Paul's doctrine, and could only be maintained by discrediting the apostle. Hence they sought to undermine his personal influence and to depreciate his apostolic authority by claiming that he had not been called of God and had received the truth at second-hand from the Twelve. It seems that Paul, when he last visited the Galatian churches, had already encountered some such enemies, 1:9, but he now heard that their influence was increasing, and that they were successful in persuading the Galatians to forsake their Christian privileges, and thus virtually though perhaps unwittingly, to deny Christ who had bought them, 3:1; 4:9-11, 17; 5:7, 8, 10. Hence he deems it imperative to write them a letter.

The purpose of the author in writing this Epistle was, of course, two-fold. In order that his words might be effective, it was necessary, first of all, that he should defend his apostolic authority by proving that God had called him and had imparted the truth of the gospel to him by means of a direct revelation. And in the second place it was incumbent on him that he should expose the Judaeistic error by which they were led astray, and should defend the doctrine of justification by faith.

2. Time and Place. There is great diversity of opinion as to the time, when the Epistle was written. Zahn, Hausrath, Baljon and Rendall (in The Exp. Gk. Test.) regard it as the earliest of Paul's Epistles, and assume that it was written during the early part of his stay in Corinth in the year 53. Ramsay thinks it was written from Antioch at the end of the second

missionary journey, i. e. according to his dating, also in A. D. 53. Weiss, Holtzmann and Godet refer it to the early part of Paul's Ephesian residence, about the year 54 or 55, while Warfield prefers to place it towards the end of this period in A. D. 57. And finally Lightfoot and Salmon agree in dating it after Paul's departure from Ephesus. This great variety of opinion proves that the data for determining the time are few and uncertain. Those accepting the North Galatian theory are virtually confined to a date after the beginning of Paul's Ephesian residence in the year 54, because the πρότερον of Gal. 4:13 seems to imply that the apostle had visited the churches of Galatia twice before he wrote his letter; while it is for the same reason most natural that they who advocate the South Galatian theory, find their terminus a quo in A. D. 52 (McGiffert notwithstanding), when Paul had paid a second visit to the South Galatian churches. Assuming, as we do, that this letter was addressed to the churches of South Galatia, we may dismiss the idea that the apostle wrote it during the third missionary journey, because this would imply that he had already visited them three times, in which case he would have used πρῶτον instead of πρότερον in 4:13. Moreover if Paul wrote it from Ephesus, the question is naturally raised, why he did not visit the Galatians rather than write to them, seeing that he had a great desire to be with them, 4:20. We are inclined to think that Paul wrote this letter on his second missionary journey, after he had passed into Europe, and probably during the first part of his residence at Corinth, for: (1) Gal. 4:20 implies that Paul was at some distance from the Galatian churches; (2) The letter presupposes that some time had elapsed between its composition and the second visit of the apostle; and (3) The letter contains no greetings from Silas and Timotheus, who were both well known to the Galatians. Evidently they had not yet reached Corinth.

CANONICAL SIGNIFICANCE

There has never been any serious doubt respecting the canonicity of this Epistle. It was received as authoritative in all sections of the Church from the very earliest times. There are allusions to its language in the apostolic fathers, Clement of Rome, Polycarp and Ignatius. Justin Martyr, Melito and Athanagoras seem to have known it; and some of the heretics, especially the Ophites, used it extensively. It is found in Marcions canon, is named in the Muratorian Fragment, and the Syriac and old Latin versions contain it. From the end of the second century the quotations multiply and increase in directness and definiteness.

This Epistle too has abiding significance for the Church of God. It is essentially a defense of the doctrine of free grace, of the Christian liberty of New Testament believers over against those that would bring them under the law in its Old Testament application, and would place them under the obligation to submit to circumcision and to participate in the shadowy ceremonies of a by-gone day. The great central exhortation of this letter is: "Stand fast in the liberty wherewith Christ has made us free, and be not tangled again with the yoke of bondage." The way of the ritualist is not the way of life, is the lesson that should be remembered by all those who are inclined to over-emphasize the outward form of religion to the neglect of its spirit and essence.

14

The Epistle to the Ephesians

CONTENTS

The Epistle to the Ephesians is naturally divided into two parts:

I. The Doctrinal Part, treating of the Unity of the Church, 1:1-3:21. After the address and salutation, 1:1, 2, the apostle praises God for the great spiritual blessings received in Christ, in whom the Ephesians have been chosen, adopted and sealed with the Holy Spirit of promise, 1:3-14. He renders thanks for these blessings and prays that God may make known to the Church, the glorious body of Christ, who filleth all in all, the glory of its heavenly calling, 1:15-23. Then he compares the past and present condition of the readers, 2:1-13, and describes Christ's work of reconciliation, resulting in the unity and glory of the Church, 2:14-22. Next he enlarges on the mystery of the Gospel and reminds his readers that he has been commissioned by God to make it known to mankind, 3:1-13. He prays that they may be strengthened and enabled to comprehend the greatness of the love of Christ to the glory of God, 3:14-21.

II. The Practical Part, containing Exhortations to a Conversation worthy of the Calling and Unity of the Readers, 4:1-6:20. The readers are exhorted to maintain the unity which God seeks to establish among them by distributing spiritual gifts and instituting different offices, 4:1-16. They should not walk as the Gentiles do, but according to the principle of their new life, shunning the vices of the old man and practicing the virtues of the new, 4:17-32. In society it must be their constant endeavor to be separate from the evils of the world and to walk circumspectly; husbands and wives should conform in their mutual relation to the image of Christ and the Church; children should obey their parents and servants their masters, 5:1-6:9. Finally Paul exhorts the readers to be strong in the Lord, having put on the whole armour of God and seeking strength in prayer and supplication;

and he closes his Epistle with some personal intelligence and a twofold salutation, 6:10–24.

CHARACTERISTICS

1. This letter is marked first of all by its general character. It has this in common with the Epistle to the Romans, that it partakes somewhat of the nature of a treatise; yet it is as truly a letter, as any one of the other writings of Paul. Deissmann correctly remarks, however, that "the personal element is less prominent in it than the impersonal." St. Paul, p. 23. The letter does not presuppose, like those to the Corinthians and to the Galatians, some special clearly marked historical situation, does not refer to any historical incidents known to us from other sources, except the imprisonment of Paul, and contains no personal greetings. The only person mentioned is Tychicus, the bearer of the letter. It treats in a profound and sublime manner of the unity of all believers in Jesus Christ, and of the holy conversation in Christ that must issue from it.

2. It is also characterized by its great similarity to the letter sent to the Colossians. This is so great that some critics have regarded it as merely a revised and enlarged edition of the latter; but this idea must be dismissed altogether, because the difference between them is too great and fundamental. The Epistle to the Colossians is more personal and controversial than that to the Ephesians; the former treats of Christ, the Head of the Church, while the latter is mainly concerned with the Church, the body of Christ. Notwithstanding this, however, the resemblance of the two is readily observed. There is good reason for calling them twin letters. In many cases the same words and forms of expression are found in both; the thought is often identical, while the language differs; and the general structure of the Epistles is very similar.

3. The style of the letter is in general very exalted, and forms a great contrast with that of the epistle to the Galatians. Dr. Sanday says: "With few exceptions scholars of all different schools who have studied and interpreted this epistle have been at one in regarding it as one of the sublimest and most profound of all the New Testament writings. In the judgment of many who are well entitled to deliver an opinion, it is the grandest of all the Pauline letters." The Exp. Gk. Test. III p. 208. The style is characterized by a succession of participial clauses and dependent sentences that flow on like a torrent, and by lengthy digressions. One is impressed by its grandeur, but often finds it difficult to follow the apostle as he soars to giddy

heights. The language is further remarkable in that it contains a series of terms with far-reaching significance, such as the council (βουλή) of God, His will (θέλημα), His purpose (πρόθεσις), His good pleasure (εὐδοκία), etc., and also a great number of ἅπαξ λεγόμενα. According to Holtzmann there are 76 words that are peculiar to this epistle, of which 18 are found nowhere else in the Bible, 17 do not occur in the rest of the New Testament, and 51 are absent from all the other Pauline letters (the Pastoral epistles being excepted). Einleitung p. 259.

AUTHORSHIP

The historical evidence for the Pauline authorship of the Epistle is exceptionally strong. Some scholars claim that Ignatius even speaks of Paul as the author, when he says in his Epistle to the Ephesians: "—who (referring back to Paul) throughout all his Epistle (ἐν πάσῃ ἐπιστολῇ) makes mention of you in Christ Jesus." But it is very doubtful, whether the rendering, "in all the Epistle," should not rather be, "in every Epistle." Marcion ascribed the letter to Paul, and in the Muratorian Fragment the church of Ephesus is mentioned as one of the churches to which Paul wrote Epistles. Irenaeus and Clement of Alexandria refer to Paul by name as the author of this letter and quote it as his, while Tertullian mentions Ephesus among the churches that had apostolic Epistles.

Internal evidence also points to Paul as the author. In the opening verse of the Epistle the writer is named, and the structure of the letter is characteristically Pauline. In the first place it contains the usual blessing and thanksgiving; this is followed in the regular way by the body of the epistle, consisting of a doctrinal and a practical part; and finally it ends with the customary salutations. The ideas developed are in perfect agreement with those found in the letters which we already discussed, although in certain particulars they advance beyond them, as f. i. in the theological conception of the doctrine of redemption; and in the doctrine of the Church as the body of Christ with its various organs. The style of the Epistle too is Pauline. It is true that it differs considerably from that of Romans, Corinthians and Galatians, but it shows great affinity with the style of Colossians and of the Pastorals.

Notwithstanding all the evidence in favor of the Pauline authorship of this Epistle, its authenticity has been questioned by several New Testament scholars. De Wette, Baur and his school, Davidson, Holtzmann and Weizsäcker are among the most prominent. The idea is that some later, probably a second century writer impersonated the great apostle. The principal grounds on which the Epistle was attacked, are the following: (1) It is so like the Epistle to the Colossians that it cannot be an original document. De Wette came to the conclusion that it was a "verbose amplification" of the Epistle to the Colossians. Holtzmann, finding that in some parts the priority must be ascribed to Ephesians rather than to Colossians, advocated the theory that Paul wrote an Epistle to the Colossians shorter than our canonical letter; that a forger, guided by this, fabricated the Epistle to the Ephesians; and that this plagiarist was so enamoured with his work that he, in turn, revised the Colossian Epistle in accordance with it. (2) The vocabulary and in general the style of the Epistle is so different from that of the other letters of Paul as to give it an un-Pauline stamp. This objection is based partly, though not primarily, on the numerous ἅπαξ λεχόμενα; but especially on the use of Pauline words in a new souse, such as μυστήριον, οἰκονομία and περιποίησις; on the expression of certain ideas by terms that differ from those employed elsewhere by the apostle for the same purpose, as f. i. ὁ θεὸς τοῦ κυρίου ἡμῶν Ἰησοῦ χριστοῦ, 1:17, and above all τοῖς ἁγίοις ἀποστόλοις κἀι προφήταις, 3:5, which, it is said, smacks of a later time, when the apostle's were held in great veneration, and does not agree with the apostle's estimate of himself in 3:8; and on the fact that, as Davidson puts it, "there is a fulness of expression which approaches the verbose." (3) The line of thought in this letter is very different from that of the recognized Pauline Epistles. The law is contemplated, not in its moral and religious value, but only as the cause of enmity and separation between Jew and Gentile; the death of Christ is not dwelt on as much as in the other Epistles, while his exaltation is made far more prominent; the parousia is placed in the distant future; and instead of the diversity the unity of the Church in Jesus Christ if emphasized. (4) The Epistle contains traces of Gnostic and even of Montanist influences in such words as αἰῶνες, πλήρωμα and γενεάι. (5) The letter, along with the writings of John, evidently aims at reconciling the Petrine and Pauline factions, and therefore emphasizes the unity of the Church. This unmistakably points to the second century as the time of its composition.

But these objections are not sufficient to discredit the Pauline authorship. Such men as Lightfoot, Ellicott, Eadie, Meyer, Hodge, Reuss, Godet, Weiss, Baljon, Zahn, Sanday and Abbot defend it. The similarity of the Epistle and that to the Colossians is most naturally explained by the fact that the two were written by the same author, at about the same time,

under similar circumstances, and to neighboring congregations. The idea
that it is but a copy of the Epistle to the Colossians is now generally given
up, since it appears that many passages favor the priority of Ephesians. The
theory of Holtzmann is too complicated to command serious consideration.
This whole argument is very peculiar in view of the following ones. While
it derives its point from the Epistle's similarity to Colossians, their cogency
depends on the unlikeness of this letter to the other Epistles of Paul. The
linguistic features to which the critics call attention are not such as to disprove the Pauline authorship. If the ἅπαξ λεγόμενα found in this letter prove
that it is un Pauline, we must come to a similar conclusion with respect
to the Epistle to the Romans, for this contains a hundred words that are
peculiar. The terms that are said to be used in a new sense dwindle into
insignificance on closer inspection. And of the expressions that are held
to be unusual only the one in 3:5 has any argumentative force. And even
this need not cause surprise, especially not, if we take in consideration
that Paul designates believers in general as ἅγιοι, and that in this place he
applies this epithet at once to the apostle's and to the prophets. And further
we may ask, whether it is reasonable to demand that such a fertile mind as
that of Paul should always express itself in the same way. The argument
derived from the line of thought in this Epistle simply succeeds in proving,
what is perfectly obvious, that the apostle looks at the work of redemption
from a point of view different from that of the other letters, that he views
it sub specie aeternitatis. It is now generally admitted that the supposed
traces of Gnosticism and Montanism have no argumentative value, since
the terms referred to do not have the second century connotation in this
Epistle. Similarly that other argument of the Tübingen school, that the
letter was evidently written to heal the breach between the Judæistic and
the liberal factions of the Church, is now discarded, because it was found
to rest on an unhistorical basis.

DESTINATION

There is considerable uncertainty respecting the destination of this
Epistle. The question is whether the words ἐν Ἐφέσῳ in 1:1 are genuine. They are indeed found in all the extant MSS. with the exception of
three, viz. the important MSS. Aleph and B and codex 67. The testimony
of Basil is that the most ancient MSS. in his day did not contain these
words. Tertullian informs us that Marcion gave the Epistle the title ad
Laodicenos; and Origen apparently did not regard the words as genuine.

All the old Versions contain them; but, on the other hand, Westcott and Hort say: "Transcriptional evidence strongly supports the testimony of documents against ἐν Ἐφέσῳ." New Testament in Greek, Appendix p. 123. Yet there was in the Church an early and, except as regards Marcion, universal tradition that the Epistle was addressed to the Ephesians. Present day scholars quite generally reject the words, although they are still defended by Meyer, Davidson, Eadie and Hodge. The conclusion to which the majority of scholars come is, either that the Epistle was not written to the Ephesians at all, or that it was not meant for them only, but also for the other churches in Asia.

Now if we examine the internal evidence, we find that it certainly favors the idea that this Epistle was not intended for the Ephesian church exclusively, for (1) It contains no references to the peculiar circumstances of the Ephesian church, but might be addressed to any of the churches founded by Paul. (2) There are no salutations in it from Paul or his companions to any one in the Ephesian church. (3) The Epistle contemplates only heathen Christians. while the church at Ephesus was composed of both Jews and Gentiles, 2:11, 12; 4:17; 5:8. (4) To these proofs is sometimes added that 1:15 and 3:2 make it appear as if Paul and his readers were not acquainted with each other; but this is not necessarily implied in these passages.

In all probability the words ἐν Ἐφέσῳ were not originally in the text. But now the question naturally arises, how we must interpret the following words τοῖς ἁγίοις τοῖς οὖσιν κὰι πιστοῖς etc. Several suggestions have been made. Some would read: "The saints who are really such;" others: "the saints existing and faithful in Jesus Christ;" still others: "the saints who are also faithful." But none of these interpretations is satisfactory: the first two are hardly grammatical; and the last one implies that there are also saints who are not faithful, and that the Epistle was written for a certain select view. Probably the hypothesis first suggested by Ussher is correct, that a blank was originally left after τοῖς οὖσιν, and that Tychicus or someone else was to make several copies of this Epistle and to fill in the blank with the name of the church to which each copy was to be sent. The fact that the church of Ephesus was the most prominent of the churches for which it was intended, will account for the insertion of the words ἐν Ἐφέσῳ in transcribing the letter, and for the universal tradition regarding its destination. Most likely, therefore, this was a circular letter, sent to several churches in Asia, such as those of Ephesus, Laodicea, Hierapolis, e. a. Probably it is identical with the Epistle ἐκ Λαοδικίας, Col. 4:16.

COMPOSITION

1. Occasion and Purpose. There is nothing in the Epistle to indicate that it was called forth by any special circumstances in the churches of Asia. To all appearances it was merely the prospective departure of Tychicus and Onesimus for Colossæ, 6:21, 22; Col. 4:7-9, combined with the intelligence that Paul received as to the faith of the readers in the Lord Jesus, and regarding their love to all the saints, 1:15, that led to its composition.

Since the Epistle was not called forth by any special historical situation, the purpose of Paul in writing it was naturally of a general character. It seems as if what he had heard of "the faith of the readers in the Lord Jesus, and of their love to all the saints," involuntarily fixed his thought on the unity of believers in Christ, and therefore on that grand edifice,—the Church of God. He sets forth the origin, the development, the unity and holiness, and the glorious end of that mystical body of Christ. He pictures the transcendent beauty of that spiritual temple, of which Christ is the chief cornerstone and the saints form the superstructure.

2. Time and Place. From 3:1 and 4:1 we notice that Paul was a prisoner, when he wrote this Epistle. From the mention of Tychicus as the bearer of it in 6:21, compared with Col. 4:7 and Philemon 13, we may infer that these three letters were written at the same time. And it has generally been thought that they were composed during the Roman imprisonment of Paul. There are a few scholars, however, such as Reuss and Meyer, who believe that they date from the imprisonment at Cæsarea, A. D. 58-60. Meyer urges this view on the following grounds: (1) It is more natural and probable that the slave Onesimus had run away as far as Cæsarea than that he had made the long journey to Rome. (2) If these Epistles had been sent from Rome, Tychicus and Onesimus would have arrived at Ephesus first and then at Colossæ. But in that case the apostle would most likely have mentioned Onesimus along with Tychicus in Ephesians, like he does in Collossians 4:9, to insure the runaway slave a good reception; which was not necessary however, if they reached Colossæ first, as they would in coming from Cæsarea, since Onesimus would remain there.

(3) In Eph. 6:21 the expression, "But that ye also may know my affairs," implies that there were others who had already been informed of them, viz. the Collossians, Col. 4:8, 9. (4) Paul's request to Philemon in Philem. 22, to prepare a lodging for him, and that too, for speedy use, favors the idea that the apostle was much nearer Colossæ than the far distant Rome.

Moreover Paul says in Phil. 2:24 that he expected to proceed to Macedonia after his release from the Roman imprisonment.

But these arguments are not conclusive. To the first one we may reply that Onesimus would be far safer from the pursuit of the fugitivarii in a large city like Rome than in a smaller one such as Cæsarea. The second argument loses its force, if this Epistle was a circular letter, written to the Christians of Asia in general. The καί in Eph. 6:21 is liable to different interpretations, but finds a sufficient explanation in the fact that the Epistle to the Colossians was written first. And in reply to the last argument we would say that Philem. 22 does not speak of a speedy coming, and that the apostle may have intended to pass through Macedonia to Colossæ.

It seems to us that the following considerations favor the idea that the three Epistles under consideration were written from Rome: (1) From Eph. 6:19, 20 we infer that Paul had sufficient liberty during his imprisonment to preach the gospel. Now this ill accords with what we learn of the imprisonment at Cæsarea from Acts 24:23, while it perfectly agrees with the situation in which Paul found himself at Rome according to Acts 28:16. (2) The many companions of Paul, viz. Tychicus, Aristarchus, Marcus, Justus, Epaphras, Luke and Demas, quite different from those that accompanied him on his last journey to Jerusalem (cf. Acts 20:4), also point to Rome, where the apostle might utilize them for evangelistic work. Cf. Phil. 1:14. (3) In all probability Philippians belongs to the same period as the other Epistles of the imprisonment; and if this is the case, the mention of Cæsar's household in Phil. 4:22 also points to Rome. (4) Tradition also names Rome as the place of composition. Ephesians must probably be dated about A. D. 62.

CANONICAL SIGNIFICANCE

The early Church leaves no doubt as to the canonicity of this Epistle. It is possible that we have the first mention of it in the New Testament itself, Col. 4:16. The writings of Igpatius, Polycarp, Herman and Hippolytus contain passages that seem to be derived from our Epistle. Marcion the Muratorian Canon, Irenaeus, Clement of Alexandria and Tertullian clearly testify to its early recognition and use. There is not a dissentient voice in all antiquity.

The particular significance of the Epistle lies in its teaching regarding the unity of the Church: Jews and Gentiles are one in Christ. It constantly emphasizes the fact that believers have their unity in the Lord and therefore contains the expression "in Christ" about twenty times. The unity of the faithful originates in their election, since God the Father chose them in Christ before the foundation of the world, 1:4; it finds expression in a holy conversation, sanctified by true love, that naturally results from their living relation with Christ, in whom they are builded together for a habitation of God in the Spirit; and it issues in their coming in the "unity of the faith, and of the knowledge of the Son of God, unto a perfect man, unto the measure of the stature of the fulness of Christ." The great practical exhortation of the Epistle is that believers live worthily of their union with Christ, since they were sometime darkness, but are now light in the Lord, and should therefore walk as children of light, 5:8.

15

The Epistle to the Philippians

CONTENTS

In the Epistle to the Philippians we may distinguish five parts:

I. Paul's Account of his Condition, 1:1-26. The apostle addresses the Philippians in the usual way, 1, 2; and then informs them of his gratitude for their participation in the work of the Gospel, of his prayer for their increase in spiritual strength and labor, of the fact that even his imprisonment was instrumental in spreading the Gospel, and of his personal feelings and desires, 3-26.

II. His Exhortation to Imitate Christ, 1:27-2:18. He exhorts the Philippians to strive after unity by exercising the necessary self-denial, 1:27-2:4; points them to the pattern of Christ, who humiliated himself and was glorified by God, 2:5-11; and expresses his desire that they follow the example of their Lord, 12-18.

III. Information respecting Paul's Efforts in behalf of the Philippians, 2:19-30. He intends to send Timotheus to them that he may know of their condition, and therefore commends this worthy servant of Christ to them, 19-23; and though he trusted that he himself would come shortly he now sends Epaphroditus back to them, and bespeaks a good reception for him, 24-30.

IV. Warnings against Judaeism and Antinomian Error, 3:1-21. The apostle warns his readers against Judæistic zealots that boasted in the flesh, pointed to his own example in renouncing his fleshly prerogatives that he might gain Christ and experience the power of His resurrection, and in striving after perfection, 1:15. By way of contrast this induces him to warn them also for the example of those whose lives are worldly and licentious, 16-21.

V. Final Exhortations and Acknowledgment, 4:1-23. He urges the Philippians to avoid all dissension, 1-3; exhorts them to joyfulness, freedom from care, and the pursuit of all good things, 4-9; gratefully acknowledges their gifts, invoking a blessing on their love, 10-20; and closes his Epistle with salutation and benediction, 21-23.

CHARACTERISTICS

1. The Epistle to the Philippians is one of the most personal of Paul's letters, resembling in that respect II Corinthians. It has been called the most letter-like of all the writings of Paul, and may be compared in this respect with I Thessalonians and Philemon. The personal note is very marked throughout the Epistle. There is not much dogma, and what little is found is introduced for practical purposes. This holds true even with reference to the classical passage in 2:6-11. The apostle, with the prospect of an early martyrdom before him, yet not without hope of a speedy release, opens his heart to his most beloved congregation. He speaks of the blessings that attend his labors at Rome, of the strait in which he finds himself, and expresses his desire to remain with them. He manifests his love for the Philippians, shows himself concerned for their spiritual welfare, and expresses his profound gratitude for their support. Though in bonds, he rejoices, and bids the readers be joyful. The tone of joyous gratitude rings through the entire Epistle.

2. The letter is in no sense a controversial one. There are in it no direct polemics; there is very little that has to any degree a polemical character. The apostle warns against errorists that are without the church, but might disturb its peace, and forestalls their attacks; he hints at dissensions, most likely of a practical nature, in the congregation, and admonishes the readers to be peaceful and self-denying; but he never once assumes a polemical attitude, like he does in Corinthians or Galatians. Stronger still, the Epistle is singularly free from all denunciation and reproof; it is written throughout in a lauditory spirit. The apostle finds little to chide and much to praise in the Philippian church.

3. The address of the Epistle is peculiar in that it names not only, "the saints in Christ Jesus which are at Philippi," but adds, "with the bishops and deacons." In that respect it stands in a class by itself. The greetings at the end of the Epistle are also unique. On the one hand they are very general, while, on the other, "the household of Cæsar" is singled out for special mention.

4. As to style, Alford reminds us, that this letter, like all those in which Paul writes with fervor, "is discontinuous and abrupt, passing rapidly from

one theme to another; full of earnest exhortation, affectionate warnings, deep and wonderful settings-forth of his individual spiritual condition and feelings, of the state of the Christian and of the sinful world, of the loving councils of our Father respecting us, and the self-sacrifice and triumph of our Redeemer." Prolegomena Sec. IV. There are constant expressions of affection, such as ἀγαπητοί and ἀδελφοί. Notice especially 4:1, "Therefore my brethren, my dearly beloved and longed for, my joy and crown, so stand fast in the Lord, my dearly beloved."

AUTHORSHIP

The Pauline authorship of this Epistle is established as well as anything can be. We probably find the first reference to it in the epistle of Polycarp to the Philippians, where we read: "The glorious Paul who, being personally among you, taught you exactly and surely the word of truth; who also, being absent, wrote you letters (or, a letter) which you have only to study to be edified in the faith that has been given you." The passage does not necessarily refer to more than one letter. Our Epistle formed a part of Marcion's collection, is mentioned in the Muratorian canon, is found in the Syriac and old Latin Versions, and is quoted by Irenaeus, Clement of Alexandria, Tertullian and many others.

And this testimony of antiquity is clearly borne out by the evidence furnished by the Epistle itself. It is self-attested and has, at the beginning, the usual Pauline blessing and thanksgiving. Above all, however, it is like II Corinthians in that the personality of the apostle is so strongly stamped on it as to leave little room for doubt. The historical circumstances which the Epistle presupposes, the type of thought which it contains, the language in which it is couched, and the character which it reveals,—it is all Pauline.

The evidence in its favor is so strong that its authenticity has been generally admitted, even by radical critics. Of course, Baur and the majority of his school rejected it, but even Hilgenfeld, Jülicher and Pfleiderer accept it as Pauline. The great majority of New Testament scholars regard the objections of Baur as frivolous, as f. i. that the mention of bishops and deacons points to a post-Pauline stage of ecclesiastical organization; that there is no originality in the Epistle; that it contains evident traces of Gnosticism; that the doctrine of justification which it sets forth is not that of Paul; and that the Epistle aims at reconciling the opposing parties of the second century, typified by Euodia and Syntyche.

Of late Holsten has taken up the cudgels against the genuineness of this letter. Dismissing several of the arguments of Baur as irrelevant, he bases his attack especially on the Christological and Soteriological differences that he discerns between this Epistle and the other writings of Paul. The most important points to which he refers are these: (1) The idea of the pre-existent Christ in 2:6–11 does not agree with that found in 1 Cor. 15:45–49. According to the first passage the manhood of Christ begins with his incarnation; according to the second, He was even in his pre-existence "a heavenly man." (2) There is a glaring contradiction between 3:6, where the writer says that he was blameless as touching the righteousness which is in the law, and Rom. 7:21, where the apostle declares: "—when I would do good, evil is present." (3) The doctrine of forensic, imputed righteousness is replaced by that of an infused righteousness in 3:9–11. (4) The writer shows a singular indifference to the objective truth of his Gospel in 1:15–18, an attitude which compares strangely with that of Paul in 2 Cor. 11:1–4, and especially in Gal. 1:8, 9.

But these objections are not of sufficient weight to disprove the Pauline authorship. In 1 Cor. 15 the apostle does not speak of the pre-existent Christ, but of Christ as he will appear at the parousia in a glorified body. With what Paul says in 3:6 we may compare Gal. 1:14. In both places he speaks of himself from the standpoint of the Jew who regards the law merely as an external carnal commandment. From that point of view he might consider himself blameless, but it was quite different, if he contemplated the law in its deep spiritual sense. It is not true that Paul substitutes an infused for an imputed righteousness in this Epistle. He clearly speaks of the latter in 2:9, and then by means of an infinitive of purpose passes on to speak of the subjective righteousness of life. The persons spoken of in 1:15–18 are not said to preach a Gospel different from that of the apostle; they preached Christ, but from impure motives. Hence they can not be compared with the adversaries of whom Paul speaks in Corinthians and Galatians. To these he probably refers in 3:2. Schürer says: "The arguments of Holsten are such that one might sometimes believe them due to a slip of the pen."

THE CHURCH AT PHILIPPI

The city of Philippi was formerly called Crenides, and derived its later name from Philip, the king of Macedonia, who rebuilt it and made it a frontier city between his kingdom and Thrace. It was situated on the river Gangites and on the important Egnatian highway that connected the Adriatic with the Hellespont. After the defeat of his enemies Octavius about 42 B. C. determined on Philippi as one of the places, where Roman soldiers who had served their time were to dwell. He constituted it a Roman colony, with the special privilege of the jus Italicum, which included "(1) exemption from the oversight of the provincial governors; (2) immunity from the poll and property taxes; and (3) right to property in the soil regulated by Roman law." These privileges, no doubt, attracted many colonists, so that Philippi soon became a city of considerable size. It is described in Acts 16:12 as, "the chief city of that part of Macedonia and a colony."

To that city Paul first came, when about the year 52, in obedience to the vision of the Macedonian man, he passed from Asia into Europe. This was in harmony with his general policy of preaching in the main centers of the Roman empire. Apparently the Jews were not numerous in Philippi: there was no synagogue, so that the small band of Jews and proselytes simply repaired to the river side for prayer; and one of the charges brought against Paul and Silas was that they were Jews. At the place of prayer the missionaries addressed the assembled women, and were instrumental in converting Lydia who, with characteristic generosity, immediately received them in her house. We read no more of the blessings that crowned their labors there, but find that on their departure there was a company of brethren to whom they spoke words of comfort.

Little can be said regarding the composition of the Philippian church. In the narrative of its founding we find no specific mention of Jews, although the assembly by the river points to their presence. However the fact that there was no synagogue, and that the enemies contemptuously emphasized the Jewish nationality of the missionaries leads us to think that they were few and greatly despised. It may be that those who did live there had, under the pressure of their environment, already lost many of their distinctive features. The presumption is that some of them accepted the teaching of Paul and Silas, but we cannot tell how large a proportion of the church they formed. In all probability they were a small minority and caused no friction in the congregation. Paul does not even refer to them in his letter, much less condemn their Jewish tenets, like he does the errors of the false brethren at Corinth and in the Galatian churches. The adversaries of whom he speaks in 3:2 were evidently outside of the church. On the whole the Philippian church was an ideal one, consisting of warmhearted people, diligent in the work of the Lord, and faithfully devoted to their apostle.

COMPOSITION

1. Occasion and Purpose. The immediate occasion of this Epistle was a contribution brought by Epaphroditus from the Philippian church. They had often sent the apostle similar tokens of their love (cf. 4:15, 16; 2 Cor. 11:9), and now, after they had for some time lacked the opportunity to communicate with him, 4:10, they again ministered to his wants. From over-exertion in the work of Gods Kingdom their messenger was taken sick at Rome. On his recovery Paul immediately sends him back to Philippi, in order to allay all possible fears as to his condition; and utilizes this opportunity to send the Philippians a letter.

His purpose in writing this Epistle was evidently fourfold. In the first place he desired to express his gratitude for the munificence of the Philippians, especially because it testified to the abundance of their faith. In the second place he wished to give utterance to his sincere love for the Philippian church that constituted his crown in the Lord. In the third place he felt it incumbent on him to warn them against the dangers that were present within the fold, and the enemies that were threatening them from without. Apparently there was some dissension in the church, 1:27-2:17; 4:2, 3, but, in all probability this was not of a doctrinal character, but rather consisted of personal rivalries and divisions among some of the church members. In 3:2 the apostle most likely referred to the Judæizing Christians that traveled about to make proselytes, and also threatened the church of Philippi. Finally he desires to exhort his most beloved church to be joyful, notwithstanding his imprisonment, and to lead a truly Christian life.

2. Time and Place. Like the Epistle to the Ephesians that to the Philippians was written at Rome. While several scholars assign the former to the Cæsarean captivity, very few refer the latter to that period. The apostle's evident residing in some great center of activity, the many friends that surrounded him, his joyful expectation of being set free soon, his mention of the prætorium, 1:13, which may be the praetorian guard (so most commentators), or the supreme imperial court (so Mommsen and Ramsay), and the greetings of Cæsar's household,—all point to Rome.

The Epistle was written, therefore, between the years 61-63. The only remaining question is, whether it was composed before or after the other three Epistles of the captivity. The prevailing view is that Philippians is the last of the group. This view is supported by the following arguments: (1) The apostle's words in 1:12 seem to imply that a long period of imprisonment has already elapsed. (2) A rather long time was required in the communications between Rome and Philippi indicated in the letter. The Philippians had heard of Paul's imprisonment, had sent Epaphroditus to Rome, had heard of the latter's illness there, and of this their messenger, in turn, had received intelligence. Four journeys are, therefore, implied. (3) Paul anticipates that his case will soon come up for decision, and although uncertain as to the outcome, he somewhat expects a speedy release. These arguments are not absolutely conclusive, but certainly create a strong presumption in favor of dating the Epistle after the other three.

Bleek was inclined to regard Philippians as the earliest of the Epistles of the captivity. This view found a strong defender in Lightfoot, who is followed by Farrar in his St. Paul. Lightfoot defends his position by pointing to the similarity of this Epistle to Romans, which implies, according to him, that it immediately follows this in order of time; and to the fact that in this Epistle we have the last trace of Paul's Judæistic controversy, while in Ephesians and Colossians he begins to deal with an incipient Gnosticism, and his teachings respecting the Church bear a close resemblance and are intimately related to the views presented in the pastorals. These Epistles, therefore, represent a further development in the doctrine of the Church. But these proofs do not carry conviction, since the character of Paul's Epistles was not necessarily determined by the order in which they were written, and the apostle did not write as one who is presenting his system of thought to the world in successive letters. His Epistles were called forth and determined by special situations. And the question may be asked, whether it seems plausible that any considerable development of doctrine should take place within the course of at most a year and a half.

CANONICAL SIGNIFICANCE

The Epistle to the Philippians is not quoted as much as some of the preceding ones, which is probably due to the fact that it contains little doctrinal matter. Notwithstanding this its canonicity is well established. There are traces of its language in Clement of Rome and Ignatius. Polycarp, addressing the Philippians, speaks more than once of Paul's writing to them. The Epistle to Diognetus, Justin Martyr and Theophilus contain references to our letter. In the Epistle of the churches of Vienne and Lyons Phil. 2:6 is quoted. Marcion has it and the Muratorian canon speaks of it. And it is often directly quoted and ascribed to Paul by Irenaeus, Clement of Alexandria and Tertullian.

Though the Epistle is primarily of a practical nature, it has also great and abiding dogmatic significance. It contains the classical passage on the important doctrine of the kenosis of Christ, 2:6–11. Aside from this, however, its great permanent value is of a practical character. It reveals to us the ideal relation between Paul and his Philippian church, a relation such as the church of God should constantly seek to realize: he, sedulously seeking to promote the spiritual welfare of those entrusted to his care, even in a time of dire distress; and they, though possessing no great wealth, willingly and lovingly ministering to the natural wants of their beloved apostle. It points us to Christ as the pattern of that self-denial and humiliation that should always characterize his followers. It comes to us with the grand exhortation, enforced by the example of the great apostle, to press forward for "the prize of the high calling of God in Christ Jesus." And finally it pictures us the Christian satisfied and joyful, even when the shades of night are falling.

16

The Epistle to the Colossians

CONTENTS

The Epistle to the Colossians may best be divided into two parts:

I. The Doctrinal Part, emphasizing the unique Significance of Christ, 1:1–2:23. Paul begins the letter with the apostolic blessing, the usual thanksgiving and a prayer for his readers, 1:1–13. Then he describes the pre-eminence of Christ as the Head of both the natural and the spiritual creation, who has reconciled all things to God, 14–23, of which mystery the apostle himself was made a minister, 24–29. He warns his readers against the inroads of a false philosophy that dishonored Christ. Since the Colossians have all the fulness of the Godhead in their Lord and Saviour, are rooted in him, and have arisen with him to a new life, they should walk in him and avoid semi-Jewish practices and the worship of angels, 2:1–19. This was all the more necessary, because they had died with Christ to their old life and to the beggarly elements of the world, 20–23.

II. The Practical Part, containing divers Directions and Exhortations, 3:1–4:18. Where believers have risen with Christ to newness of life, they must part with the vices of the old man and clothe themselves with Christian virtues, 3:1–17. Wives should submit themselves to their husbands and husbands should love their wives; children must obey their parents and parents must beware of discouraging their children; servants should obey their masters and these should give the servants their due, 18–4:1. The duty of prayer and thanksgiving is urged, and directions are given for the right behavior of believers toward the unconverted, 2–6. With a few personal notices, several greetings and a salutation the apostle closes his Epistle, 7–18.

CHARACTERISTICS

1. On its formal side this Epistle differs from that to the Ephesians in its polemical character. It is not a general exposition of the truth that is in

Christ Jesus, without reference to antagonistic principles, but a statement of it with a special view to the errors that were gradually creeping into the Colossian church, insidious errors of which the Colossians, so it seems, little realized the danger. It is true that we find none of the fiery polemics of the Epistle to the Galatians here, nor any of the sharp invective of II Corinthians;—yet the controversial character of this letter is very evident.

2. On its material side it exhibits great affinity with the Epistle to the Ephesians. Hence the contention of the critics that the one is but a copy of the other. We should not infer from this, however, that the teaching of these Epistles is identical. While that contained in Ephesians is in the main Theological, that found in Colossians is primarily Christological, the summing up of all things in Christ, the Head. Essentially the Christology of this letter is in perfect harmony with that of previous Epistles, but there is a difference of emphasis. The writer here places prominently before his readers, not only the Soteriological, but also the Cosmical significance of Christ. He is the Head both of the Church and of the new creation. All things were created by him, and find the purpose of their existence in him.

3. In point of style and language too this Epistle shows great similarity to its twin-letter. Of the 155 verses in Ephesians 78 contain expressions that find parallels in Colossians. There are the same involved sentences of difficult interpretation, and also a great number of ἅπαξ λεγόμενα. The letter contains 34 words that are absent from all the other writings of Paul, 12 of which are found in other New Testament books, however, (cf. lists of these words in Alford and in Abbotts Comm.) Of these 34 words at least 18, and therefore more than half, are found in the second chapter. Owing to the polemical character of this letter the author is generally speaking in a more matter-of-fact manner than he is in Ephesians, and it is only, when he sets forth the majesty of Christ, that he soars to sublime heights. Comparing this Epistle with those to the Corinthians and the Philippians, Lightfoot says: "It is distinguished from them by a certain ruggedness of expression, a want of finish often bordering on obscurity." Comm. p. 123.

AUTHORSHIP

There are no good reasons to doubt the Pauline authorship of this Epistle. Marcion and the school of Valentinus recognized it as genuine. And the great witnesses of the end of the second century, Irenaeus, Clement of Alexandria and Tertullian repeatedly quote it by name.

Moreover the internal evidence decidedly favors the authenticity of the letter. It claims to be written by the apostle in 1:1; the line of thought developed in it is distinctly Pauline and is in striking harmony with that of the Epistle to the Ephesians; and if we do not first rule out several of the Pauline Epistles and then compare the style of this letter with those that remain, we may confidently assert that the style is Pauline. Moreover the persons named in 4:7-17 are all, with but a couple exceptions (viz. Jesus called Justus and Nymphas) known to have been companions or fellow-laborers of Paul.

Yet the Epistle did not go unchallenged. Mayerhoff began the attack on it is 1838, rejecting it, because its vocabulary, style and thought were not Pauline; it was so similar to Ephesians; and it contained references to the heresy of Cerinthus. The school of Baur and many other critics, such as Hoekstra, Straatman, Hausrath, Davidson, Schmiedel e. a., followed his lead and considered this Epistle as a second century production. Holtzmann, as we have already seen, found a genuine nucleus in it.

There are especially three objections that are urged against the Pauline authorship of this letter. (1) The style is not that of the apostle. The fact that the letter contains 34 ἅπαξ λεγόμενα; that characteristically Pauline terms, such as δικαιοσύνη, σωτηρία, ἀποκάλυψις and καταργεῖν are absent, while some of the particles often employed by the apostle, as γάρ, οὖν, διότι and ἄρα are rarely found; and that the construction is often very involved and characterized by a certain heaviness, is urged against its genuineness. (2) The error combated in this Epistle, it is said, shows clear traces of second century Gnosticism. These are found in the use of the terms σοφία, γνῶσις, 2:3, μυστήριον, 1:26, 27; 2:2, πλήρωμα, 1:19, ἀιῶνες, 1:26, etc.; in the series of angels named in 1:16; and in the conception of Christ in 1:15. It is held that they point to the Valentinian system. (3) Closely related to the preceding is the objection that the Christology of this Epistle is un-Pauline. Davidson regards this as the chief feature that points to the Gnostics, Introd. I p. 246, but it is also thought to conflict with the representation of Paul in his other writings, and to approach very closely the Johannine doctrine of the Logos. Christ is represented as the image of the invisible God, 1:15, the central Being of the universe, absolutely pre-eminent above all visible and invisible beings, 1:16-18, the originator and the goal of creation, and the perfect Mediator, who reconciles not only sinners but all things in heaven and on earth to God, 1:16-20.

In answer to the first objection we may say that the argument derived from the ἅπαξ λεγόμενα is irrelevant and would apply with equal force in the case of the Epistle to the Romans. From the fact that more than half of them are found in the second chapter it is quite evident that they are due to the special subject-matter of this letter. The difference between Colossians and some of the other Pauline writings also explains why the character-istically Pauline terms referred to above are absent from our Epistle. Had Paul used exactly the same words that he employs elsewhere, that would also, in all probability, have been proof positive for many critics that the letter was a forgery. Moreover it should not be regarded as very strange that a person's vocabulary changes somewhat in the course of time, espe-cially not, when he is placed in an altogether different environment, as was the case with Paul. We fully agree with Dr. Salmon, when he says: "I cannot subscribe to the doctrine that a man, writing a new composition, must not, on pain of losing his identity, employ any word that he has not used in a former one." Introd. p. 148.

As to the second objection we would reply that there is absolutely no proof that the Epistle presupposes second century Gnosticism. The Gnostics evidently did not regard it as a polemic directed against their tenets, for Marcion and the Valentinians made extensive use of it. Moreover some of the most important elements of Gnosticism, such as the creation of the world by a demiurge, ignorant of the supreme God or opposed to Him, are not referred to in the Epistle. An incipient Gnosticism there may have been in Paul's time; but it is also possible that the error of the Colossian church is in no way to be identified with the Gnostic heresy. Present day scholarship strongly inclines to the view that it is not Gnosticism at all to which Paul refers in this letter.

And with respect to the third argument, we do not see why the further development of the Pauline Christology cannot have been the work of Paul himself. There is nothing in the Christology of this Epistle that conflicts with the recognized representation of Paul. We clearly find the essence of it in Rom. 8:19–22; 1 Cor. 8:6; 2 Cor. 4:4; Phil, 2:5–11. These passages prepare us for the statement of Paul regarding the Cosmical significance of Christ, 1:16, 17. And the representation that all the forces of creation culminate in the glory of Christ does not necessarily run counter to Rom. 11:36 and 1 Cor. 15:28, according to which all things exist to the praise of God, their Creator.

THE CHURCH AT COLOSSAE

Colossæ was one of the cities of the beautiful Lycus Valley in Phrygia, situated but a short distance from Laodicea and Hierapolis. Herodotus speaks of it as a great city, but it did not retain its magnitude until New Testament times, for Strabo only reckons it as a πόλισμα. We have no information respecting the founding of the Colossian church. From the Acts of the Apostles we learn that Paul passed through Phrygia twice, once at the start of his second, and again at the beginning of his third missionary journey, Acts 16:6; 18:23. But on the first of these journeys he remained well to the East of Western Phrygia, where Colossæ was situated; and though on the second he may have gone into the Lycus Valley, he certainly did not find nor found the Colossian church there, since he himself says in Col. 2:1 that the Colossians had not seen his face in the flesh. In all probability Paul's prolonged residence at Ephesus and his preaching there for three years, so that "all those in Asia heard the word of the Lord Jesus," Acts 19:10, was indirectly responsible for the founding of the churches in the Lycus Valley. The most plausible theory is that Epaphras was one of Paul's Ephesian converts and became the founder of the Colossian church. This is favored by 1:7, where the correct reading is καθὼς ἐμάθατε, and not καθὼς κὰι ἐμάθετε.

The church consisted, so it seems, of Gentile Christians, 1:21, 27; 2:11-13; the Epistle certainly does not contain a single hint that there were Jews among them. Yet they were clearly exposed to Jewish influences, and this need not cause surprise in view of the fact that Antiochus the Great transplanted two thousand families of Jews from Babylonia into Lydia and Phrygia, Jos. Ant. XII 6. 4. This number had, of course, greatly increased by the time the Epistle was written. Lightfoot estimates that the number of Jewish freemen was more than eleven thousand in the single district of which Laodicea was the capital. Cf. his essay on The Churches of the Lycus Valley in his Comm. p. 20.

According to the Epistle the Colossians were in danger of being misled by certain false teachings. As to the exact nature of the Colossian heresy there is a great variety of opinion. Some regard it as a mixture of Judæistic and theosophic elements; others dub it Gnosticism or Gnostic Ebionism; and still others consider it to be a form of Essenism. We can infer from the Epistle that the errorists were members of the congregation, for they are described as those "not holding the head," 2:19, an expression that is applicable only to those that had accepted Christ. And it seems perfectly clear that their error was primarily of a Jewish character, since they urged circumcision, not, indeed, as an absolute necessity, but as a means to perfection, 2:10–13; they appealed to the law and emphasized its ceremonial requirements and probably also the ordinances of the rabbi's, 2:14–17, 20–23. Yet they clearly went beyond the Judæism that Paul encountered in his earlier Epistles, falsely emphasizing certain requirements of the law and adjusting their views to those of their Gentile neighbors. Their dualistic conception of the world led them, on the one hand, to an asceticism that was not demanded by the law. They regarded it as essential to abstain from the use of meat and wine, not because these were Levitically unclean, but since this abstinence was necessary for the mortification of the body, which they regarded as the seat of sin. They neglected the body and apparently aspired after a pure spiritual existence; to be like the angels was their ideal. On the other hand the consciousness of their great sinfulness as material beings made them hesitate to approach God directly. And the Jewish doctrine that the law was mediated by the angels, in connection with the influence that was ascribed to the spirits in their heathen environment, naturally led them to a worship of the angels as intermediaries between God and man. Among the higher spirits they also ranked Christ and thus failed to recognize his unique significance. The Colossian error was, therefore, a strange mixture of Jewish doctrines, Christian ideas and heathen speculation; and this composite character makes it impossible to identify it with any one heretical system of the apostolic time. Cf. especially Zahn, Einl. I p. 329 ff.; Holtzmann, Einl. p. 248 ff.; Lightfoot, Comm. pp. 71–111; Biesterveld, Comm. pp. 18–28.

COMPOSITION

1. Occasion and Purpose. From the Epistle itself we can readily infer what gave Paul occasion to write it. Epaphras, the founder and probably also the minister of the congregation, had evidently seen the danger, gradually increasing, that was threatening the spiritual welfare of the church. The errorists did not directly antagonize him or Paul; yet their teaching was a subversion of the Pauline gospel. Hence he informed the apostle of the state of affairs, and this information led to the composition of the Epistle.

The object Paul has in view is the correction of the Colossian heresy. Hence he clearly sets forth the unique significance of Christ, and the all-sufficient character of his redemption. Christ is the image of the invisible God, the Creator of the world, and also of the angels, and the only Mediator between God and man. He in whom all the fulness of the Godhead dwells, has reconciled all things to God and has delivered men from the power of sin and death. In his death He abrogated the shadows of the Old Testament and terminated the special ministry of the angels that was connected with the law, so that even this vestige of a supposed Biblical foundation for the worship of angels has been removed. In him believers are perfect and in him only. Hence the Colossians should not fall back on the beggarly elements of the world, nor in sham humility worship the angels. Having their life in Christ, they should conform to his image in all their domestic and social relations.

2. Time and Place. For the discussion of these we refer to what we have said in connection with the Epistle to the Ephesians. The letter was written at Rome about A. D. 61 or 62. Of course the majority of those who reject this Epistle date it somewhere in the second century.

CANONICAL SIGNIFICANCE

The canonical character of this Epistle has never been doubted by the Church. There are slight but uncertain indications of its use in Clement of Rome, Barnabas and Ignatius. More important references to it are found in Justin Martyr and Theophilus. Marcion gave it a place in his canon, and in the Muratorian Fragment it is named as one of the Pauline Epistles. With Irenaeus, Clement of Alexandria and Tertullian the quotations increase both in number and definiteness. That the Epistle is not quoted as often as Ephesians is probably due to its polemical character.

The permanent value of this letter is found primarily in its central teaching, that the Church of God is made perfect in Christ, its glorious Head. Since He is a perfect Mediator and the complete redemption of his people, they grow into him, as the Head of the body, they find the fulfillment of all their desires in him, as their Saviour, and they reach their perfection in him, as the Goal of the new creation. His perfect life is the life of the entire Church. Hence believers should seek to realize ever more in every atom of their existence the complete union with their divine Head. They should avoid all arbitrary practices, all human inventions and all will-worship that is derogatory to the only Mediator and Head of the Church, Jesus Christ.

17

The First Epistle to the Thessalonians

CONTENTS

In the first Epistle to the Thessalonians we distinguish two parts:

I. Paul's Apologia, 1:1-3:13. The letter opens with the usual apostolic blessing and thanksgiving, 1:1-4. This thanksgiving was called forth by the fact that the apostle's work in Thessalonica had not been in vain, but had resulted in a faith that was spoken of throughout Macedonia and Achaia, 5-10. The writer reminds the readers of his labors among them, emphasizing his suffering, good moral behavior, honesty, faithfulness, diligence and love, 2:1-12. He thanks God that they had received him and his message and had suffered willingly for the cause of Christ at the hands of the Jews, and informs them that he had often intended to visit them, 13-20. His great love to them had induced him to send Timothy to establish them and to strengthen them in their affliction, 3:1-5; who had now returned and gladdened his heart by a report of their steadfastness, 6-10. He prays that the Lord may strengthen them, 11-13.

II. Practical Exhortations and Instruction regarding the Parousia, 4:1-5:28. The apostle exhorts the Thessalonians that they follow after sanctification, abstaining from fornication and fraud, and exercising love, diligence and honesty, 4:1-12. He allays their fears respecting the future of those that have died in Christ, 13-8, and admonishes the Thessalonians in view of the sudden coming of Christ to walk as children of the light that they may be prepared for the day of Christ's return, 5:1-11. After exhorting the brethren to honor their spiritual leaders, and urging them to warn the unruly, to comfort the feeble-minded, to support the weak, and to practice all Christian virtues, the apostle closes his Epistle by invoking on the Thessalonians the blessing of God, by expressing his desire that the Epistle be read to all the brethren, and with the usual salutations, 12-28.

CHARACTERISTICS

1. This Epistle is like that to the Philippians one of the most letterlike of all the writings of Paul. It is, as Deissmann says, 'full of moving personal reminiscences." The practical interest greatly predominates over the doctrinal; and though the polemical element is not altogether absent, it is not at all prominent. The letter is primarily one of practical guidance, instruction and encouragement, for a faithful, persecuted church, whose knowledge is still deficient, and whose weak and faint-hearted and idlers greatly need the counsel of the apostle.

2. Doctrinally I Thessalonians is one of the eschatological Epistles of Paul. It refers very little to Christ's coming in the flesh to give himself a ransom for sin, but discusses all the more his future coming as the Lord of Glory. There are at least six references to the parousia in this short letter, two of which are rather extensive passages, 1:10; 2:19; 3:13; 4:13-18; 5:1-11, 23. This doctrine is at once the impelling motive for the exhortations of the apostle, and the sufficient ground for the encouragement of his readers, who expected the return of Christ in the near future.

3. The Epistle never appeals to the Old Testament as an authority, and contains no quotations from it. We find a reference to its history, however, in 2:15, and probable reminiscences of its language in 2:16; 4:5, 6, 8, 9; 5:8. The language of 4:15-17 shows some similarity to 2 Esdras 5:42, but the thought is quite different.

4. The style of this letter is thoroughly Pauline, containing an abundance of phrases and expressions that have parallels in the other Epistles of Paul, especially in those to the Corinthians. Comparing it with the other polemical writings of the apostle, we find that it is written in a quiet unimpassioned style, a style, too, far more simple and direct than that of Ephesians and Colossians. There are 42 words peculiar to it, of which 22 are not found elsewhere in the New Testament, and 20 are, but not in the writings of Paul.

AUTHORSHIP

The external testimony in favor of the Pauline authorship is in no way deficient. Marcion included the letter in his canon, and the Muratorian Fragment mentions it as one of the Pauline writings. It is contained in the old Latin and Syriac Versions; and from the time of Irenaeus, Clement of Alexandria and Tertullian it is regularly quoted by name.

The internal evidence also clearly points to Paul as the writer. The Epistle comes to us under the name of Paul; and those that were associated with him in writing it, viz. Silvanus (Silas) and Timotheus, are known to have been Paul's companions on the second missionary journey. It is marked by the usual Pauline blessing, thanksgiving and salutation, and clearly reflects the character of the great apostle to the Gentiles. Although it has been subject to attack, it is now defended by critics of nearly every school as an authentic production of Paul.

Schrader and Baur were the first ones to attack it in 1835. The great majority of critics, even those of Baur's own school, turned against them; such men as Hilgenfeld, Pfleiderer, Holtzmann, Davidson, Von Soden and Jülicher defending the genuineness of the letter. They found followers, however, especially in Holsten and Van der Vies.

Of the objections brought against the Epistle the following deserve consideration: (1) As compared with the other writings of Paul, the contents of this Epistle are very insignificant, not a single doctrine, except that in 4:13-18, being made prominent. In the main it is but a reiteration of Paul's work among the Thessalonians, and of the circumstances attending their conversion, all of which they knew very well. (2) The letter reveals a progress in the Christian life that is altogether improbable, if a period of only a few months had elapsed between its composition and the founding of the church, cf. 1:7, 8; 4:10. (3) The passage 2:14-16 does not fit in the mouth of him who wrote Rom. 9-11 and who was himself at one time a fierce persecutor of the Church. Moreover it implies that the destruction of Jerusalem was already a thing of the past. (4) The Epistle is clearly dependent on some of the other Pauline writings, especially I and II Corinthians. Compare 1:5 with 1 Cor. 2:4;—1:6 with 1 Cor. 11:1;—2:4 ff. with 1 Cor. 2:4; 4:3 ff.; 9:15 ff.; 2 Cor. 2:17; 5:11.

The cogency of these arguments is not apparent. Paul's letters have an occasional character, and the situation at Thessalonica did not call for an exposition of Christian doctrine, save a deliverance on the parousia; but did require words of encouragement, guidance and exhortation, and also, in view of the insinuations against the apostle, a careful review of all that he had done among them. Looked at from that point of view the Epistle is in no sense insignificant. The words of 1:7, 8 and 4:10 do not imply a long existence of the Thessalonian church, but simply prove the intensity of its faith and love. Three or four months were quite sufficient for the report of their great faith to spread in Macedonia and Achaia. Moreover the very shortcomings of the Thessalonians imply that their religious experience was as yet of but short duration. In view of what Paul writes in II Corinthians

and Galatians respecting the Judæizers, we certainly need not be surprised
at what he says in 2:14-16. If the words are severe, let us remember that
they were called forth by a bitter and dogged opposition that followed the
apostle from place to place, and on which he had brooded for some time.
The last words of this passage do not necessarily imply that Jerusalem had
already been destroyed. They are perfectly intelligible on the supposition
that Paul, in view of the wickedness of the Jews and of the calamities that
were already overtaking them, Jos. Ant. XX 2, 5, 6, had a lively presentiment of their impending doom. The last argument is a very peculiar one.
It is tantamount to saying that the Epistle cannot be Pauline, because there
are so many Pauline phrases and expressions in it. Such an argument is
its own refutation, and is neutralized by the fact that in the case of other
letters dissimilarity leads the critics to the same conclusion.

THE CHURCH AT THESSALONICA

Thessalonica, originally called Thermae (Herodotus), and now bearing the slightly altered name Saloniki, a city of Macedonia, has always
been very prominent in history and still ranks, after Constantinople, as
the second town in European Turkey. It is situated on what was formerly
known as the Thermaic gulf, and is built "in the form of an amphithe-
ater on the slopes at the head of the bay." The great Egnatian highway
passed through it from East to West. Hence it was of old an important
trade center and as such had special attraction for the Jews, who were
found there in great numbers. Cassander, who rebuilt the city in 315 B. C.
in all probability gave it the name Thessalonica in honor of his wife. In
the time of the Romans it was the capital of the second part of Macedonia
and the seat of the Roman governor of the entire province.

Paul, accompanied by Silas and Timothy, came to that city, after they
had left Philippi about the year 52. As was his custom, he repaired to the
synagogue to preach the gospel of Jesus Christ. The result of this work was
a spiritual harvest consisting of some Jews, a great number of proselytes
(taking the word in its widest significance) and several of the city's chief
women. From the Acts of the Apostles we get the impression (though it
is not definitely stated) that Paul's labors at Thessalonica terminated at
the end of three weeks; but the Epistles rather favor the idea that his stay
there was of longer duration. They pre-suppose a flourishing, well organized congregation, 5:12, whose faith had become a matter of common comment, 1:7-9; and show us that Paul, while he was in Thessalonica, worked

for his daily bread, 2:9; 2 Thess. 3:8, and received aid at least twice from the Philippians, Phil. 4:16.

His fruitful labor was cut short, however, by the malign influence of envious Jews, who attacked the house of Jason, where they expected to find the missionaries, and failing in this, they drew Jason and some of the brethren before the rulers, πολιτάχας (a name found only in Acts 17:6, 8, but proved absolutely correct by inscriptions, cf. Ramsey, St. Paul the Traveler and the Roman Citizen p. 227) and charged them with treason. "The step taken by the politarchs was the mildest that was prudent in the circumstances; they bound the accused over in security that peace should be kept." (Ramsay) As a result the brethren deemed it advisable to send Paul and his companions to Berea, where many accepted the truth, but their labors were again interrupted by the Jews from Thessalonica. Leaving Silas and Timothy here, the apostle went to Athens, where he expected them to join him shortly. From the narrative in the Acts it seems that they did not come to the apostle until after his arrival at Corinth, but 1 Thess. 3:1 implies that Timothy was with him at Athens. The most natural theory is that both soon followed the apostle to Athens, and that he sent Timothy from there to Thessalonica to establish and comfort the church, and Silas on some other mission, possibly to Philippi, both returning to him at Corinth.

From the data in Acts 17:4 and 1 Thess. 1:9; 2:14 we may infer that the church of Thessalonica was of a mixed character, consisting of Jewish and Gentile Christians. Since no reference is made in the Epistles to the tenets of the Jews and not a single Old Testament passage is quoted, it is all but certain that its members were mostly Christians of the Gentiles. Only three of them are known to us from Scripture, viz. Jason, Acts 17:5-9, and Aristarchus and Secundus, Acts 20:4. The congregation was not wealthy, 2 Cor. 8:2, 3; with the exception of a few women of the better class, it seems to have consisted chiefly of laboring people that had to work for their daily bread, 4:11; 2 Thess. 3:6-12. They had not yet parted company with all their old vices, for there was still found among them fornication 4:3-5, fraud 4:6 and idleness 4:11. Yet they were zealous in the work of the Lord and formed one of the most beloved churches of the apostle.

COMPOSITION

1. Occasion and Purpose. What led Paul to write this letter, was undoubtedly the report Timothy brought him respecting the condition of the Thessalonian church. The apostle felt that he had been torn away from

them all too soon and had not had sufficient time to establish them in the truth. Hence he was greatly concerned about their spiritual welfare after his forced departure. The coming of Timothy brought him some relief, for he learnt from that fellow-laborer that the church, though persecuted, did not waver, and that their faith had become an example to many. Yet he was not entirely at ease, since he also heard that the Jews were insinuating that his moral conduct left a great deal to be desired, while he had misled the Thessalonians for temporal gain and vainglory, 2:3-10; that some heathen vices were still prevalent in the church; and that the doctrine of the parousia had been misconstrued, giving some occasion to cease their daily labors, and others, to feel concerned about the future condition of those who had recently died in their midst. That information led to the composition of our Epistle.

In view of all these things it was but natural that the apostle should have a threefold purpose in writing this letter. In the first place he desired to express his gratitude for the faithful perseverance of the Thessalonians. In the second place he sought to establish them in faith, which was all the more necessary, since the enemy had sown tares among the wheat. Hence he reminds them of his work among them, pointing out that his conversation among them was above reproach, and that as a true apostle he had labored among them without covetousness and vainglory. And in the third place he aimed at correcting their conception of the Lord's return, emphasizing its importance as a motive for sanctification,

2. Time and Place. There is little uncertainty as to the time and place of composition, except in the ranks of those who regard the Epistle as a forgery. When Paul wrote this letter, the memory of his visit to Thessalonica was still vivid, chs. 1 and 2; and he was evidently in some central place, where he could keep posted on the state of affairs in Macedonia and Achaia, 1:7, 8, and from where he could easily communicate with the Thessalonian church. Moreover Silas and Timothy were with him, of which the former attended the apostle only on his second missionary journey, and the latter could not bring him a report of conditions at Thessalonica, until he returned to the apostle at Corinth, Acts 18:5. Therefore the Epistle was written during Paul's stay in that city. However it should not be dated at the beginning of Paul's Corinthian residence, since the faith of the Thessalonians had already become manifest throughout Macedonia and Achaia, and some deaths had occurred in the church of Thessalonica. Neither can we place it toward the

end of that period, for II Thessalonians was also written before the apostle left Corinth. Most likely it was composed towards the end of A. D. 52.

CANONICAL SIGNIFICANCE

The canonicity of this Epistle was never questioned in ancient times. There are some supposed references to it in the apostolic fathers, Clement of Rome, Barnabas, Ignatins and Polycarp, but they are very uncertain. Marcion and the Muratorian Fragment and the old Latin and Syriac Versions testify to its canonicity, however, and from the end of the second century its canonical use is a well established fact.

In this letter we behold Paul, the missionary, in the absence of any direct controversy, carefully guarding the interest of one of his most beloved churches, comforting and encouraging her like a father. He strengthens the heart of his persecuted spiritual children with the hope of Christ's return, when the persecutors shall be punished for their evil work, and the persecuted saints, both the dead and the living, shall receive their eternal reward in the Kingdom of their heavenly Lord. And thus the apostle is an example worthy of imitation; his lesson is a lesson of permanent value. The glorious parousia of Christ is the cheering hope of the militant church in all her struggles to the end of time.

18

The Second Epistle to the Thessalonians

CONTENTS

The contents of the letter naturally falls into three parts:

I. Introduction, ch. 1. The apostle begins his letter with the regular blessing, 1, 2. He thanks God for the increasing faith and patience of the Thessalonians, reminding them of the fact that in the day of Christ's coming God will provide rest for his persecuted church and will punish her persecutors; and prays that God may fulfil his good pleasure in them to the glory of his Name, 3-12.

II. Instruction respecting the Parousia, ch. 2. The church is warned against deception regarding the imminence of the great day of Christ and is informed that it will not come until the mystery of iniquity has resulted in the great apostasy, and the man of sin has been revealed whose coming is after the work of satan, and who will utterly deceive men to their own destruction, 1-12. The Thessalonians need not fear the manifestation of Christ, since they were chosen and called to everlasting glory; and it is the apostle's wish that the Lord may comfort their hearts and establish them in all good work, 13-17.

III. Practical Exhortations, ch. 3. The writer requests the prayer of the church for himself that he may be delivered from unreasonable and wicked men, and exhorts her to do what he commanded, 1-5. They should withdraw from those who are disorderly and do not work, because each one should labor for his daily bread and thus follow the example of the apostle, 6-12. Those who do not heed the apostolic word should be censured, 13-15. With a blessing and a salutation the apostle closes his letter, 16-18.

CHARACTERISTICS

1. The main characteristic of this letter is found in the apocalyptic passage, 2:1-12. In these verses, that contain the most essential part of the Epistle, Paul speaks as a prophet, revealing to his beloved church that the

return of Christ will be preceded by a great final apostacy and by the revelation of the man of sin, the son of perdition who, as the instrument of satan, will deceive men, so that they accept the lie and are condemned in the great day of Christ. II Thessalonians, no doubt, was written primarily for the sake of this instruction.

2. Aside from this important doctrinal passage the Epistle has a personal and practical character. It contains expressions of gratitude for the faith and endurance of the persecuted church, words of encouragement for the afflicted, fatherly advice for the spiritual children of the apostle, and directions as to their proper behavior.

3. The style of this letter, like that of I Thessalonians, is simple and direct, except in 2:1–12, where the tone is more elevated. This change is accounted for by the prophetic contents of that passage. The language clearly reveals the working of the vigorous mind of Paul, who in the expression of his thoughts was not limited to a few stock phrases. Besides the many expressions that are characteristically Pauline the Epistle contains several that are peculiar to it, and also a goodly number which it has in common only with I Thessalonians. Of the 26 ἅπαξ λεγόμενα in the letter 10 are not found in the rest of the New Testament, and 16 are used elsewhere in the New Testament but not in the writings of Paul.

AUTHORSHIP

The external testimony for the authenticity of this Epistle is just as strong as that for the genuineness of the first letter. Marcion has it in his canon, the Muratorian Fragment names it, and it is also found in the old Latin and Syriac Versions. From the time of Irenaeus it is regularly quoted as a letter of Paul, and Origen and Eusebius claim that it was universally received in their time.

The Epistle itself claims to be the work of Paul, 1:1; and again in 3:17, where the apostle calls attention to the salutation as a mark of genuineness. The persons associated with the writer in the composition of this letter are the same as those mentioned in I Thessalonians. As in the majority of Paul's letters the apostolic blessing is followed by a thanksgiving. The Epistle is very similar to I Thessalonians and contains some cross-references to it, as f. i. in the case of the parousia and of the idlers. It clearly reveals the character of the great apostle, and its style may confidently be termed Pauline.

Nevertheless the genuineness of the Epistle has been doubted far more than that of I Thessalonians. Schmidt was the first one to assail it in 1804; in this he was followed by Schrader, Mayerhof and De Wette, who afterwards changed his mind, however. The attack was renewed by Kern and Baur in whose school the rejection of the Epistle became general. Its authenticity is defended by Reuss, Sabatier, Hofmann, Weiss, Zahn, Jülicher, Farrar, Godet, Baljon, Moffat e. a.

The principal objections urged against the genuineness of this letter are the following: (1) The teaching of Paul regarding the parousia in 2:1-12 is not consistent with what he wrote in 1 Thessalonians 4:13-18; 5:1-11. According to the first letter the day of Christ is imminent and will come suddenly and unexpectedly; the second emphasizes the fact that it is not close at hand and that several signs will precede it. (2) The eschatology of this passage 2:1-12 is not Paul's but clearly dates from a later time and was probably borrowed from the Revelation of John. Some identify the man of sin with Nero who, though reported dead, was supposed to be hiding in the East and was expected to return; and find the one still restraining the evil in Vespasian. Others hold that this passage clearly refers to the time of Trajan, when the mystery of iniquity was seen in the advancing tide of Gnosticism. (3) This letter is to a great extent but a repitition of I Thessalonians, and therefore looks more like the work of a forger than like a genuine production of Paul. Holtzmann says that, with the exception of 1:5, 6, 9, 12; 2:2-9, 11, 12, 15; 3:2, 13, 14, 17, the entire Epistle consists of a reproduction of parallel passages from the first letter. Einl. p. 214. (4) The Epistle contains a conspicuously large number of peculiar expressions that are not found in the rest of Paul's writings, nor in the entire New Testament. Cf. lists in Frame's Comm. pp. 28-34, in the Intern. Crit. Comm. (5) The salutation in 3:17 has a suspicious look. It seems like the attempt of a later writer to ward off objections and to attest the Pauline authorship.

But the objections raised are not sufficient to discredit the authenticity of our Epistle. The contradictions in Paul's teaching regarding the parousia of Christ, are more apparent than real. The signs that precede the great day will not detract from its suddenness any more than the signs of Noah's time prevented the flood from taking his contemporaries by surprise. Moreover these two features, the suddenness of Christ's appearance and the portentous facts that are the harbingers of his coming, always go hand in hand in the eschatological teachings of Scripture. Dan. 11:1-12:3; Mt. 24:1-44; Lk. 17:20-37. As to the immediacy of Christ's coming we can at most say that the first Epistle intimates that the Lord might appear during that generation (though possibly it does not even imply that), but it certainly does not teach that Christ will presently come.

The eschatology of the second chapter has given rise to much discussion and speculation regarding the date and authorship of the Epistle, but recent investigations into the conditions of the early church have clearly brought out that the contents of this chapter in no way militate against the genuineness of the letter. Hence they who deny the Pauline authorship have ceased to place great reliance on it. There is nothing improbable in the supposition that Paul wrote the passage regarding the man of sin. We find similar representations as early as the time of Daniel (cf. Dan. 11), in the pseudepigraphic literature of the Jews (cf. Schürer, Geschichte des Jüdischen Volkes II p. 621 f.), and in the eschatological discourses of the Lord. The words and expressions found in this chapter are very well susceptible of an interpretation that does not necessitate our dating the Epistle after the time of Paul. We cannot delay to review all the preterist and futurist expositions that have been given (for which cf. Alford, Prolegomena Section V), but can only indicate in a general way in what direction we must look for the interpretation of this difficult passage. In interpreting it we should continually bear in mind its prophetic import and its reference to something that is still future. No doubt, there were in history prefigurations of the great day of Christ in which this prophecy found a partial fulfilment, but the parousia of which Paul speaks in these verses is even now only a matter of faithful expectation. The history of the world is gradually leading up to it. Paul was witnessing some apostasy in his day, the μυστή-ριον τῆς ἀνομίας was already working, but the great apostasy (ἡ ἀποστασία) could not come in his day, because there had been as yet but a very partial dissemination of the truth; and will not come until the days immediately preceding the second coming of Christ, when the mystery of godlessness will complete itself, and will finally be embodied in a single person, in the man of sin, the son of perdition, who will then develop into a power antagonistic to Christ (anti-christ, ὁ ἀντικείμενος), yea to every form of religion, the very incarnation of satan. Cf. vs. 9. This can only come to pass, however, after the restraining power is taken out of the way, a power that is at once impersonal (κατέχον) and personal (κατέχων), and which may refer first of all to the strict administration of justice in the Roman empire and to the emperor as the chief executive, but certainly has a wider signification and probably refers in general to "the fabric of human polity and those who rule that polity." (Alford). For a more detailed exposition cf. especially, Alford,

Prolegomena Section V; Zahn, Einleitung I p. 162 ff.; Godet, Introduction p. 171 ff.; and Eadie, Essay on the Man of Sin in Comm. p. 329 ff.

We fail to see the force of the third argument, unless it is an established fact that Paul could not repeat himself to a certain degree, even in two Epistles written within the space of a few months, on a subject that engaged the mind of the apostle for some time, to the same church and therefore with a view to almost identical conditions. This argument looks strange especially in view of the following one, which urges the rejection of this letter, because it is so unlike the other Pauline writings. The points of difference between our letter and I Thessalonians are generally exaggerated, and the examples cited by Davidson to prove the dissimilarity are justly ridiculed by Salmon, who styles such criticism "childish criticism, that is to say, criticism such as might proceed from a child who insists that a story shall always be told to him in precisely the same way." Introd. p. 398. The salutation in 3:17 does not point to a time later than that of Paul, since he too had reason to fear the evil influence of forged Epistles, 2:2. He merely states that, with a view to such deception, he would in the future authenticate all his letters by attaching an autographic salutation.

COMPOSITION

1. Occasion and Purpose. Evidently some additional information regarding the state of affairs at Thessalonica had reached Paul, it may be through the bearers of the first Epistle, or by means of a communication from the elders of the church. It seems that some letter had been circulated among them, purporting to come from Paul, and that some false spirit was at work in the congregation. The persecution of the Thessalonians still continued and had probably increased in force, and in some way the impression had been created that the day of the Lord was at hand. This led on the one hand to feverish anxiety, and on the other, to idleness. Hence the apostle deemed it necessary to write a second letter to the Thessalonians.

The purpose of the writer was to encourage the sorely pressed church; to calm the excitement by pointing out that the second advent of the Lord could not be expected immediately, since the mystery of lawlessness had to develop first and to issue in the man of sin; and to exhort the irregular ones to a quiet, industrious and orderly conduct.

2. Time and Place. Some writers, such as Grotius, Ewald, Vander Vies and Laurent advocated the theory that II Thessalonians was written before I Thessalonians, but the arguments adduced to support that position cannot

bear the burden. Moreover 2 Thess. 2:15 clearly refers to a former letter of the apostle. In all probability our Epistle was composed a few months after the first one, for on the one hand Silas and Timothy were still with the apostle, 1:1, which was not the case after he left Corinth, and they were still antagonized by the Jews so that most likely their case had not yet been brought before Gallio, Acts 18:12–17; and on the other hand a change had come about both in the sentiment of the apostle, who speaks no more of his desire to visit the Thessalonians, and in the condition of the church to which he was writing, a change that would necessarily require some time. We should most likely date the letter about the middle of A. D. 53.

CANONICAL SIGNIFICANCE

The early Church found no reason to doubt the canonicity of this letter. Little stress can be laid, it is true, on the supposed reference to its language in Ignatius, Barnabas, the Didache and Justin Martyr. It is quite evident, however, that Polycarp used the Epistle. Moreover it has a place in the canon of Marcion, is mentioned among the Pauline letters in the Muratorian Fragment, and is contained in the old Latin and Syriac Versions. Irenaeus, Clement of Alexandria, Tertullian and others since their time, quote it by name.

The great permanent value of this Epistle lies in the fact that it corrects false notions regarding the second advent of Christ, notions that led to indolence and disorderliness. We are taught in this Epistle that the great day of Christ will not come until the mystery of iniquity that is working in the world receives its full development, and brings forth the son of perdition who as the very incarnation of satan will set himself against Christ and his Church. If the Church of God had always remembered this lesson, she would have been spared many an irregularity and disappointment. The letter also reminds us once more of the fact that the day of the Lord will be a day of terror to the wicked, but a day of deliverance and glory for the Church of Christ.

CHAPTER

19

The Pastoral Epistles

AUTHORSHIP

In the case of these Epistles it seems best to consider the question of authorship first, and to treat them as a unity in the discussion of their authenticity. When we examine the external testimony to these letters we find that this is in no way deficient. If many have doubted their genuineness, it was not because they discovered that the early Church did not recognize them. It is true that some early heretics, who acknowledged the genuineness of the other letters attributed to Paul, rejected these, such as Basilides and Marcion, but Jerome says that their adverse judgment was purely arbitrary. From the time of Irenaeus, Clement of Alexandria and Tertullian, who were the first to quote the New Testament books by name, until the beginning of the nineteenth century, no one doubted the Pauline authorship of these letters. The Muratorian Fragment ascribes them to Paul, and they are included in all MSS., Versions and Lists of the Pauline letters, in all of which (with the single exception of the Muratorian Fragment) they are arranged in the same order, viz. I Timothy, II Timothy, Titus.

As far as the internal evidence is concerned we may call attention in a preliminary way to a few facts that favor the authenticity of these letters and take up the consideration of other features in connection with the objections that are urged against them. They are all self-attested; they contain the characteristic Pauline blessing at the beginning, end with the customary salutation, and reveal the usual solicitude of Paul for his churches and for those associated with him in the work; they point to the same relation between Paul and his spiritual sons Timothy and Titus that we know from other sources; and they refer to persons (cf. 2 Tim. 4. Titus 3) that are also mentioned elsewhere as companions and co-laborers of Paul.

Yet it is especially on the strength of internal evidence that these Epistles have been attacked. J. E. C. Schmidt in 1804, soon followed by Schleiermacher, was the first one to cast doubt on their genuineness. Since that time they have been rejected, not only by the Tübingen school and by practically all negative critics, but also by some scholars that usually incline to the conservative side, such as Neander (rejecting only I Timothy), Meyer; (Introd. to Romans) and Sabatier. While the majority of radical critics reject these letters unconditionally, Credner, Harnack, Hausrath and McGiffert believe that they contain some genuine Pauline sections; the last named scholar regarding especially the passages that contain personal references, such as 2 Tim. 1:15-18; 4:9-21; Titus 3:12, 13, as authentic, and surmising that some others may be saved from the ruins, The Apostolic Age p. 405 ff. The genuineness of the Pastorals is defended by Weiss, Zahn, Salmon, Godet, Barth, and nearly all the Commentators, such as Huther, Van Oosterzee, Ellicott, Alford, White (in The Exp. Gk. Test.) e. a.

Several arguments are employed to discredit the authenticity of these letters. We shall briefly consider the most important ones. (1) It is impossible to find a place for their composition and the historical situation which they reflect in the life of Paul, as we know it from the Acts of the Apostles. Reuss, who provisionally accepted their Pauline authorship in his, History of the New Testament I pp. 80-85; 121-129, did so with the distinct proviso that they had to fit into the narrative of Acts somewhere. Finding that his scheme did not work out well, he afterwards rejected I Timothy and Titus. Cf. his Commentary on the Pastorals. (2) The conception of Christianity found in these letters is un-Pauline and clearly represents a later development. They contain indeed some Pauline ideas, but these are exceptional. "There is no trace whatever," says McGiffert, "of the great fundamental truth of Paul's gospel,—death unto the flesh and life in the Spirit." Instead of the faith by which we are justified and united to Christ, we find piety and good works prominently in the foreground. Cf. 1 Tim. 1:5; 2:2, 15; 4:7 f.; 5:4; 6:6;—2 Tim. 1:3; 3:5, 12;—Titus 1:1; 2:12. Moreover the word faith does not, as in the letters of Paul, denote the faith that believes, but rather the sum and substance of that which is believed, 1 Tim. 1:19; 3:9; 4:1, 6; 5:8. And sound doctrine is spoken of in a way that reminds one of the characteristic esteem in which orthodoxy was later held, cf. 1 Tim. 1:10; 4:6; 6:3;—2 Tim. 4:3;—Titus 1:9; 2:1, 7. (3) The church organization that is reflected in these letters points to a later age. It is unlikely that Paul, believing as he did in the speedy second coming of Christ, would pay so much attention to details of organization; nor does it seem probable that he would lay such stress on the offices received by ecclesiastical appointment, and have so little regard to the spiritual gifts that are independent of official position and that occupy a very prominent place in the undoubted writings of the apostle. Moreover the organization assumed in these letters reveals second century conditions. Alongside of the πρεσβύτεροι the ἐπίσκοπος is named as a primus inter pares (notice the singular in 1 Tim. 3:1; Titus 1:7); and the office-bearers in general are given undue prominence. There is a separate class of widows, of which some held an official position in the Church, just as there was in the second century, 1 Tim. 5. Ecclesiastical office is conferred by the laying on of hands, 1 Tim. 5:22; and the second marriage of bishops, deacons, and ministering widows was not to be tolerated, 1 Tim. 3:2, 12; 5:9-11; Tit. 1:6. (4) The false teachers and teachings to which the Epistles refer are evidently second century Gnostics and Gnosticism. The term ἀντιθέσεις, 1 Tim. 6:20, according to Baur, contains a reference to the work of Marcion which bore that title. And the endless genealogies of 1 Tim. 1:4 are supposed to refer to the Aeons of Valentinus. (5) The most weighty objection is, however, that the style of these letters differs from that of the Pauline Epistles to such a degree as to imply diversity of authorship. Says Davidson: "The change of style is too great to comport with identity of authorship. Imitations of phrases and terms occurring in Paul's authentic Epistles are obvious; inferiority and feebleness show dependence; while the new constructions and words betray a writer treating of new circumstances and giving expression to new ideas, yet personating the apostle all the while. The change is palpable; though the author throws himself back into the situation of Paul the prisoner." Introd. II p. 66. Holtzmann claims that of the 897 words that constitute these letters (proper names excepted) 171 (read 148) are ἅπαξ λεγόμενα, of which 74 are found in I Timothy, 46 in II Timothy, and 28 in Titus. Besides these there is a great number of phrases and expressions that are peculiar and point away from Paul, such as διώκειν δικαιοσύνην, 1 Tim. 6:11; 2 Tim. 2:22; φυλάσσειν τὴν παραθήκην, 1 Tim. 6:20; 2 Tim. 1:12, 14; παρακολουθεῖν τῇ διδασκαλίᾳ, 1 Tim. 4:6; 2 Tim. 3:10; βέβηλοι κενοφωνίαι, 1 Tim. 6:20; 2 Tim. 2:16; ἄνθρωπος θεοῦ, 1 Tim. 6:11; 2 Tim. 3:17; etc. On the other hand many expressions that play a prominent part in Pauline literature are absent from these letters, as ἄδικος, ἀκροβυστία, γνωρίζειν, δικαιοσύνη θεοῦ, δικαίωμα, ἔργα νόμου, ὁμοίωμα, παράδοσις, etc.

As far as the first argument is concerned, it must be admitted that these Epistles do not fit in the life of Paul, as we know it from the Acts of the

Apostles. Their genuineness depends on the question, whether or not Paul was set free again after the imprisonment described in Acts 28. Now we have reasons, aside from the contents of these Epistles, to believe that he was liberated and resumed his missionary labors. In view of the fact that Felix, Festus and Agrippa found no guilt in Paul, and that the apostle was sent to Rome, only because he appealed to Cæsar, the presumption is that he was not condemned at Rome. This presumption is greatly strengthened by the fact that, when the apostle wrote his letters to the Philippians and to Philemon, the prospect of his release seemed favorable, Phil. 1:25; 2:24; Philem. 22; compare 2 Tim. 4:6-8. It is objected to this that Paul, in taking his farewell of the Ephesan elders, says to them: "I know (οἶδα) that ye all— shall see my face no more," Acts 20:25. But it may be doubted, whether we have the right to press this οἶδα so that it becomes prophetic; if we have, it is counterbalanced by the οἶδα in Phil. 1:25. The most natural infer- ence from the data of Scripture (outside of these Epistles) is that Paul was set free; and this is confirmed by the tradition of the early Church, as it is expressed by Eusebius, Church Hist. II 22: Paul is said (λόγος ἔχει), after having defended himself to have set forth again upon the ministry of preaching, and to have entered the same city a second time, and to have ended his life by martyrdom. Whilst then a prisoner, he wrote the second Epistle to Timothy, in which he both mentions his first defense, and his impending death." Moreover the Muratorian Fragment speaks of a visit that Paul paid to Spain, which cannot be placed before the first Roman imprisonment. And Clement of Rome states in his letter to the Corinthians, after relating that the apostle labored in the East and in the West, that he came to "the bounderies of the West." Now it does not seem likely that he, who himself lived in Rome, would refer to the city on the Tiber in those terms. And if this is not the import of those words, the presumption is that he too has reference to Spain.

Paul's movements after his release are uncertain, and all that can be said regarding, them is conjectural. Leaving Rome he probably first repaired to Macedonia and Asia Minor for the intended visits, Phil. 1:23-26; Philem. 22, and then undertook his long looked for journey to Spain, Rom. 15:24. Returning from there, he possibly went to Ephesus, where he had a dispute with Hymenaeus and Alexander, 1 Tim. 1:20, and engaged the services of Onesiphorus, 2 Tim. 1:16-18. Leaving Timothy in charge of the Ephesian church, he departed for Macedonia, 1 Tim. 1:3, from where he most likely wrote I Timothy. After this he may have visited Crete with Titus, leaving the latter there to organize the churches, Tit. 1:5, and returning to Ephesus according to his wishes, 1 Tim. 3:14; 4:13, where Alexander the coppersmith did him great evil, 2 Tim. 4:14. From here he probably wrote the Epistle to Titus, for he was evidently in some center of missionary enterprise, when he composed it, Tit. 3:12-15. Departing from Ephesus, he went through Miletus, 2 Tim. 4:20 to Troas, 2 Tim. 4:13, where he was probably re-arrested, and whence he was taken to Rome by way of Corinth, the abode of Erastus, 2 Tim. 4:20; Rom. 16:23. In that case he did not reach Nicopolis, where he intended to spend the winter. In this statement we proceed on the assumption that the winter mentioned in 2 Tim. 4:21 is the same as that of Titus 3:12. The second imprisonment of Paul was more severe than the first, 2 Tim. 1:16, 17; 2:9. His first defense appears to have been successful, 2 Tim. 4:16, 17, but as his final hearing drew nigh, he had a presentiment of approaching martyrdom. According to the Chronicles of Eusebius Paul died as a martyr in the thirteenth year of Nero, or A. D. 67.

The objection that the theological teaching of these Epistles is different from that of Paul, must be taken cum grano salis, because this teaching merely complements and in no way contradicts the representation of the undoubted Epistles. We find no further objective development of the truth here, but only a practical application of the doctrines already unfolded in previous letters. And it was entirely fitting that, as every individual letter, so too the entire cycle of Pauline Epistles should end with practical admonitions. Historically this is easily explained, on the one hand, by the fact that the productive period of the apostle's life had come to an end, and it is now Paul the aged—for all the vicissitudes of a busy and stormy life must greatly have sapped his strength—that speaks to us, cf. Philem. 9; and, on the other hand, by the fact that the heresy which the apostle here encounters had developed into ethical corruption. If it is said that the writer of these Epistles ascribes a meritorious character to good works, we take exception and qualify that as a false statement. The passages referred to, such as 1 Tim. 1:15; 3:13; 4:8; 6:18 ff.; 2 Tim. 4:8, do not prove the assertion. Since a rather full statement of the Christian truth had preceded these letters, it need not cause surprise that Paul should refer to it as "the sound doctrine," Cf. Rom. 6:17. Nor does it seem strange, in view of this, that alongside of the subjective the objective sense of the word faith should begin to assert itself. We find an approach to this already in Rom. 12:6; Gal. 1:23; Phil. 1:27.

It is a mistake to think that the emphasis which these letters place on the external organization of the churches, and the particular type of

ecclesiastical polity which they reflect, precludes their Pauline authorship. There is nothing strange in the fact that Paul, knowing that the day of
Christ was not at hand (2 Thess. 2:1-12), should lay special stress on church
government now that his ministry was drawing to a close. It might rather
have caused surprise, if he had not thus made provision for the future
of his churches. And it is perfectly natural also that he should emphasize the offices in the church rather than the extraordinary spiritual gifts,
since these gradually vanished and made place for the ordinary ministry of the Word. The position that the office-bearers mentioned in these
letters prove a development beyond that of the apostolic age is not sub-
stantiated by the facts. Deacons were appointed shortly after the establishment of the Church, Acts 6; elders were chosen from place to place, as
the apostle founded churches among the Gentiles, Acts 14:23; and in Phil,
1:1 Paul addresses not only the Philippians in general, but also "the bishops and deacons." Moreover in Eph. 4:11 the apostle says: "And He gave you
some apostle's; and some prophets; and some evangelists; and some pas-
tors and teachers." Surely it does not seem that the Pastoral Epistles are
strikingly different in this respect from the others. If it be said that the
bishop becomes so prominent here as to indicate that the leaven of hierar-
chy was already working, we answer that in the New Testament the terms
ἐπίσκοπος and πρεσβύτερος are clearly synonymous. The fact that the bishop
is spoken of in the singular proves nothing to the contrary. Not once are
bishops and presbyters arranged alongside of each other as denoting two
separate classes, and in Titus 1:5-7 the terms are clearly interchangeable.
The case of Phebe, Rom. 16:1 certainly does not countenance the theory
that the office of deaconess was not called into existence until the second
century. And the passages that are supposed to prohibit the second marriage of office-bearers are of too uncertain interpretation to justify the
conclusions drawn from them.

Granted that the errors to which these letters refer were of a Gnostic
character—as Alford is willing to grant—, it by no means follows that the
Epistles are second century productions, since the first signs of the Gnostic
heresy are known to have made their appearance in the apostolic age. But it
is an unproved assumption that the writer refers to Gnosticism of any kind.
It is perfectly evident from the letters that the heresy was of a Judæistic,
though not of a Pharisæic type, resembling very much the error that threatened the Colossian church. Hort, after examining it carefully comes to the
conclusion that "there is a total want of evidence for anything pointing to

even rudimentary Gnosticism or Essenism." In view of the fact that the errorists prided themselves as being teachers of the law, 1 Tim. 1:7, and that the term γενεαλογία is brought in close connection with "strivings about the law" in Titus 3:9, the presumption is that it contains no reference whatever to the emanations of Gnostic aeons, but rather, as Zahn surmises, to rabbinic disputations regarding Jewish genealogies. And the word "antitheses," of which Hort says that it cannot refer to Marcion's work, is simply descriptive of the opposition in which the heretics that boasted of a higher knowledge placed themselves to the Gospel.

The argument from style has often proved to be a very precarious one. If a person's vocabulary were a fixed quantity, he were limited to the use of certain set phrases and expressions, and his style, once acquired, were unchangeable and necessarily wanting in flexibility, a plausible case might be made out. But as a matter of fact such is not the usual condition of things, and certainly was not the case with Paul, who to a great extent moulded the language of the New Testament. We need not and cannot deny that the language of the Pastorals has many peculiarities, but in seeking to explain these we should not immediately take refuge in a supposed difference of authorship, but rather make allowance for the influence of Paul's advancing years, of the altered conditions of his life, of the situation in which his readers were placed, and of the subjects with which he was obliged to deal in these Epistles. And let us not forget what N. J. D. White says, Exp. Gk. Test. IV p. 63, that "the acknowledged peculiarities must not be allowed to obscure the equally undoubted fact that the Epistles present not only as many characteristic Pauline words as the writer had use for, but that, in the more significant matter of turns of expression, the style of the letters is fundamentally Pauline. Cf. also the judicious remarks of Reuss on the style of these letters. History of the New Testament, I p. 123.

In concluding our discussion of the authenticity of the Pastoral Epistles we desire to remark: (1) The critics admit that the objections urged by them against the genuineness of these letters do not apply to all three of them in the same degree. According to Baur II Timothy and Titus are the least suspicious. He maintains, however, that I Timothy will always be "the betrayer of its spurious brothers." But it would be reasonable to turn the statement about with Reuss, and to say that "so long as no decisive and palpable proofs of the contrary are presented the two which are in and of themselves less suspicious ought always to afford protection to the third which is more so." Ibid. p. 84. (2) Baur and his followers rightly held that, in order to prove the spuriousness of these letters, they had to point out the positive purpose of the forgery; in which, according to Reuss, they utterly failed, when they said that it was to combat the Gnostic heresies that were prevalent after A. D. 150, Ibid. p. 124 f. (3) It looks a great deal like a confession of defeat, when several of the negative critics admit that the passages in which personal reminiscences are found, must be regarded as genuine, for it means that they yield their case wherever they can be controlled. For a broader discussion of the authenticity of these letters, cf. Alford, Prolegomena Section I; Holtzmann, Einl. pp. 274-292; Zahn, Einl. I pp. 459-491; Godet, Introd. pp. 567-611; Farrar, St. Paul, II pp. 607-622; Salmon, Introd. pp. 433-452; McGiffert, Apostolic Age pp. 399-423; Davidson, Introd. II pp. 21-76. Lock (in Hastings D. B. Artt. I Timothy, II Timothy and Titus.)

20

The First Epistle to Timothy

CONTENTS

The first Epistle to Timothy may be divided into four parts:

I. Introduction, 1:1-20. The apostle begins by reminding Timothy that he had been left at Ephesus to counteract prevalent heresies, 1-10. He directs the attention of his spiritual son to the Gospel contradicted by these errors, thanks the Lord that he was made a minister of it, and charges Timothy to act in accordance with that Gospel, 11-20.

II. General Regulations for Church Life, 2:1-4:5. Here we find first of all directions for public intercession and for the behavior of men and women in the meetings of the church, 2:1-15. These are followed by an explicit statement of the qualities that are necessary in bishops and deacons, 3:1-13. The expressed purpose of these directions is, to promote the good order of the church, the pillar and ground of the truth, essentially revealed in Christ, from which the false brethren were departing, 3:14-4:5.

III. Personal Advice to Timothy, 4:6-6:2. Here the apostle speaks of Timothy's behavior towards the false teachers, 4:6-11; of the way in which he should regard and discharge his ministerial duties, 12-16; and of the attitude he ought to assume towards the individual members of the church, especially towards the widows, the elders and the slaves, 5:1-6:2.

IV. Conclusion, 6:3-21. The apostle now makes another attack on the heretical teachers, 3-10; and exhorts Timothy to be true to his calling and to avoid all erroneous teachings, giving him special directions with respect to the rich, 11-21.

CHARACTERISTICS

1. This letter is one of the Pastoral Epistles of Paul, which are so called, because they were written to persons engaged in pastoral work and contain many directions for pastoral duties. They were sent, not to churches, but to office-bearers, instructing them how to behave in the house of God.

It is evident, however, that, with the possible exception of II Timothy, they were not intended exclusively for the persons to whom they were addressed, but also for the churches in which these labored. Cf. as far as this Epistle is concerned, 4:6, 11; 5:7; 6:17.

2. From the preceding it follows that this letter is not doctrinal but practical. We find no further objective development of the truth here, but clear directions as to its practical application, especially in view of divergent tendencies. The truth developed in previous Epistles is here represented as the "sound doctrine" that must be the standard of life and action, as "the faith" that should be kept, and as "a faithful word worthy of all acceptation." The emphasis clearly falls on the ethical requirements of the truth.

3. The letter emphasizes, as no other Epistle does, the external organization of the church. The apostle feels that the end of his life is fast approaching, and therefore deems it necessary to give more detailed instruction regarding the office-bearers in the church, in order that, when he is gone, his youthful co-laborers and the church itself may know how its affairs should be regulated. Of the office-bearers the apostle mentions the ἐπίσκο-πος and the πρεσβύτεροι, which are evidently identical, the first name indicating their work, and the second emphasizing their age; the διάκονοι, the γυναῖκες, if 3:11 refers to deaconesses, which is very probable (so Ellicott, Alford, White in Exp. Gk. Test.) and the χῆραι, ch. 5, though it is doubtful, whether these were indeed office-bearers.

4. Regarding the style of the Pastoral Epistles in general Huther remarks: "In the other Pauline Epistles the fulness of the apostle's thoughts struggle with the expression, and cause peculiar difficulties in exposition. The thoughts slide into one another, and are so intertwined in many forms that not seldom the new thought begins before a correct expression has been given of the thought that preceded. Of this confusion there is no example in the Pastoral Epistles. Even in such passages as come nearest to this confused style, such as the beginning of the first and second Epistles of Timothy (Tit. 2:11 ff.; 3:4 ff.) the connection of ideas is still on the whole simple." Comm. p. 9. This estimate is in general correct, though we would hardly speak of Paul's style in his other letters as "a confused style."

THE PERSON TO WHOM THE EPISTLE WAS WRITTEN

Paul addresses this letter to "Timothy my own son in the faith," 1:2. We find the first mention of Timothy in Acts 16:1, where he is introduced as an inhabitant of Lystra. He was the son of a Jewish mother and a Greek father, of whom we have no further knowledge. Both his mother Eunice and his grandmother Lois are spoken of as Christians in 2 Tim. 1:5. In all probability he was converted by Paul on his first missionary journey, since he was already a disciple, when the apostle entered Lystra on his second tour. He had a good report in his home town, Acts 16:2, and, being circumcised for the sake of the Jews, he joined Paul and Silas in their missionary labors. Passing with the missionaries into Europe and helping them at Philippi, Thessalonica and Berea, he remained with Silas in the last named place, while Paul pressed on to Athens and Corinth, where they finally joined the apostle again, Acts 17:14; 18:5. Cf. however also 1 Thess. 3:1 and p. 222 above. He abode there with the missionaries and his name appears with those of Paul and Silvanus in the addresses of the two Epistles to the Thessalonians. We next find him ministering to the apostle during his long stay at Ephesus, Acts 19:22, from where he was sent to Macedonia and Corinth, Acts 19:21, 22; 1 Cor. 4:17; 16:10, though it is doubtful, whether he reached that city. He was again in Paul's company, when II Corinthians was written, 2 Cor. 1:1, and accompanied the apostle to Corinth, Rom. 16:21, and again on his return through Macedonia to Asia, Acts 20:3, 4, probably also to Jerusalem, 1 Cor. 16:3. He is then mentioned in the Epistles of the imprisonment, which show that he was with the apostle at Rome, Phil. 1:1; Col. 1:1; Philem. 1. From this time on we hear no more of him until the Pastoral Epistles show him to be in charge of the Ephesian church, 1 Tim. 1:3.

From 1 Tim. 4:14, and 2 Tim. 1:6 we learn that he was set apart for the ministry by Paul with the laying on of hands, in accordance with prophetic utterances of the Spirit, 1 Tim. 1:18, when he probably received the title of evangelist, 2 Tim. 4:5, though in 1 Thess. 2:6 he is loosely classed with Paul and Silas as an apostle. We do not know when this formal ordination took place, whether at the very beginning of his work, or when he was placed in charge of the church at Ephesus.

The character of Timothy is clearly marked in Scripture. His readiness to leave his home and to submit to the rite of circumcision reveal his self-denial and earnestness of purpose. This is all the more striking, since he was very affectionate, 2 Tim. 1:4, delicate and often ill, 1 Tim. 5:23. At the same time he was timid, 1 Cor. 16:10, hesitating to assert his authority, 1 Tim. 4:12, and needed to be warned against youthful lusts, 2 Tim. 2:22, and to be encouraged in the work of Christ, 2 Tim. 1:8. Yet withal he was a worthy servant of Jesus Christ, Rom. 16:21, 1 Thess. 3:2; Phil. 1:1; 2:19–21; and the beloved spiritual son of the apostle, 1 Tim. 1:2; 2 Tim. 1:2; 1 Cor. 4:17.

COMPOSITION

1. Occasion and Purpose. This letter was occasioned by Paul's necessary departure from Ephesus for Macedonia, 1:3, the apprehension that he might be absent longer than he at first expected, 3:14, 15, and the painful consciousness that insidious errors were threatening the Ephesian church. Since Timothy was acquainted with these heresies, the apostle refers to them only in general terms which convey no very definite idea as to their real character. The persons who propagated them were prominent members of the church, possibly even office-bearers, 1:6, 7, 20; 3:1–12; 5:19–25. Their heresy was primarily of a Jewish character, 1:7, and probably resulted from an exaggeration of the demands of the law, a mistaken application of Christian ideas and a smattering of Oriental speculation. They claimed to be teachers of the law, 1:7, laid great stress on myths and genealogies, 1:4; 4:7, prided themselves like the rabbi's on the possession of special knowledge, 6:20, and, perhaps assuming that matter was evil or at least the seat of evil, they propagated a false asceticism, prohibiting marriage and requiring abstenence from certain foods, 4:3, and taught that the resurrection was already past, most likely recognizing only a spiritual resurrection, 2 Tim. 2:18. The charge entrusted to Timothy was therefore a difficult one, hence the apostle deemed it necessary to write this Epistle.

In connection with the situation described the purpose of Paul was twofold. In the first place he desired to encourage Timothy. This brother, being young and of a timid disposition, needed very much the cheering word of the apostle. And in the second place it was his aim to direct Timothy's warfare against the false doctrines that were disseminated in the church. Possibly it was also to prevent the havoc which these might work, if they who taught them were allowed in office, that he places such emphasis on the careful choice of office-bearers, and on the necessity of censuring them, should they go wrong.

2. Time and Place. The Epistle shows that Paul had left Ephesus for Macedonia with the intention of returning soon. And it was because he anticipated some delay that he wrote this letter to Timothy. Hence we may be sure that it was written from some place in Macedonia.

But the time when the apostle wrote this letter is not so easily determined. On what occasion did Paul quit Ephesus for Macedonia, leaving Timothy behind? Not after his first visit to Ephesus, Acts 18:20, 21, for on that occasion the apostle did not depart for Macedonia but for Jerusalem. Neither was it when he left Ephesus on his third missionary journey after a three years' residence, since Timothy was not left behind then, but had been sent before him to Corinth, Acts 19:22; 1 Cor. 4:17. Some are inclined to think that we must assume a visit of Paul to Macedonia during his Ephesian residence, a visit not recorded in the Acts of the Apostles. But then we must also find room there for the apostle's journey to Crete, since it is improbable that the Epistle of Paul to Titus was separated by any great interval of time from I Timothy. And to this must be added a trip to Corinth, cf. above p. 163. This theory is very unlikely in view of the time Paul spent at Ephesus, as compared with the work he did there, and of the utter silence of Luke regarding these visits. We must date the letter somewhere between the first and the second imprisonment of Paul. It was most likely after the apostle's journey to Spain, since on the only previous occasion that he visited Ephesus after his release he came to that city by way of Macedonia, and therefore would not be likely to return thither immediately. Probably the letter should be dated about A. D. 65 or 66.

CANONICAL SIGNIFICANCE

There was not the slightest doubt in the ancient church as to the canonicity of this Epistle. We find allusions more or less clear to its language in Clement of Rome, Polycarp, Ilegesippus, Athenagoras and Theophilus. It was contained in the old Latin and Syriac Versions and referred to Paul by the Muratorian Fragment. Irenaeus, Clement of Alexandria and Tertullian quote it by name, and Eusebius reckons it among the generally accepted canonical writings.

The great abiding value of the Epistle is found in the fact that it teaches the Church of all generations, how one, especially an office-bearer, should behave in the house of God, holding the faith, guarding his precious trust against the inroads of false doctrines, combating the evil that is found in the Lord's heritage, and maintaining good order in church life. "It witnesses," says Lock (Hastings D. B. Art. I Timothy) "that a highly ethical and spiritual conception of religion is consistent with and is safeguarded by careful regulations about worship, ritual and organized ministry. There is no opposition between the outward and the inward, between the spirit and the organized body."

21

The Second Epistle to Timothy

CONTENTS

The contents of this Epistle falls into three parts:

I. Considerations to strengthen Timothy's Courage, 1:1–2:13. After the greeting, 1, 2, the apostle urges Timothy to stir up his ministerial gift, to be bold in suffering, and to hold fast the truth entrusted to him, 3–14, enforcing these appeals by pointing to the deterrent example of the unfaithful and the stimulating example of Onesiphorus, 15–18. Further he exhorts him to be strong in the power of grace, to commit the true teaching to others, and to be ready to face suffering, 2:1–13.

II. Exhortations primarily dealing with Timothy's Teaching, 2:14–4:8. Timothy should urge Christians to avoid idle and useless discussions, and should rightly teach the truth, shunning vain babblings, 14–21. He must also avoid youthful passions, foolish investigations, and false teachers who, for selfish purposes, turn the truth of God into unrighteousness, 2:22–3:9. He is further exhorted to abide loyally by his past teaching, knowing that sufferings will come to every true soldier and that deceivers will grow worse, 10–17; and to fulfil his whole duty as an evangelist with sobriety and courage, especially since Paul is now ready to be offered up, 4:1–8.

III. Personal Reminiscences, 4:9–22. Paul appeals to Timothy to come to Rome quickly, bringing Mark and also taking his cloak and books, and to avoid Alexander, 9–15. He speaks of his desertion by men, the protection afforded him by the Lord, and his trust for the future, 16–18. With special greetings, a further account of his fellow-laborers, and a final salutation the apostle ends his letter, 19–22.

CHARACTERISTICS

1. II Timothy is the most personal of the Pastoral Epistles. Doctrinally it has no great importance, though it does contain the strongest proof-passage for the inspiration of Scripture. In the main the thought centers

about Timothy, the faithful co-laborer of Paul, whom the apostle gives encouragement in the presence of great difficulties, whom he inspires to noble, self-denying efforts in the Kingdom of God, and whom he exhorts to fight worthily in the spiritual warfare against the powers of darkness, that he may once receive an eternal reward.

2. It is the last Epistle of Paul, the swan-song of the great apostle, after a life of devotion to a noble cause, a life of Christian service. We see him here with work done, facing a martyr's death. Looking back his heart is filled with gratitude for the grace of God that saved him from the abyss that yawned at his feet, that called and qualified him to be a messenger of the cross, that protected him when dangers were threatening, and that crowned his work with rich spiritual fruits. And as he turns his eyes to the future, calm assurance and joyous hope are the strength of his soul, for he knows that the firm foundation of God will stand, since the Lord will punish the evil-doers and be the eternal reward of his children. He already has visions of the heavenly Kingdom, of eternal glory, of the coming righteous Judge, and of the crown of righteousness, the blessed inheritance of all those that love Christ's appearance.

COMPOSITION

1. Occasion and Purpose. The immediate occasion for writing this Epistle was the apostle's presentiment of his fast approaching end. He was anxious that Timothy should come to him soon, bringing Mark with him. In all probability he desired to give his spiritual son some fatherly advice and some practical instruction before his departure. But we feel that this alone did not call for a letter such as II Timothy really is. Another factor must be taken in consideration. Paul was not sure that Timothy would succeed in reaching Rome before his death, and yet realized that the condition of the Ephesian church, the danger to which Timothy was there exposed, and the importance of the work entrusted to this youthful minister, called for a word of apostolic advice, encouragement and exhortation. It seems that the Ephesian church was threatened by persecution, 1:8; 2:3, 12; 3:12; 4:5; and the heresy to which the apostle referred in his first epistle was evidently still rife in the circle of believers. There were those who strove about words, 2:14, were unspiritual, 2:16, corrupted in mind, 3:8, indulging in foolish and ignorant questionings, 2:23, and fables, 4:4, tending to a low standard of morality, 2:19, and teaching that the resurrection was already past, 2:18.

Hence the object of the Epistle is twofold. The writer wants to warn Timothy of his impending departure, to inform him of his past experiences at Rome and of his present loneliness, and to exhort him to come speedily. Besides this, however, he desired to strengthen his spiritual son in view of the deepening gloom of trials and persecution that were threatening the church from without; and to fore-arm him against the still sadder danger of heresy and apostasy that were lurking within the fold. Timothy is exhorted to hold fast the faith, 1:5, 13; to endure hardness as a good soldier of Jesus Christ, 2:3-10; to shun every form of heresy, 2:16-18; to instruct in meekness those that withstand the Gospel, 2:24-26; and to continue in the things he had learnt, 3:14-17.

2. Time and Place. From 1:17 it is perfectly evident that this letter was written at Rome. The apostle was again a prisoner in the imperial city. Though we have no absolute certainty, we deem it probable that he was re-arrested at Troas in the year 67. The situation in which he finds himself at Rome is quite different from that reflected in the other epistles of the captivity. He is now treated like a common criminal, 2:9; his Asiatic friends with the exception of Onesiphorus turned from him, 1:15; the friends who were with him during his first imprisonment are absent now, Col. 4:10-14; 2 Tim. 4:10-12; and the outlook of the apostle is quite different from that found in Philippians and Philemon. It is impossible to tell just how long the apostle had already been in prison, when he wrote the Epistle, but from the fact that he had had one hearing, 4:16 (which cannot refer to that of the first imprisonment, cf. Phil. 1:7, 12-14), and expected to be offered up soon, we infer that he composed the letter towards the end of his imprisonment, i. e. in the fall of A. D. 67.

CANONICAL SIGNIFICANCE

The canonicity of this Epistle has never been questioned by the Church; and the testimony to its early and general use is in no way deficient. There are quite clear traces of its language in Clement of Rome, Ignatius, Polycarp, Justin Martyr, The Acts of Paul and Thecla, and Theophilus of Antioch. The letter is included in all the MSS., the old Versions and the Lists of the Pauline Epistles. The Muratorian Fragment names it as a production of Paul, and from the end of the second century it is quoted by name.

The Epistle has some permanent doctrinal value as containing the most important proof-passage for the inspiration of Scripture, 3:16, and also

abiding historical significance in that it contains the clearest Scriptural testimony to the life of Paul after his first Roman imprisonment. But Lock truly
says that "its main interest is one of character, and two portraits emerge
from it." We have here (1) the portrait of the ideal Christian minister, busily
engaged in the work of his Master, confessing His Name, proclaiming His
truth, shepherding His fold, defending his heritage, and battling with the
powers of evil; and (2) the "portrait of the Christian minister, with his work
done, facing death. He acquiesces gladly in the present, but his eyes are
turned mainly to the past or to the future." (Lock in Hastings D. B. Art. II
Timothy) He is thankful for the work he was permitted to do, and serenely
awaits the day of his crowning.

22

The Epistle to Titus

CONTENTS

The contents of this Epistle may be divided into three parts:

I. Instruction regarding the Appointment of Ministers, 1:1–16. After the opening salutation, 1–4, the apostle reminds Titus of his past instruction to appoint presbyters, 5. He emphasizes the importance of high moral character in an overseer, in order that such an office-bearer may maintain the sound doctrine and may refute the opponents that mislead others and, claiming to know God, deny Him with their words, 6–16.

II. Directions as to the Teaching of Titus, 2:1–3:11. Paul would have Titus urge all the different classes that were found in the Cretan church, viz. the elder men and women, the younger women and men, and the slaves, to regulate their life in harmony with the teachings of the Gospel, since they were all trained by the saving grace of God to rise above sin and to lead godly lives, 2:1–14. As regards their relation to the outer world, Titus should teach believers to subject themselves to the authorities, and to be gentle towards all men, remembering that God had delivered them from the old heathen vices, in order that they should set others an example of noble and useful lives, 3:1–8. He himself must avoid foolish questionings and reject the heretics, who refused to listen to his admonition, 9–11.

III. Personal Details, 3:12–15. Instructing Titus to join him at Nicopolis after Artemus or Tychicus has come to Crete, bringing with him Zenos and Apollos, the writer ends his letter with a final salutation.

CHARACTERISTICS

1. Like the other Pastoral Epistles this letter is also of a personal nature. It was not directed to any individual church or to a group of churches, but to a single person, one of Paul's spiritual sons and co-laborers in the work of the Lord. At the same time it is not as personal as II Timothy, but has distinctly a semi-private character. It is perfectly evident from the Epistle

itself (cf. 2:15) that its teaching was also intended for the church in Crete to which Titus was ministering.

2. This letter is in every way very much like I Timothy, which is due to the fact that the two were written about the same time and were called forth by very similar situations. It is shorter than the earlier Epistle, but covers almost the same ground. We do not find in it any advance on the doctrinal teachings of the other letters of Paul; in fact it contains very little doctrinal teaching, aside from the comprehensive statements of the doctrine of grace in 2:11–14 and 3:4–8. The former of these passages is a locus classicus. The main interest of the Epistle is ecclesiastical and ethical, the government of the church and the moral life of its members receiving due consideration.

THE PERSON TO WHOM THE EPISTLE WAS WRITTEN

Paul addressed the letter to "Titus mine own son after the common faith," 1:4. We do not meet with Titus in the Acts of the Apostles, which is all the more remarkable, since he was one of the most trusted companions of Paul. For this reason some surmised that he is to be identified with some one of the other co-laborers of Paul, as f. i. Timothy, Silas or Justus, Acts 18:7. But neither of these satisfy the conditions.

He is first mentioned in Gal. 2:1, 3, where we learn that he was a Greek, who was not compelled to submit to circumcision, lest Paul should give his enemies a handle against himself. From Titus 1:4 we infer that he was one of the apostle's converts, and Gal. 2:3 informs us that he accompanied Paul to the council of Jerusalem. According to some the phrase ὁ σύν ἐμόι in this passage implies that he was also with Paul, when he wrote the Epistle to the Galatians, but the inference is rather unwarranted. He probably bore I Corinthians to its destination, 2 Cor. 2:13, and after his return to Paul, was sent to Corinth again to complete the collection for the saints in Judæa, 2 Cor. 8:16 ff. Most likely he was also the bearer of II Corinthians. When next we hear of him, he is on the island of Crete in charge of the church (es) that had been founded there. Titus 1:4, 5, and is requested to join Paul at Nicopolis, 3:12. Evidently he was with the apostle in the early part of his second imprisonment, but soon left him for Dalmatia, either at the behest, or against the desire of Paul. The traditions regarding his later life are of doubtful value.

If we compare 1 Tim. 4:12 with Titus 2:15, we get the impression that Titus was older than his co-laborer at Ephesus. The timidity of the latter did not characterize the former. While Timothy went to Corinth, so it seems, with some hesitation, 1 Cor. 16:10, Titus did not flinch from the delicate task of completing the collection for the saints in Judæa, but undertook it of his own accord, 2 Cor. 8:16, 17. He was full of enthusiasm for the Corinthians, was free from wrong motives in his work among them, and followed in the footsteps of the apostle, 2 Cor. 12:18.

COMPOSITION

1. Occasion and Purpose. The occasion for writing this Epistle is found in the desire of Paul that Titus should come to him in the near future, and in the condition of the Cretan church (es), whose origin is lost in obscurity. Probably the island was evangelized soon after the first Pentecost by those Cretans that were converted at Jerusalem, Acts 2:11. During the last part of his life Paul visited the island and made provision for the external organization of the church (es) there. When he left, he entrusted this important task to his spiritual son, Titus, 1:5. The church (es) consisted of both Jews and Gentiles, 1:10, of different ages and of various classes, 2:1–10. The Cretans did not have a very good reputation, 1:12, and some of them did not belie their reputed character, even after they had turned to Christ. Apparently the errors that had crept into the church (es) there were very similar to those with which Timothy had to contend at Ephesus, though probably the Judæistic element was still more prominent in them, 1:10, 11, 14; 3:9.

The object of Paul in writing this letter is to summon Titus to come to him, as soon as another has taken his place; to give him directions regarding the ordination of presbyters in the different cities; to warn him against the heretics on the island; and guide him in his teaching and in his dealing with those that would not accept his word.

2. Time and Place. Respecting the time when this Epistle was written there is no unanimity. Those who believe in the genuineness of the letter, and at the same time postulate but one Roman imprisonment, seek a place for it in the life of Paul, as we know it from the Acts. According to some it was written during the apostle's first stay at Corinth, from where, in that case, he must have made a trip to Crete; others think it was composed at Ephesus, after Paul left Corinth and had on the way visited Crete. But the word "continued" in Acts 18:11 seems to preclude a trip from Corinth to Crete. Moreover both of these theories leave Paul's acquaintance with Apollos, presupposed in this letter, unexplained, 3:13. Still others would

date the visit to Crete and the composition of this letter somewhere between the years 54–57, when the apostle resided at Ephesus, but this hypothesis is also burdened with insuperable objections. Cf. above p. 249. The Epistle must have been composed in the interval between the first and the second imprisonment of the apostle, and supposing the winter of 3:13 to be the same as that of 2 Tim. 4:21, probably in the early part of the year 67. We have no means to determine, where the letter was written, though something can be said in favor of Ephesus, cf. p. 239 above.

CANONICAL SIGNIFICANCE

The Church from the beginning accepted this Epistle as canonical. There are passages in Clement of Rome, Ignatius, Barnabas, Justin Martyr and Theophilus that suggest literary dependence. Moreover the letter is found in all the MSS. and in the old Latin and Syriac Versions; and is referred to in the Muratorian Fragment. Irenaeus, Clement of Alexandria and Tertullian quote it by name.

The permanent value of the letter is in some respects quite similar to that of I Timothy. It has historical significance in that it informs us of the spread of Christianity on the island of Crete, a piece of information that we could not gather from any other Biblical source. Like I Timothy it emphasizes for all ages to come the necessity of church organization and the special qualifications of the officebearers. It is unique in placing prominently before us the educative value of the grace of God for the life of every man, of male and female, young and old, bond and free.

23

The Epistle to Philemon

CONTENTS

We can distinguish three parts in this brief letter:

I. The Introduction, 1–7. This contains the address, the customary blessing, and a thanksgiving of the apostle for the charity of Philemon, for the increase of which Paul hopes, because it greatly refreshes the saints.

II. The Request, 8–21. Rather than command Philemon the apostle comes to him with a request, viz. that he receive back the converted slave Onesimus and forgive him his wrong-doing. Paul enforces his request by pointing to the conversion of Onesimus, and to his own willingness to repay Philemon what he lost, though he might ask retribution of him; and trusts that Philemon will do more than he asks.

III. Conclusion, 22–25. Trusting that he will be set free, the apostle requests Philemon to prepare for him lodging. With greetings of his fellow-laborers and a final salutation he ends his letter.

CHARACTERISTICS

1. This letter is closely related to the Epistle that was sent to the Colossian church. They were composed at the same time, were sent to the same city and, with a single exception (that of Justus), contain identical greetings. At the same time it is distinguished from Colossians in that it is a private letter. Yet it is not addressed to a single individual, but to a family and to the believers at their house.

2. The letter is further characterized by its great delicacy and tactfulness. It bears strong evidence to Christian courtesy, and has therefore been called "the polite epistle." In it we see Paul, the gentleman, handling a delicate question with consummate skill. Though he might command, he prefers to request that Philemon forgive and receive again his former slave. Tactfully he refers to the spiritual benefit that accrued from what might be called material loss. In a delicate manner he reminds Philemon of the

debt the latter owed him, and expresses his confidence that this brother in Christ would even do more than he requested.

AUTHORSHIP

Marcion included this letter in his Pauline collection, and the Muratorian Fragment also ascribes it to Paul. Tertullian and Origen quote it by name, and Eusebius reckons it among the Pauline letters.

Moreover the Epistle has all the marks of a genuine Pauline production. It is self-attested, contains the usual Pauline blessing, thanksgiving and salutation, reveals the character of the great apostle and clearly exhibits his style.

Yet even this short and admirable Epistle has not enjoyed universal recognition. Baur rejected it because of its close relation to Colossians and Ephesians, which he regarded as spurious. He called it "the embryo of a Christian romance," like that of the Clementine Recognitions, its tendency being to show that what is lost on earth is gained in heaven. He also objects to it that it contains seven words which Paul uses nowhere else. Weizsäcker and Pfleiderer are somewhat inclined to follow Baur. They find proof for the allegorical character of the letter in the name Onesimus = profitable, helpful. The latter thinks that this note may have accompanied the Epistle to the Colossians, to illustrate by a fictitious example the social precepts contained in that letter. Such criticism need not be taken seriously. Hilgenfeld's dictum is that Baur has not succeeded in raising his explanation to the level of probability. And Renan says: "Paul alone can have written this little masterpiece."

THE PERSON TO WHOM THE LETTER IS WRITTEN

The letter is addressed to "Philemon our dearly beloved and fellow-laborer, and to our beloved Apphia, and Archippus, our fellow-soldier, and to the church in thy house," 1, 2. Little is known of this Philemon. He was evidently an inhabitant of Colossæ, Col. 4:9, and apparently belonged to the wealthy class. He had slaves, received a circle of friends in his house, and was able to prepare a lodging for Paul, 22. His munificence was generally known, 5-7, and he made himself useful in Christian service. He was converted by Paul, 19, most likely during the apostle's three years residence at Ephesus. Apphia is generally regarded as the wife of Philemon, while many consider Archippus as their son. We notice from Col. 4:17 that the latter had an office in the church. Probably he was temporarily taking the place of Epaphras. The expression "the church in thy house" undoubtedly refers to the Christians of Colossæ that gathered in the dwelling of Philemon for worship.

COMPOSITION

1. Occasion and Purpose. The occasion for writing this Epistle is clearly indicated in the letter itself. Onesimus, the slave of Philemon absconded and, so it seems, defrauded his master, 18, 19. He fled to Rome, where in some way—it is useless to guess just how—he fell in with Paul, whom he may have known from the time of his Ephesian residence. The apostle was instrumental in converting him and in showing him the evil of his way, 10, and although he would gladly have retained him for the work, sent him back to Colossæ in deference to the claims of Philemon. He did not send him empty-handed, however, but gave him a letter of recommendation, in which he informs Philemon of the change wrought in Onesimus by which the former slave became a brother, bespeaks for him a favorable reception in the family of his master and in the circle that gathered at their house for worship, and even hints at the desirability of emancipating him.

2. Time and place. For the discussion of the time and place of composition cf. what was said respecting the Epistle to the Ephesians.

CANONICAL SIGNIFICANCE

This Epistle is rarely quoted by the early church fathers, which is undoubtedly due to its brevity and to its lack of doctrinal contents. The letter is recognized by Marcion and the Muratorian Fragment, and is contained in the old Latin and Syriac Versions. Tertullian quotes it more than once, but no trace of it is found in Irenaeus and Clement of Alexandria. Eusebius classes it with the Homologoumena and Jerome argues at length against those who refused to accept it as Pauline. The Church never doubted its canonicity.

The permanent value of this little letter is both psychological and ethical. It shows us Paul as he corresponds in a friendly way with a brother in Christ, and thus gives us a new glimpse of his character, the character of a perfect gentleman, unobtrusive, refined, skillful and withal firm,—a character worthy of imitation. Moreover it reveals to us how Paul, in view of the unity of bond and free in Jesus Christ, deals with the perplexing question of slavery. He does not demand the abolishment of the institution, since the time for such a drastic measure had not yet come; but he does clearly hint at emancipation as the natural result of the redemptive work of Christ.

24

The Epistle to the Hebrews

CONTENTS

In this Epistle we may distinguish five parts.

I. The Superiority of Christ as Mediator, 1:1-4:16. The writer begins by saying that the New Testament revelation was mediated by the very Son of God, who is far superior to the angels, 1:1-14; whose revelation one can only neglect to the peril of one's soul, 2:1-4, and in whom and through whom the ideal of man is realized through suffering, 5-18. Then he points out that Christ is greater than Moses, as the builder is greater than the house and the son is superior to the servant, 3:1-6, wherefore it is necessary that we should listen to his voice, since unbelief deprives us of the blessings of salvation, as is clearly seen in the history of Israel, 7-19. They were not brought into the rest by Joshua, so that the promise remains to be fulfilled, and we should labor to enter into that rest, seeking strength in our great High Priest, 4:1-16.

II. Christ the true High Priest, 5:1-7:28. Like every high priest Christ was taken from among men to represent them in worship, and was called by God, 5:1-5; but in distinction from these He was made a Priest after the order of Melchizedek, and thus became the author of eternal salvation for those that obey him, 6-10. Since the readers were not yet able to understand all that might be said regarding the Priesthood of Christ after the order of Melchizedek, the author exhorts them to press on to more perfect knowledge, to beware of apostasy, and to be diligent to inherit, through faith and patience, the promises of the ever faithful God, 5:11-6:20. Returning now to the subject in hand, the writer describes the unique character of Melchizedek, 7:1-10, and contrasts the priesthood of Christ with that of the order of Aaron with respect to fleshly descent (Levi—Judah), 11-14; endurance (temporal—eternal) 15-19; solemnity and weight (without oath—with oath) 20-22; number (many—one) 23-24; and then argues the necessity of such a High Priest for us, 25-28.

III. Pre-eminence of the New Covenant mediated by Jesus Christ, 8:1-10:18. As High Priest Christ is now ministering in heaven, of which the tabernacle on earth was but a shadow, since He is the Mediator, not of the Old, but of the New Covenant, 8:1-13. The ordained services and the sanctuary of the old dispensation were merely figures for the time then present, and pointed to the better services which Christ, the Mediator of the New Covenant would render at the heavenly sanctuary, since He would not enter with the blood of bulls and goats, but with his own blood, thus bringing eternal redemption, 9:1-28. The sacrifices of the old dispensation could not take away sin, and therefore Christ offered himself for our purification and to give us access to the throne of God, 10:1-18.

IV. Application of the Truths presented and Personal Epilogue, 10:19-13:25. The writer exhorts the readers to draw near to God with confidence, and warns them against apostasy, reminding them of its dire consequences and of their former endurance, and assuring them that the just shall live by faith, 10:19-39. He illustrates this point by presenting to their view a long line of heroes that triumphed in faith, 11:1-40. In view of these examples he urges them to endure chastening which is a sign of their sonship and ministers to their sanctification, and warns them against despising the grace of God, 12:1-17. Since they have received far greater privileges than Old Testament saints, they should strive to serve God acceptably with reverence and godly feat, 18-29. Then follow some general exhortations respecting hospitality, marriage, contentment, the following in the footsteps of their teachers, and the necessity of guarding against strange doctrines, 13:1-17; after which the writer closes the letter with a few personal notices and salutations, 18-25.

CHARACTERISTICS

1. The Epistle to the Hebrews has not the letter-like appearance of the confessedly Pauline writings. It does not contain the name of the author, nor that of the addressees. And if it were not for a few stray personal notes, 10:34; 13:18, 25, and for the greetings and salutations found at the end, we might regard this writing as a treatise rather than an Epistle. Deissmann, who emphasizes the non literary character of the admittedly Pauline compositions, and insists that they be looked upon as real letters, considers this writing to be an Epistle as distinguished from a letter, and

thinks it is very important to recognize its literary character. According to him "it is historically the earliest example of Christian artistic literature." Light from the Ancient East p. 64 f.; 236 f.; 243.

2. The relation in which the teaching of this book stands to that of the Old Testament is unique. It does not view the Law as a body of commandments imposed on the obedience of man, but as a system of ritual provided by the mercy of God; and clearly reveals its insufficiency as an institution for the removal of sin, since it could only remove ceremonial defilement and could not purify the heart. In harmony with this divergence from the prevailing Pauline conception of the Law, it does not, like the undoubted letters of Paul, regard the Law as an episode temporarily intervening, on account of sin, between the promise and its fulfilment; but as a typical representation, as a primitive revelation of the blessings to which the promise pointed. In it the image of the New Testament realities is dimly seen; it is the bud that gradually develops into a beautiful flower. The realities that answer to the shadows of the Old Testament are pointed out in detail, and thereby this Epistle is for all ages the inspired commentary on the ritual of the Old Covenant, making the pages of Leviticus luminous with heavenly light. We should bear in mind that the terms type and antitype are employed in a rather unusual sense in this letter; their meaning is in a way reversed. The holy places of the earthly tabernacle are called the ἀντίτυπα of the true and heavenly, 9:24, according to which usage the latter are, of course, the types of the former, cf. 8:5.

3. This letter is peculiar also in the way in which it quotes the Old Testament. While in the writings that bear Paul's name the quotations are partly from the Hebrew and partly from the Septuagint, in this Epistle they are uniformly derived from the Greek. Moreover the formulae of quotation are different from those in the other letters. While these generally refer the passages quoted to their human authors, except in cases where God speaks in the first person in the Old Testament, our Epistle with but few exceptions refers them to the primary author, i. e. to God or to the Holy Spirit, thus offering indubitable proof of the author's belief in the inspiration of the Scriptures.

4. The language of this Epistle is the best literary Greek of the New Testament. We do not find the author struggling, as it were, with a scanty language to express the abundance of the thoughts that are crowding in upon him. There are no broken constructions, no halting sentences, and, although a few parentheses are introduced, they do not disturb the thought,

cf. 11:38; 12:20, 21. The sentences are all evenly balanced and the style flows on with great regularity. The writer seems to have given special attention to the rhetorical rhythm and equilibrium of words and sentences. Westcott says: "The style of the book is characteristically Hellenistic, perhaps we may say, as far as our scanty knowledge goes, Alexandrian." Comm. p. LXI.

AUTHORSHIP

The authorship of the Epistle to the Hebrews constitutes a very diffi-cult question. The external testimony is of a conflicting character. The oldest and most explicit tradition is that of Alexandria, where Clement testified that the Epistle was written by Paul in the Hebrew language and was translated by Luke into Greek. Origen regards the thoughts of the Epistle as Paul's, but the language as that of a disciple of the great apostle, and finally comes to the conclusion that God only knows who wrote this letter. He does not make mention of a Hebrew original. Both Clement and Origen agree, however, in regarding the Greek Epistle as Pauline only in a secondary sense. In Italy and Western Europe generally the letter was not held to be Paul's. This is the more remarkable, since we find the first trace of its existence in the West, in the writings of Clement of Rome. Hippolytus and Irenaeus were acquainted with it, but did not accept it as Paul's; Cajus reckoned only thirteen Pauline Epistles and Eusebius says that even in his time the negative opinion was still held by some Romans. In North Africa, where the Roman tradition is usually followed, the letter was not regarded as the work of Paul. Tertullian ascribes it to Barnabas. In the fourth century the Eastern tradition gradually prevailed over the Western, especially through the influence of Augustine and Jerome, though they felt by no means certain that Paul was the author. During the Middle Ages this mooted question hardly ever came up for discus-sion, but when the light of the Reformation dawned, doubts were again expressed as to the authorship of Paul. Erasmus questioned whether Paul had written the letter; Luther conjectured that Apollos was the writer; Calvin thought that it might be the work of Luke or of Clement; and Beza held that it was written by a disciple of Paul. At present there are compar-atively few that maintain the authorship of Paul.

And if we examine the internal evidence of the Epistle, we find that it points away from Paul. It must be admitted that its teaching is in a gen-eral sense Pauline, but this does not prove that Paul was the author. There are also some expressions in the letter to which parallels are found in the

Epistles of Paul. Compare f. i. 2:14 with 2 Tim. 1:10; 1 Cor. 15:26;—2:8 with 1 Cor. 15:27. But this similarity may find its explanation in the author's acquaintance with the Pauline writings. The statement in 10:34 cannot be urged in favor of Paul, especially not, if we adopt the reading τοῖς δεσμίοις συνεπαθήσατε, in which almost all the critical editors concur, and which is certainly favored by the context. The expression in 13:19 does not prove that the writer was a prisoner, when he wrote these words, much less that he was Paul. Neither does the notice respecting Timothy in 13:23 necessarily point to the apostle, for some of the older companions of Paul might have made that same statement. Moreover we know of no time in the life of Paul when Timothy was a prisoner. If there were other positive evidence for the Pauline authorship, some of these supposed criteria might serve as corroborative proofs, but such evidence is not forthcoming. The main features of the Epistle are such as to discredit the authorship of Paul: (1) The letter, in distinction from the Pauline Epistles, is entirely anonymous. It contains neither the name of the author nor that of the addressees. Moreover the customary blessing and thanksgiving are altogether wanting. (2) In 2:3 the writer clearly distinguishes himself and his hearers from those who heard the Lord, i. e. from his immediate disciples and apostle's. Would Paul say that he had heard the word of the Gospel only from the immediate followers of the Lord, and not of the Lord himself? The assumption does not seem reasonable in view of Gal. 1:12. (3) Though the teaching of the Epistle is in full harmony with that of Paul, yet it does not reveal the usual trend of Paul's reasoning. As Bruce points out (Hastings D. B. Art. Hebrews, Epistle to), there is an entire absence of the Pauline antitheses law and grace, faith and works, flesh and spirit; while there are found instead the antitheses of shadow and reality, type and antitype. (4) While Paul is wont to take some of his quotations from the Hebrew and often quotes from memory, the writer of this Epistle always derives his quotations from the Septaugint, and with such exactness that he seems to have had the manuscript before him. He does not like Paul refer his quotations to the human author, but to the auctor primarius. And instead of the Pauline formulæ of quotation, γέγραπται or ἡ γραφή λέγει, he often employs μαρτυρεῖ or φησί. (5) There is also a great difference in the names ascribed to the Mediator. In the writings of Paul we find the names, Christ, the Lord, the Lord Jesus Christ, Jesus Christ our Lord, our Lord Jesus Christ, and very seldom the simple Jesus. In our Epistle, on the other hand, Jesus is the regular name for the Saviour; Jesus Christ is used three times, the Lord, twice, but the full Pauline name, our Lord Jesus Christ is wanting altogether. (6) The strongest proof against the Pauline authorship is generally considered to be the argument from style. Says Dr. Salmon: "There is here none of the ruggedness of St. Paul, who never seems to be solicitous about forms of expression, and whose thoughts come pouring out so fast as to jostle one another in the struggle for utterance. This is a calm composition, exhibiting sonorous words and well balanced sentences.—I have already shown that I do not ascribe to Paul any rigid uniformity of utterance, and that I am not tempted to deny a letter to be his merely because it contains a number of words and phrases which are not found in his other compositions; but in this case I find myself unable to assert the Pauline authorship in the face of so much unlikeness, in the structure of sentences, in the general tone of the Epistle, in the general way of presenting doctrines, and in other points that I will not delay to enumerate." Introd. p. 464 f.

In view of all the foregoing it is all but certain that Paul did not write the Epistle to the Hebrews. But now the question naturally arises: Who did? Several answers have given, as Barnabas (Tertullian), Luke or Clement (Calvin), Apollos (Luther), Silas (Böhme, Godet), (Aquila and) Priscilla (Harnack), of which only two are at present seriously considered, viz. Barnabas and Apollos, though the suggestion of Harnack has found favor with some. Renan, Hausrath, Weiss, Salmon and Barth accept the authorship of Barnabas, relying especially on the facts: (1) that Tertullian points to him as the author, thereby transmitting not only his own private opinion, but the North African tradition; (2) that Barnabas was an apostolic man and as a Levite would be well acquainted with the Jewish ritual; and (3) that, as an inhabitant of the island Cyprus, he would in all probability have been subject to the influence of Alexandrian culture. On the other hand, Lünemann, Farrar, Alford and Zahn hold that Apollos best answers the requirements, since (1) he was a man of fine Greek culture; (2) was well acquainted with the writings of Paul; and (3) as a native of Alexandria was deeply embued with the thoughts of the Alexandrian school. But it has been objected to Barnabas that he could not reckon himself to the second generation of Christians, 2:3; and that he certainly knew Hebrew, with which, so it seems, the author of this Epistle was not acquainted;—and to Apollos, that there is no tradition whatever connecting his name with the Epistle; and that the historical allusions in 13:18-24 have no point of contact in the life of Apollos as we know it from the Acts of the Apostles. If we had to choose between the two, Barnabas would be our choice, but we prefer with Moll, Westcott, Dods, Baljon and Bruce (Hastings D. B.) to confess our ignorance on this point and to abide by the dictum of Origen. The general thought of the Epistle is Pauline, but God only knows who wrote it.

DESTINATION

Under this head we must consider two questions: 1. Was the letter written for Jewish or for Gentile Christians? 2. Where were the first readers located?

1. Until a comparatively recent date the general opinion was that this Epistle was composed for Jewish Christians. Of late, however, some scholars, as Schürer, Weizsäcker, Von Soden, Jülicher and McGiffert reached the opposite conclusion. They argue that the fundamentals enumerated in 6:1, 2 are such as were suitable only to Gentile catechumens; that the expression "the living God" in 9:14 implies a contrast between the true God and pagan idols; and that the exhortations at the end of the Epistle were more appropriate to Gentile than to Jewish Christians. From these passages it has been argued with great ingenuity that the original readers were Christians of the Gentiles; but they are also susceptible of a plausible interpretation on the opposite view. Cf. the Commentaries and also Dods, Exp. Gk. Test. IV p. 231. It seems preferable to hold that the first readers were of Jewish extraction. In support of this theory we cannot rely on the title πρός Ἑβραίος, because the presumption is that this, though it can be traced to the second century, is not original. Yet it does express the early conviction of the Church that the letter was destined first of all for Jewish Christians. The general features of the letter point in the same direction. The Epistle presupposes that its readers are in danger of a relapse into Judæism; and its symbolism, based entirely on the tabernacle and its services, is peculiarly adapted to converted Jews. The whole Epistle has a Jewish physiognomy. With Bruce we say: "If the readers were indeed Gentiles, they were Gentiles so completely disguised in Jewish dress and wearing a mask with so pronounced Jewish features, that the true nationality has been hidden for nineteen centuries. Hastings D. B.

2. But where must we look for the first readers? Some scholars, regarding this writing as a treatise, are of the opinion that it was not intended for any definite locality, but for Christians in general, (Lipsius, Reuss); this opinion cannot pass muster, however, in view of the many passages that have no meaning unless they are addressed to a definite circle of Christians, f. i. 5:11, 12; 6:9, 10; 10:32; 12:4. At the same time it is impossible to determine

with certainty the exact locality in which the readers were found. The four places that received the most prominent consideration in this connection are Alexandria, Antioch (in Syria), Rome and Jerusalem, of which, it would appear, the choice really lies between the last two. The position that the letter was sent to the Jewish Christians of Jerusalem or of entire Judæa, is defended by Moll, Lünemann, Salmon, Weiss and Westcott, and is supported by the following considerations: (1) The name Ἑβραῖος, embodying an early tradition, certainly fits them better than it does Christians of any other community. (2) They were the most likely to develop great love for the Jewish ritual and to be exposed to danger from these quarters. (3) Their church (es) was (were) well nigh purely Jewish, which best accords with the total absence of any reference to Gentile Christians in the Epistle. (4) They would certainly understand the symbolism of the letter far better than the Christians of the diaspora. (5) A passage like 13:12, 13 has a peculiar appropriateness, if it was written to them. The objections are urged against this hypothesis, however, that the passages 3:2 and 5:12 are hardly applicable to the Christians of Jerusalem or Judæa; that these, rather than exercise liberality, 6:10, were continually the objects of charity; that the letter was written in Greek and not in Hebrew; and that, as far as we know, Timothy stood in no particular relation to the Jerusalem church. Many present day scholars, such as Alford, Zahn, Baljon, Dods, Holtzmann, Jülicher and Von Soden fixed on Rome as the destination of this letter. In favor of this they urge: (1) The greeting of 13:24 is evidently one of such as had gone forth from Italy, to their old friends at home. (2) The first traces of the use of this Epistle are found in the writings of Clement and in the Shepherd of Hermas, both issuing from Rome. (3) The term ἡγούμενοι, 13:7, 17, 24 was not in vogue in the Pauline churches, but was used at Rome, since Clement speaks of προηγούμενοι. (4) The persecutions mentioned in 10:32–34 probably refer to those of Nero and his predecessors. But this theory is burdened with the objections; that it was exactly at Rome that the canonicity of the letter was questioned for centuries; that the congregation at Rome was primarily Gentile-Christian (which Zahn denies, however); and that the words of 12:4 were hardly applicable to the Christians at Rome after the Neronian persecution. To our mind the first theory deserves the preference, unless we are prepared to admit that the Epistle was written to Gentile Christians.

COMPOSITION

1. Occasion and Purpose. This letter was occasioned by the danger of apostasy that threatened the readers. For a time they had professed Christianity, 5:12, and for the sake of it had endured persecution, and had even joyfully borne the spoiling of their goods, 10:32-34. But they were disappointed, so it seems, in two respects. In the first place in their expectation of the speedy return of Christ to trimph over his enemies and to transform the affliction of his followers into everlasting bliss. Christ remained hidden from their view and their sufferings continued, yea even increased in severity. In the encircling gloom they had no visible support for their faith. And in the second place they were disappointed in the attitude their own people took to the new religion. For a time they had combined their Christian services with the worship of their fathers, but it became ever increasingly evident that the Jews as a people would not accept Christ. Their brethren according to the flesh persisted in their opposition and waxed ever more intolerant of the followers of Jesus. The time was fast approaching, when these would have to break with the ministrations of the temple and look elsewhere for the support of their faith. Hence they had become feeble, 12:12, had ceased to make progress, 5:12, were inclined to unbelief, 3:12, and in danger of falling away, 6:4-6. Returning to Jewry, they might escape the persecution to which they were subjected, and enjoy their former privileges.

The writer desires to warn them against the danger to which they were exposed, and to exhort them to remain loyal to their Christian standard. In order to do this he points out by way of contrast the true nature and intrinsic worth of the Christian religion. The Old Testament service of God contained but the shadows of the New Testament realities. Christ is higher than the angels, ch. 1, is greater than Moses, ch. 3, is our only true High Priest, who through suffering opened up the way to heaven and gives us free unrestricted access to God, chs. 5-10. He was perfected through sufferings, that He might sympathize with his followers in their trials and afflictions, 2:10, 17, 18; 4:15, and might lead them through suffering to glory. If He is now invisible to the eye, it is only because He has entered the sanctuary, where He continually ministers to the spiritual needs of his followers, and insures them free access to the throne of God, 4:16; 6:18-20; 9:24; 10:18-22. He may seem distant, yet He is near, and they who believe can enjoy his presence and strength through faith. That is their true support in time of need, ch. 11, 12:1, 2. And though He tarry for a while, He will surely come in due time to lead his children to glory. They should willingly go forth without the camp, bearing his reproach, since they enjoy far greater privileges than the Old Testament saints and will at last enter their eternal inheritance.

2. Time and Place. It is not easy to determine the date of this letter, since it contains no definite notes of time. The majority of scholars agree in placing it before the destruction of Jerusalem. Thus Moll, Kurtz, Hilgenfeld, Reuss, Davidson, Weiss, Godet, Westcott, Salmon, Bruce, Barth, Dods. Others, however, as Baur, Kluge, Zahn, Meijboom, Volkmar and Hausrath bring it down to a later date. To our mind the evidence favors a date before the destruction of the temple, for (1) Though it is true that the author does not speak of the temple but of the tabernacle, the danger to which the Hebrew Christians were exposed seems to imply that the temple services were still carried on. (2) If the Jewish ritual had already ceased, it is strange that the writer does not refer to this, when he describes the transitory character of the old dispensation. And (3) the present tense used by the writer in the description of the Jewish services, 8:4 f.; 9:6, 9 (cf. Gk.); 10:1 ff.; 13:10 creates the presumption that the ministry of the temple was still continued. It is true that parallels to such presents use of past events can be pointed out in Clement of Rome. But as a rule the use of the present implies the existence of the subject spoken of, at the time of the speaker; and the question of 10:2, "Else would they not have ceased to be offered?" is certainly difficult to interpret on any other view. It is not possible to say, how long before the destruction of Jerusalem the Epistle was written, but from the solemn tone of the writer, and from the fact that, according to him, the readers saw the day of the Lord approaching, 10:25, we infer that it was but shortly before that great catastrophe. Cf. also 12:26, 27. We shall not go far wrong, if we date the Epistle about the year 69.

CANONICAL SIGNIFICANCE

The letter was not regarded as canonical in the Western church until the fourth century; in the Eastern church, however, the recognition of its apostolicity and canonicity went hand in hand. Clement of Alexandria often quotes the letter as canonical, and Origen does sometimes, though he felt uncertain as to its Pauline authorship. The Epistle is found in the Peshito, but it is uncertain, whether it also had a place in the earliest Syriac translation. From the fourth century the Western church also admitted its canonical authority. The intrinsic value of the letter naturally commended it as authoritative and as a part of the Word of God. Augustine and Jerome regarded it as canonical, though they still had scruples about the authorship of Paul; and it was included in the Lists authorized by the Councils of Hippo in 393 and of Carthage in 397 and 419. From that time the Church did not again question the canonical authority of the Epistle until the time of the Reformation, when some Lutheran theologians had serious doubts.

The permanent value of this Epistle lies especially in two facts, which may be said to imply a third. In the first place it brings out, as no other New Testament book does, the essential unity of both the Old and the New Testament religions. They are both from God; they both center in Christ; they both pertain to the same spiritual verities; and they both aim at bringing man to God. In the second place the Epistle emphasizes the difference between the two dispensations, the one containing the shadows, the other the corresponding realities; the services of the one being earthly and therefore carnal and temporal, those of the other being heavenly and therefore spiritual and abiding; the ministry of the one effecting only ceremonial purity and union with God, that of the other issuing in the purification of the soul and in spiritual communion with God in heaven. And because the letter so presents the relation of the Old Covenant to the New, it is an inspired commentary on the entire Mosaic ritual.

25

The General Epistle of James

CONTENTS

There are no clearly defined parts in this Epistle; hence no classification of its contents is attempted. After the opening salutation the writer points out the significance of temptation in the life of his readers, exhorts them to ask in faith for the wisdom needed in bearing them and warns them not to refer their inward temptations to God, 1:1-18. Then he admonishes them to receive the Word in all humility and to carry it out in action, 19-27. He warns them against that respect of persons that reveals itself in favoring the rich at the expense of the poor, reminding them of the fact that he who violates the law in one point breaks the whole law; 2:1-13; and asserts that it is foolish to trust to a faith without works, since this is dead, 14-26. A warning against rash teaching and reproving follows, based on the difficulty of controlling the tongue, which is yet of the very greatest importance, 3:1-12. Wisdom from above is commended to the readers, since the wisdom of this world is full of bitter envy and works confusion and evil, while heavenly wisdom is plenteous in mercy and yields good fruits, 13-18. The author then reprimands the readers for their quarrelsomeness, which results from a selfishness and lust that infects even one's prayers and renders them futile; and exhorts them to humble themselves before God, 4:1-12. He condemns those who, in the pride of possession, forget their dependence on God, and denounces the rich that oppress and rob the poor, 4:13-5:6; after which he urges the brethren to be patient, knowing the Lord is at hand, 7-11. Finally he warns his readers against false swearing, gives special advice to the sick, exhorts them all to pray for one another, reminding them of the efficacy of prayer, and of the blessedness of turning a sinner from his sinful way, 12-20.

CHARACTERISTICS

1. From a literary point of view the Epistle of James is quite different from those of Paul. The latter are real letters, which cannot be said of this Epistle. There is no benediction at the beginning, nor any salutation or greeting at the end. Moreover it contains very little that points to definite historical circumstances such as are known to us from other sources. Zahn calls this Epistle, "eine ... in schriftliche Form gefasste Ansprache." Einl. I p. 73. Barth speaks of it as, "eine Sammlung von Ansprachen des Jakobus an die Gemeinde zu Jerusalem," which, he thinks were taken down by a hearer and sent to the Jewish Christians of the diaspora. Einl. p. 140. And Deissmann says: "The Epistle of James is from the beginning a little work of literature, a pamphlet addressed to the whole of Christendom, a veritable Epistle (as distinguished from a letter). The whole of the contents agrees therewith. There is none of the unique detail peculiar to the situation, such as we have in the letters of Paul, but simply general questions, most of them still conceivable under the present conditions of church life." Light from the Ancient East p. 235.

2. The contents of the Epistle are not doctrinal but ethical. The writer does not discuss any of the great truths of redemption, but gives moral precepts for the life of his readers. There is no Christological teaching whatever, the name of Christ being mentioned but twice, viz. 1:1; 2:1. Beischlag correctly remarks that it is "so wesentlich noch Lehre Christi und so wenig noch Lehre von Christo." The letter may be called, the Epistle of the Royal Law, 2:8. The emphasis does not rest on faith, but on the works of the law, which the writer views, not in its ceremonial aspect, but in its deep moral significance and as an organic whole, so that transgressing a single precept is equivalent to a violation of the whole law. The essential element of life according to the law is a love that reveals itself in grateful obedience to God and in self-denying devotion to one's neighbor.

3. Some scholars, as f. i. Spitta, claim that this Epistle is really not a Christian but a Jewish writing; but the contents clearly prove the contrary. Yet it must be admitted that the Epistle has a somewhat Jewish complexion. While the writer never once points to the examplary life of Christ, he does refer to the examples of Abraham, Rahab, Job and Elijah. In several passages he reveals his dependence on the Jewish Chokmah literature, on the Sermon on the Mount, and on the words of Jesus generally; compare 1:2 with Matt. 5:12;—1:4 with Matt. 5:48;—1:5 with Matt. 7:7;—1:6 with Mark 11:23;—1:22 with Matt. 7:24;—2:8 with Mark 12:31;—2:13 with Matt.

5:7; 18:33;—4:10 with Matt. 23:12; etc. Moreover the author does not borrow his figurative language from the social and civil institutions of the Greek and Roman world, as Paul often does, but derives it, like the Lord himself had done, from the native soil of Palestine, when he speaks of the sea, 1:6; 3:4; of the former and the latter rain, 5:7; of the vine and the fig-tree, 3:12; of the scorching wind, 1:11; and of salt and bitter springs, 3:11, 12.

4. The Epistle is written in exceptionally good, though Hellenistic Greek. The vocabulary of the author is rich and varied, and perfectly adequate to the expression of his lofty sentiments. His sentences are not characterized by great variation; yet they have none of the utter simplicity, bordering on monotony, that marks the writings of John. The separate thoughts are very clearly expressed, but in certain instances there is some difficulty in tracing their logical sequence. We find some examples of Hebrew parallelism especially in the fourth chapter; downright Hebraisms, however are very few, cf. the adjectival genitive in 1:25, and the instrumental ev in 3:9.

AUTHORSHIP

According to external testimony James, the brother of the Lord, is the author of this Epistle. Origen is the first one to quote it by name, and it is only in Rufinus Latin translation of his works that the author is described as, "James, the brother of the Lord." Eusebius mentions James, the brother of Christ, as the reputed author, remarking, however, that the letter was considered spurious. Jerome, acknowledging its authenticity, says: "James, called the Lord's brother, surnamed the Just, wrote but one Epistle, which is among the seven catholic ones.

The author simply names himself, "James a servant of God and of the Lord Jesus Christ," 1:1, thus leaving the question of his identity still a matter of conjecture, since there were other persons of that name in the apostolic Church. It is generally admitted, however, that there is but one James that meets the requirements, viz. the brother of the Lord, for: (1) The writer was evidently a man of great authority and recognized as such not only by the Jews in Palestine but also by those of the diaspora. There is only one James of whom this can be said. While James, the brother of John, and James the son of Alphæus soon disappear from view in the Acts of the Apostles, this James stands out prominently as the head of the Jerusalem church. During the Lord's public ministry he did not yet believe in Christ, John 7:5. Probably his conversion was connected with the special appearance of the Lord to him after the resurrection, 1 Cor. 15:7. In the Acts we soon meet him as a man of authority. When Peter had escaped out of prison, after James the brother of John had been killed, he says to the brethren: "Go, show these things to James," Acts 12:17. Paul says that he, on his return from Arabia, went to Jerusalem and saw only Peter and James, the Lord's brother, Gal. 1:18, 19. On the following visit James, Cephas and John, who seemed to be pillars, gave Paul and Barnabas the right hand of fellowship, Gal. 2:9. Still later certain emissaries came from James to Antioch and apparently had considerable influence, Gal. 2:12. The leading part in the council of Jerusalem is taken by this James, Acts 15:13 ff. And when, at the end of his third missionary journey, Paul comes to Jerusalem, he first greeted the brethren informally, and on the following day "went unto James, and all the elders were present," Acts 21:18. (2) The authorship of this James is also favored by a comparison of the letter, Acts 15:23-29, very likely written under the inspiring influence of James, together with his speech at the council of Jerusalem, and certain parts of our Epistle, which reveals striking similarities. The salutation χαίρειν, Acts 15:23, Jas. 1:1 occurs elsewhere in the New Testament only in Acts 23:26. The words τὸ καλὸν ὄνομα τὸ ἐπικληθὲν ἐφ' ὑμᾶς, 2:7, can only be paralleled in the New Testament in Acts 15:17. Both the speech of James and the Epistle are characterized by pointed allusions to the Old Testament. The affectionate term ἀδελφός, of frequent occurrence in the Epistle (cf. 1:2, 9, 16, 19; 2:5, 15; 3:1; 4:11; 5:7, 9, 10, 12, 19), is also found in Acts 15:13, 23; compare especially Jas. 2:5 and Acts 15:13. Besides these there are other verbal coincidences, as ἐπισκέπτεσθαι, Jas. 1:27; Acts 15:14; τηρεῖν and διατηρεῖν, Jas. 1:27, Acts 15:29; ἐπιστρέφειν, Jas. 5:19, 20; Acts 15:19; ἀγαπητός, Jas. 1:16, 19; 2:5; Acts 15:25. (3) The words of the address are perfectly applicable to this particular James. He does not claim that he is an apostle, as do Paul and Peter in their Epistles. It might be objected, however, that if he was the brother of the Lord, he would have laid stress on that relation to enhance his authority. But does it not seem far more likely, in view of the fact that Christ definitely pointed out the comparative insignificance of this earthly relationship, Matt. 12:46-50, that James would be careful not to make it the basis of any special claim, and therefore simply speaks of himself as a servant of God and of the Lord Jesus Christ?

Now the question comes up, whether this James cannot be identified with James, the son of Alphæus, one of the Lord's apostle's, Mt. 10:3; Mk. 3:18; Lk. 6:15; Acts 1:13. This identification would imply that the so-called brethren of the Lord were in reality his cousins, a theory that was broached by Jerome about A. D. 383, and which, together with the view of Epiphanius (that these brethren were sons of Joseph by a former marriage) was urged especially in the interest of the perpetual virginity. But this theory is not borne out by the data of Scripture, for: (1) The brethren of the Lord are distinguished from his disciples in John 2:12, and from the twelve after their calling in Mt. 12:46 ff.; Mk. 3:31 ff.; Lk. 8:19 ff.; and John 7:3. It is stated that they did not belong to the circle of his disciples, indirectly in Mt. 13:55; Mk. 6:3, and directly in John 7:5. (2) Although it is true that cousins are sometimes called brethren in Scripture, cf. Gen. 14:16; 29:12, 15, we need not assume that this is the case also in the instance before us. Moreover it is doubtful whether James the son of Alphæus was a cousin of Jesus. According to some this relationship is clearly implied in John 19:25; but it is by no means certain that in that passage, "Mary the wife of Clopas", stands in apposition with, "his mother's sister." If we do accept that interpretation, we must be ready to believe that there were two sisters bearing the same name. It is more plausible to think that John speaks of four rather than of three women, especially in view of the fact that the gospels speak of at least five in connection with Jesus' death and resurrection, cf. Mt. 27:56; Mk. 16:1; Lk. 24:10. But even if we suppose that he speaks of but three, how are we going to prove the identity of Alphæus and Clopas? And in case we could demonstrate this, how must we account for the fact that only two sons are named of Mary, the wife of Clopas, viz. James and Joses, Mt. 27:56; Mk. 15:40; Lk. 24:10, comp. John 19:25, while there are four brethren of the Lord, Mt. 13:55; Mk. 6:3, viz. James, Joses, Judas and Simon? It has been argued that Judas is indicated as a brother of James the less in Lk. 6:16; Acts 1:13, where we read of a Ἰούδας Ἰακώβου. But it is contrary to analogy to supply the word brother in such cases. (3) We repeatedly find the brethren of the Lord in the company of Mary, the mother of Jesus, just as we would expect to find children with their mother. Moreover in passages like Mt. 12:46; Mk. 3:31, 32; and Lk. 8:19 it is an exegetical mistake to take the word mother in its literal sense, and then to put a different interpretation on the word brother. We conclude, therefore, that James, the brother of the Lord and the author of this Epistle, was not an apostle. There are two passages that seem to point in a different direction, viz. Gal. 1:19 and 1 Cor. 15:7; but in the former passage ἐι μὴ may be adversative rather than exceptive, as in Lk. 4:26, 27, cf. Thayer in loco; and the name apostle was not limited to the twelve. The considerations of Lange in favor of identifying the author with James, the son of Alphæus, are rather subjective.

James seems to have been a man of good common sense, with a well balanced judgment, who piloted the little vessel of the Jerusalem church through the Judæistic breakers with a skillful hand, gradually weaning her from ceremonial observances without giving offense and recognizing the greater freedom of the Gentile churches. He was highly respected by the whole Church for his great piety and whole-hearted devotion to the saints. The account of Hegesippus with respect to his paramount holiness and ascetic habits is in all probability greatly overdrawn. Cf. Eusebius II 23.

The authorship of James has been called in question by many scholars during the last century, such as DeWette, Schleiermacher, Baur, Hilgenfeld, Holtzmann, Harnack, Spitta, Baljon e. a. The main reasons for regarding the Epistle as spurious, are the following: (1) The condition of the church reflected in it reminds one of the church at Rome in the time of Hermas, when the glowing love of the first time had lost its fervency. (2) The Greek in which the Epistle is written is far better than one could reasonably expect of James, who always resided in Palestine. (3) The writer does not mention the law of Moses, nor refer to any of its precepts, but simply urges the readers to keep the perfect law that requires love, charity, peacefulness, etc., just as a second century writer would do; while James believed in the permanent validity of the Mosaic law, at least for the Jews. (4) The Epistle bears traces of dependence on some of the Epistles of Paul, especially Romans and Galatians, on the Epistle to the Hebrews and on I Peter; and clearly contradicts the Pauline doctrine of justification by faith.

But these arguments need not shake our conviction as to the authorship of James. The condition implied in this letter may very well and, at least in part, is known to have existed about the middle of the first century. Jos. Ant. XX 8.8; 9.2 Cf. especially Salmon, Introd, p. 501 f. With respect to the second argument Mayor remarks that, accepting the view that Jesus and his brethren usually spoke Aramaeic, "we are not bound to suppose that, with towns like Sepphoris and Tiberius in their immediate vicinity, with Ptolomais, Scythopolis and Gadara at no great distance, they remained ignorant of Greek." Hastings D. B. Art. James, the General Epistle of. The idea that James was a fanatic Judæist and therefore could not but insist on keeping the Mosaic law, is not borne out by Scripture. He was a Jewish Christian and reveals himself as such f. i. in Acts 15:14–29; 21:20–25 and in his Epistle, cf. 2:5 ff.; 3:2; 4:7, 14. His insistence on the spirit of the law, not at all Judæistic, is in perfect harmony with the teaching of the Lord. The literary dependence to which reference has been made may, in so far as any really exists, just as well be reversed, and the contradiction between James and Paul is only apparent. Cf. the larger Introductions and the Commentaries.

DESTINATION

The Epistle is addressed to "the twelve tribes which are in the dispersion," 1:1. Who are indicated by these words? The adverbial phrase, "in the dispersion" excludes the idea that the writer refers to all the Jewish Christians, including even those in Palestine (Hofmann, Thiersch); and the contents of the letter forbid us to think that he addresses Jews and Jewish Christians jointly (Thiele, Guericke, Weiss). There are, however, two interpretations that are admissible. The expression may designate the Jewish Christians that lived outside of Palestine (the great majority of scholars); but it may also be a description of all the believers in Jesus Christ that were scattered among the Gentiles, after the analogy of 1 Pet. 1:1 and Gal. 6:16 (Koster, Hilgenfeld, Hengstenberg, Von Soden). Zahn is rather uncertain in his interpretation. He finds that the twelve tribes mentioned here form an antithesis to the twelve tribes that were in Palestine, and refer either to Christianity as a whole, or to the totality of Jewish Christians; and reminds us of the fact that there was a time, when the two were identical. Einl. I p. 55. We prefer to think of the Jewish Christians of the diaspora in Syria and neighboring lands, which were probably called "the twelve tribes" as representing the true Israel, because (1) the Epistle does not contain a single reference to Gentile Christians; (2) James was pre-eminently the leader of the Jewish Church; (3) the entire complexion of the Epistle points to Jewish readers.

The Epistle being of an encyclical character, naturally does not have reference to the situation of any particular local church, but to generally prevailing conditions at that time. The Jewish Christians to whom the Epistle is addressed were subject to persecutions and temptations, and the poor were oppressed by the rich that, possibly, did not belong to their circle. They did not bear these temptations with the necessary patience, but were swayed by doubt. They even looked with envy at the glitter of the world and favored the rich at the expense of the poor. In daily life they did not follow the guidance of their Christian principles, so that their faith was barren. There may have been dead works, but the fruits of righteousness were not apparent.

COMPOSITION

1. Occasion and Purpose. The occasion for writing this Epistle is found in the condition of the readers which we just described. James, the head of the Jerusalem church, would naturally be informed of this, probably in part by his own emissaries to the various churches of the diaspora, Acts 15:22; 2 Cor. 3:1; Gal. 2:12, and in part by those Jewish Christians that came from different lands to join in the great festivals at Jerusalem.

The object of the Epistle was ethical rather than didactic; it was to comfort, to reprove and to exhort. Since the readers were persecuted to the trial of their faith, and were tempted in various ways, the writer comes to them with words of consolation. Feeling that they did not bear their trials with patience, but were inclined to ascribe to God the temptations that endangered them as a result of their own lust and worldliness, he reproves them for the error of their way. And with a view to the blots on their Christian life, to their worldliness, their respect of persons, their vainglory and their envy and strife, he exhorts them to obey the royal law, that they may be perfect men.

2. Time and Place. The place of composition was undoubtedly Jerusalem, where James evidently had his continual abode. It is not so easy to determine when the letter was written. We have a terminus ad quem in the death of James about the year 62, and a terminus a quo in the persecution that followed the death of Stephen about A. D. 35, and that was instrumental in scattering the Jewish church. Internal evidence favors the idea that it was written during this period, for (1) There is no reference in the Epistle to the destruction of Jerusalem either as past or imminent; but the expectation of the speedy second coming of Christ, that was characteristic of the first generation of Christians, was still prevalent, 5:7-9. (2) The picture of the unbelieving rich oppressing the poor Christians and drawing them before tribunals, is in perfect harmony with the description Josephus gives of the time immediately after Christ, when the rich Sadducees tyrannized over the poor to such a degree that some starved. Ant. XX 8.8; 9.2. This condition terminated with the destruction of Jerusalem. (3) The indistinctness of the line of separation between the converted and the unconverted Jews also favors the supposition that the letter was composed during this period, for until nearly the end of that time these two classes freely intermingled both at the temple worship and in the synagogues. In course of time, however, and even before the destruction of Jerusalem, this condition was gradually changed.

But the question remains, whether we can give a nearer definition of the time of composition. In view of the fact that the Christian Jews addressed in this letter must have had time to spread and to settle in the dispersion so that they already had their own places of worship, we cannot date the Epistle in the very beginning of the period named. Neither does it seem likely that it was written after the year 50, when the council of Jerusalem was held, for (1) the Epistle does not contain a single allusion to the existence in the church of Gentile Christians; and (2) it makes no reference whatever to the great controversy respecting the observance of the Mosaic law, on which the council passed a decision. Hence we are inclined to date the Epistle between A. D. 45 and 50.

Some have objected to this early date that the Epistle is evidently dependent on Romans, Galatians, Hebrews and I Peter; but this objection is an unproved assumption. It is also said that the πρεσβύτεροι mentioned in 5:14 imply a later date. We should remember, however, that the Church, especially among the Jews, first developed out of the synagogue, in which presbyters were a matter of course. Moreover some urge that the Christian knowledge assumed in the readers, as in 1:3; 3:1, does not comport with such an early date. It appears to us that this objection is puerile.

Of those who deny the authorship of James some would date the Epistle after the destruction of Jerusalem, Reuss, Von Soden, and Hilgenfeld in the time of Domitian (81–96); Blom in A. D. 80; Brückner and Baljon in the time of Hadrian (117–138).

CANONICAL SIGNIFICANCE

There was considerable doubt as to the canonicity of this Epistle in the early church. Some allusions to it have been pointed out in Clement of Rome, Hermas and Irenaeus, but they are very uncertain indeed. We cannot point to a single quotation in Irenaeus, Clement of Alexandria and Tertullian, though some are inclined to believe on the strength of a statement made by Eusebius, Ch. Hist. VI 14 that Clement commented on this Epistle, just as he did on the other general Epistles. There are reasons, however, to doubt the correctness of this statement, cf. Westcott, on the Canon p. 357. The letter is omitted from the Muratorian Fragment, but is contained in the Peshito. Eusebius classes it with the Antilegomena, though he seems uncertain as to its canonicity. Origen was apparently the first to quote it as Scripture. Cyril of Jerusalem, Athanasius and Gregory of Nazianze recognized it, and it was finally ratified by the third council of Carthage in A. D. 397. During the Middle Ages the canonicity of the Epistle was not doubted, but Luther for dogmatical reasons called it "a right strawy Epistle." Notwithstanding the doubts expressed in the course of time, the Church continued to honor it as a canonical writing ever since the end of the fourth century.

The great permanent value of this Epistle is found in the stress it lays on the necessity of having a vital faith, that issues in fruits of righteousness. The profession of Christ without a corresponding Christian life is worthless and does not save man. Christians should look into the perfect law, and should regulate their lives in harmony with its deep spiritual meaning. They should withstand temptations, be patient under trials, dwell together in peace without envying or strife, do justice, exercise charity, remember each other in prayer, and in all their difficulties be mindful of the fact that the coming of the Lord is at hand.

CHAPTER

26

The First General Epistle of Peter

CONTENTS
The contents of the Epistle can be divided into four parts:

I. Introduction, 1:1–12. After the greeting, 1, 2, the apostle praises God for the blessings of salvation, which should raise the readers above all temporal sufferings, since they are so great that the prophets searched them, and the angels were desirous to understand their mystery, 3–12.

II. General Exhortations to a worthy Christian Conversation, 1:13–2:10. The writer exhorts the readers to become ever more firmly grounded in their Christian hope. To that end the holiness of God should be the standard of their life, 1:13–16; they must fear God, and as regenerated persons, love the brethren and seek to increase in spiritual life, 1:17–2:3. This growth should not only be individual, however, but also communal, a developing into a spiritual unity, 4–10.

III. Particular Directions for the special Relations of Life, 2:11–4:6. The author urges the readers to be dutiful to the authorities, 2:11–17; more particularly he exhorts the servants among them to follow the example of Christ in self-denying service, 18–25; the wives to submit themselves to their husbands, and the husbands to love their wives and to treat then with consideration, 3:1–7. Then he admonishes them all to do good and to refrain from evil, that in their sufferings they may be like their Master, whom they should also follow in their Christian conversation, 3:8–4:6.

IV. Closing Instructions for the present Needs of the Readers, 4:7–5:14. The apostle exhorts the readers to prayer, brotherly love, hospitality, and conscientiousness in the exercise of their official duties, 4:7–11. He warns them not to be discouraged by persecutions, but to regard these as necessary to the imitation of Christ, 12–19. Further he exhorts the elders to rule the flock of Christ wisely, the younger ones to submit to the elder; and all to humble themselves and to place their trust in God, 5:1-9; and ends the letter with good wishes and a salutation, 10-14.

CHARACTERISTICS

1. Though there are some doctrinal statements in the Epistle, its chief interest is not theoretical but practical, not doctrinal but ethical. It has been said that, while Paul represents faith and John love, Peter is the apostle of hope. This distinction, which may easily be misconstrued, nevertheless contains an element of truth. The basic idea of the Epistle is that the readers are begotten again unto a lively hope, the hope of an incorruptable, undefiled and unfading inheritance. This glorious expectation must be an incentive for them to strive after holiness in all the relations of life, and to bear patiently the reproach of Christ, mindful of the fact that He is their great prototype, and that suffering is the pre-requisite of everlasting glory.

2. The Epistle has a characteristic impress of Old Testament modes of thought and expression. Not only does it, comparatively speaking, contain more quotations from and references to the Old Testament than any other New Testament writing, cf. 1:16, 24, 25; 2:3, 4, 6, 7, 9, 10, 22-24; 3:10-12, 13, 14; 4:8, 17, 18; 5:5, 7; but the entire complexion of the letter shows that the author lived and moved in Old Testament conceptions to such an extent, that he preferably expresses his thoughts in Old Testament language.

3. On the other hand, there is great similarity between this Epistle and some of the New Testament writings, notably the Epistles of Paul to the Romans and to the Ephesians, and the Epistle of James. And this likeness is of such a character as to suggest dependence of the one on the other. Nearly all the thoughts of Rom. 12 and 13 are also found in this letter; compare 2:5 with Rom. 12:1;—1:14 with Rom. 12:2;—4:10 with Rom. 12:3-8;—1:22 with Rom. 12:9;-2:17 with Rom. 12:10, etc. The relationship between it and the Epistle to the Ephesians is evident not only from single passages, but also from the structure of the letter. There is a certain similarity in the general and special exhortations, which is probably due to the fact that both Epistles are of a general character. Compare also the passages 1:3 and Eph. 1:3;—1:5 and Eph. 1:19;—1:14 and Eph. 2:3;—1:18 and Eph. 4:17;—2:4, 5 and Eph. 2:20-22. There are also points of resemblance between this Epistle and that of James, and though not so numerous, yet they indicate a relation of dependence; compare 1:6, 7 with Jas. 1:2, 3;—2:1 with Jas. 1:21;-5:5-9 with Jas. 4:6, 7, 10.

4. The Greek in which this letter is written is some of the best that is found in the New Testament. Though the language is simple and direct, it is not devoid of artistic quality. Simcox, comparing it with the language of James, says: "St. Peter's language is stronger where St. James is weak, and weaker where he is strong—it is more varied, more classical, but less eloquent and of less literary power." The Writers of the New Testament p. 66. The authors vocabulary is very full and rich, and his sentences flow on with great regularity, sometimes rising to grandeur. It is noticeable, however, that the writer, though having a good knowledge of Greek in general, was particularly saturated with the language of the Septuagint.

AUTHORSHIP

The external authentication of this Epistle is very strong. Irenaeus, Clement of Alexandria, Tertullian, Origen and Cyprian all quote it by name and without expressing the slightest doubt as to its canonicity. And Eusebius says: "One Epistle of Peter called his first is universally received." Salmon suggests that, in view of what Westcott says, its omission from the Muratorian Canon may be due to the error of a scribe, who left out a sentence. Cf. Westcott, The canon of the N. T., Appendix C.

Aside from the fact that the letter is self-attested there is very little internal evidence that can help us to determine who the author was. There is nothing that points definitely to Peter, which is in part due to the fact that we have no generally recognized standard of comparison. The speeches in Acts may not have been recorded literally by Luke; and II peter is one of the most doubted Epistles of the New Testament, partly because it is so dissimilar to our letter. If we leave the first verse out of consideration, we can only say on the strength of internal evidence that the writer was evidently an eyewitness of the sufferings of Christ, 3:1; that the central contents of his teaching is, like that of Peter in the Acts of the Apostles, the death and the resurrection of Christ; and that his attitude toward the Christians of the Gentiles is in perfect harmony with that of the apostle of the circumcision. Moreover the persons mentioned in 5:12, 13 are known to have been acquaintances of Peter, cf. Acts 12:12; 15:22.

The apostle Peter, originally called Simon, was a native of Bethsaida, John 1:42, 44. When the Lord entered on his public ministry, Peter was married and dwelt at Capernaum, Lk. 4:31, 38. He was the son of Jonas, Mt. 16:17 and was, with his father and his brother, by occupation a fisherman, Mk. 1:16. We find him among the first that were called to follow the Lord,

Mt. 4:18, 19, and he soon received a certain prominence among the disciples of Jesus. This was in harmony with the new name, Πέτρος, which the Lord gave him, John 1:42. With John and James he formed the inner circle of the disciples; together they were the most intimate followers of the Saviour and as such enjoyed special privileges. They only entered with the Lord into the house of Jairus, Lk. 8:51; none but they witnessed his glory on the Mount of Transfiguration, Mt. 17:1; and they alone beheld him in his hour of great grief in the garden of Gethsemane, Mt. 26:37. The trial of Jesus was also the hour of Peter's deepest fall, for on that occasion he thrice denied his Master, Mt. 26:69-75. He truly repented of his deed, however, and was restored to his former position by the Lord, John 21:15-17. After the ascension he is found at the head of the disciples at Jerusalem, guiding them in the choice of an apostle in the place of Judas, Acts 1:15-26, and preaching the Pentecostal sermon, Acts 2:14-36. Laboring at first in connection with John, he healed the lame man, repeatedly addressed the people in the temple, executed judgment on Ananias and Sapphira, and once and again defended the cause of Christ before the Sanhedrin, Acts 3-5. During the time of persecution that followed the death of Stephen, they together went to Samaria to establish the work of Philip, Acts 8:14 ff. In Lydda he healed Aeneas, Acts 9:22 f. and raised up Tabitha in Joppa, Acts 9:36 f. By means of a vision he was taught that the Gentiles too were to be admitted to the Church, and was prepared to go and preach Christ to the household of Cornelius, Acts 10:1-48. After James, the brother of John was killed, Peter was cast in prison, but, being delivered by an angel, he left Jerusalem, Acts 12:1-17. Later he returned thither and was present at the council of Jerusalem, Acts 15. Nothing certain is known of his movements after this time. From 1 Cor. 9:5 we infer that he labored at various places. On one occasion Paul rebuked him for his dissimulation, Gal. 2:11 ff. From all the traditions regarding his later life we can gather only one piece of reliable information, to the effect that towards the end of his life he came to Rome, where he labored for the propagation of the Gospel and suffered martyrdom under Nero.

Peter was a man of action rather than of deep thought. He was always eager and impulsive, but, as is often the case with such persons, was wanting in the necessary stability of character. Burning with love towards the Saviour, he was always ready to defend his cause, Mt. 17:24, 25; 16:22; Lk. 22:33; John 18:10, and to confess his name, John 6:68 f.; Mt. 16:16. But his action was often characterized by undue haste, as f. i. when he rebuked

Christ, Mt. 16:22, smote the servant of the high priest, John 18:10, and refused to let the Saviour wash his feet, John 13:6; and by too much reliance on his own strength, as when he went out upon the sea, Mt. 14:28–31, and declared himself ready to die with the Lord, Mt. 26:35. It was this rashness and great self-confidence that led to his fall. By that painful experience Peter had to be taught his own weakness before he could really develop into the Rock among the apostle's. After his restoration we see him as a firm confessor, ready, if need be, to lay down his life for the Saviour.

Until the previous century the Epistle was generally regarded as the work of Peter, and even now the great majority of New Testament scholars have reached no other conclusion. Still there are several, especially since the time of Baur, that deny its authenticity, as Hilgenfeld, Pfleiderer, Weizsäcker, Hausrath, Keim, Schürer, Von Soden e. a. The most important objections urged against the traditional view, are the following: (1) The Epistle is clearly dependent on Pauline letters, while it contains very few traces of the Lord's teaching. This is not what one would expect of Peter, who had been so intimate with the Lord and had taken a different stand than Paul, Gal. 2:11ff. Harnack regards this argument as decisive, for he says: "Were it not for the dependence (of I Peter) on the Pauline Epistles, I might perhaps allow myself to maintain its genuineness; that dependence, however, is not accidental, but is of the essence of the Epistle." Quoted by Chase, Hastings D. B. Art. I Peter. (2) It is written in far better Greek than one can reasonably expect of a Galilean fisherman like Peter, of whom we know that on his missionary journeys he needed Mark as an interpreter. Davidson regards it as probable that he never was able to write Greek. (3) The Epistle reflects conditions that did not exist in the lifetime of Peter. The Christians of Asia Minor were evidently persecuted, simply because they were Christians, persecuted for the Name, and this, it is said, did not take place until the time of Trajan, A. D. 98–117. (4) It is very unlikely that Peter would write a letter to churches founded by Paul, while the latter was still living.

As to the first argument, we need not deny with Weiss and his pupil Kühl that Peter is dependent on some of the writings of Paul, especially on Romans and Ephesians. In all probability he read both of these Epistles, or if he did not see Ephesians, Paul may have spoken to him a good deal about its contents. And being the receptive character that he was, it was but natural that he should incorporate some of Paul's thoughts in his Epistle. There was no such antagonism between him and Paul as to make him averse to the teachings of his fellow-apostle. The idea of an evident hostility between the two is exploded, and the theory of Baur that this letter is a Unionsschrift, is destitute of all historical basis and is burdened with a great many, improbabilities. Moreover it need not cause surprise that the teaching of this Epistle resembles the teaching of Paul more than it does that of Christ, because the emphasis had shifted with the resurrection of the Lord, which now, in connection with his death, became the central element in the teaching of the apostle's. Compare the sermons of Peter in the Acts of the Apostles.

With respect to the objection that Peter could not write, such Greek as we find in this Epistle, we refer to what Mayor says regarding James, cf. p. 286 above. The fact that Mark is said to have been the interpreter of Peter does not imply that the latter did not know Greek, cf. p. 80 above. It is also possible, however, that the Greek of this Epistle is not that of the apostle. Zahn argues with great plausibility from 5:12, Διὰ Σιλουανοῦ, that Silvanus took an active part in the composition of the letter, and in all probability wrote it under the immediate direction rather than at the verbal dictation of Peter, Einl. II p. 10 f. Cf. also Brown on I Peter in loco,, and J. H. A. Hart, Exp. Gk. Test. IV p. 13 f. Against this, however, cf. Chase, Hastings D. B. Art. I Peter. It is possible that Silvanus was both the amanuensis of Peter and the bearer of the Epistle.

The third argument is open to two objections. On the one hand it rests on a faulty interpretation of the passages that speak of the sufferings endured by the Christians of Asia Minor, as 1:6; 3:9-17; 4:4 f., and especially 4:12-19; 5:8-12. And on the other hand it is based on a misunderstanding of the correspondence between Pliny and Trajan A. D. 112. The passages referred to do not imply and do not even favor the idea that the Christians were persecuted by the state, though they do point to an ever increasing severity of their sufferings. There is no hint of judicial trials, of the confiscation of property, of imprisonments or of bloody deaths. The import of the Epistle is that the readers were placed under the necessity of bearing the reproach of Christ in a different form. As Christians they were subject to ridicule, to slander, to ill treatment, and to social ostracism; they were the outcasts of the world, 4:14. And this, of course, brought with it manifold temptations, 1:6. At the same time the correspondence of Pliny and Trajan does not imply that Rome did not persecute Christians as such until about A. D. 112. Ramsay says that this state of affairs may have arisen as early as the year 80; and Mommsen, the greatest authority on Roman history, is of the opinion that it may have existed as early as the time of Nero.

The last objection is of a rather subjective character. Peter was undoubtedly greatly interested in the work among the Christians of Asia Minor; and it is possible that he himself had labored there for some time among the Jews and thus became acquainted with the churches of that region. And does it not seem likely that he, being informed of their present sufferings, and knowing of the antagonism of the Jews, who had occasionally used his name to undermine the authority and to subvert the doctrine of Paul, would consider it expedient to send them a letter of exhortation, urging them to abide in the truth in which they stood, and thus indirectly strengthening their confidence in his fellow-apostle?

DESTINATION

The letter is addressed to "the elect who are sojourners of the dispersion in Pontus, Galatia, Cappadocia, Asia and Bithynia," 1:1. The use of the strictly Jewish term διασπορά is apt to create the impression that the letter was sent to Jewish Christians. Origen said, presumably on the strength of this superscription, that Peter seems to have preached to the Jews in the dispersion. And Eusebius felt sure that this letter was sent to Hebrews or to Jewish Christians. The great majority of the church fathers agreed with them. Among recent scholars Weiss and Kühl defend the position that the letter was addressed to Jewish congregations founded in Asia Minor by Peter. But the idea that the original readers of this Epistle were Christians of Jewish extraction is not favored by internal evidence. Notice especially (1) the passages that point to the past moral condition of the readers, as 1:14 (comp. Gal. 4:8; Eph. 4:18); 1:18 (comp. Eph. 1:17); 4:2-4 (comp. 1 Thess. 4:5; Eph. 2:11); and (2) the emphatic use of "you" as distinguished from the "us" found in the context, to mark the readers as persons that were destined to receive the blessings of the gospel and to whom these at last came. Moreover this is in perfect agreement with what we know of the churches of Asia Minor; they certainly consisted primarily of Gentile Christians. But the question is naturally asked, whether this view is not contradicted by the address. And to that question we answer that it certainly is, if the word διασπορᾶς must be taken literally; but this will also bear, and, in harmony with the contents of the Epistle, is now generally given a figurative interpretation. The word διαπορᾶς is a Genitivus appostitivus (for which cf. Blass, Grammatik p. 101) with παρεπιδήμοις. Taken by itself the address is a figurative description of all believers, whether they be Jewish or Gentile Christians, as sojourners on earth, who have here no abiding dwellingplace, but look for a heavenly city; and who constitute a dispersion, because they are separated from that eternal home of which the earthly Jerusalem was but a symbol. In agreement with this the apostle elsewhere addresses the readers as "pilgrims and strangers," 2:11, and exhorts them "to pass the time of their sojourning here in fear," 1:17. Cf. the Comm. of Huther, Brown, and Hart (Exp. Gk. Test.), and the Introductions of Zahn, Holtzmann, Davidson and Barth. Salmon admits the possibility of this interpretation, but is yet inclined to take the word διασπορᾶς literally, and to believe that Peter wrote his letter to members of the Roman church that were scattered through Asia Minor as a result of Nero's persecution. Introd. p. 485.

As to the condition of the readers, the one outstanding fact is that they were subject to hardships and persecutions because of their allegiance to Christ, 1:17; 2:12-19. There is no sufficient evidence that they were persecuted by the state; they suffered at the hands of their associates in daily life. The Gentiles round about them spoke evil of them, because they did not take part in their revelry and idolatry, 4:2-4. This constituted the trial of their faith, and it seems that some were in danger of becoming identified with the heathen way of living, 2:11, 12, 16. They were in need of encouragement and of a firm hand to guide their feeble steps.

COMPOSITION

1. Occasion and Purpose. In a general way we can say that the condition just described led Peter to write this Epistle. He may have received information regarding the state of affairs from Mark or Silvanus, who is undoubtedly to be indentified with Paul's companion of that name, and was therefore well acquainted with the churches of Asia Minor. Probably the direct occasion for Peter's writing must be found in a prospective journey of Silvanus to those churches.

The writer's purpose was not doctrinal but practical. He did not intend to give an exposition of the truth, but to emphasize its bearings on life, especially in the condition in which the Christians of Asia Minor were placed. The Tübingen critics are mistaken, however, when they hold that the unknown writer, impersonating Peter, desired to make it appear as if there was really no conflict between the apostle of the circumcision and the apostle of the Gentiles, and to unite the discordant factions in the

Church; for (1) such antagonistic parties did not exist in the second century, and (2) the Epistle does not reveal a single trace of such a tendency. The writer incidentally and in a general way states his aim, when he says in 5:12, "By Silvanus—I have written briefly, exhorting and testifying that this is the true grace of God wherein ye stand." The main purpose of the author was evidently to exhort the readers to suffer, not as evil-doers, but as well-doers, to see to it that they should suffer for the sake of Christ only; to suffer patiently, remaining steadfast in spite of all temptations; and to bear their sufferings with a joyful hope, since they would issue in a glory that never fades away. And because these sufferings might lead them to doubt and discouragement, the writer makes it a point to testify that the grace in which they stand, and with which the sufferings of this present time are inseparably connected, is yet the true grace of God, thus confirming the work of Paul.

2. Time and Place. There are especially three theories regarding the place of composition, viz. (1) that the Epistle was sent from Babylon on the Euphrates; (2) that it was composed at Rome; and (3) that it was written from Babylon near Cairo in Egypt. The last hypothesis found no support and need not be considered. The answer to the question respecting the place of composition depends on the interpretation of 5:13, where we read: "She (the church) that is in Babylon, elect together with you, saluteth you." The prima facie impression made by these words is that the writer was at ancient Babylon, the well known city on the Euphrates. Many of the early church fathers, however, (Papias, Clement of Alexandria, Hippolytus, Eusebius, Jerome) and several later commentators and writers on Introduction (Bigg, Hart, Salmon, Holtzmann, Zahn, Chase) regard the name Babylon as a figurative designation of Rome, just as it is in the Apocalypse, 17:5; 18:2, 10. In favor of the literal interpretation it is argued, (1) that its figurative use is very unlikely in a matter-of-fact statement; and (2) that in 1:1 the order in which the provinces of Asia Minor are named is from the East to the West, thus indicating the location of the writer. Aside from the fact, however, that the last argument needs some qualification, these considerations seem to be more than off-set by the following facts: (1) An old and reliable tradition, that can be traced to the second century, informs us that Peter was at Rome towards the end of his life, and finally died there as a martyr. This must be distinguished from that fourth century tradition to the effect that he resided at Rome for a period of twenty-five years as its first bishop. On the other hand there is not the slightest

record of his having been at Babylon. Not until the Middle Ages was it inferred from 5:13 that he had visited the city on the Euphrates. (2) In the Revelation of John Rome is called Babylon, a terminology that was likely to come into general use, as soon as Rome showed herself the true counterpart of ancient Babylon, the representative of the world as over against the Church of God. The Neronian persecution certainly began to reveal her character as such. (3) The symbolical sense is in perfect harmony with the figurative interpretation of the address, and with the designation of the readers as "pilgrims and strangers in the earth." (4) In view of what Josephus says in Ant. XVIII 9. it is doubtful, whether Babylon would offer the apostle a field for missionary labors at the time, when this Epistle was composed. We regard it as very likely that the writer refers to Rome in 5:13.

With respect to the time when this Epistle was written, the greatest uncertainty prevails. Dates have been suggested all the way from 54 to 147 A. D. Of those who deny the authorship of Peter the great majority refer the letter to the time of Trajan after A. D. 112, the date of Trajan's rescript, for reasons which we already discussed. Thus Baur, Keim, Lipsius, Pfleiderer, Hausrath, Weizsäcker, Hilgenfeld, Davidson e. a. In determining the time of writing we must be guided by the following data: (1) The Epistle cannot have been written later than A. D. 67 or 68, the traditional date of Peter's death, which some, however place in the year 64. Cf. Zahn Einl. II p. 19. (2) Peter had evidently read the Epistles of Paul to the Romans (58) and that to the Ephesians (62), and therefore cannot have written his letter before A. D. 62. (3) The letter makes no mention whatever of Paul, so that presumably it was written at a time when this apostle was not at Rome. (4) The fact that Peter writes to Pauline churches favors the idea that Paul had temporarily withdrawn from his field of labor. We are inclined to think that he composed the Epistle, when Paul was on his jojurney to Spain, about A. D. 64 or 65.

CANONICAL SIGNIFICANCE

The canonicity of the letter has never been subject to doubt in the opening centuries of our era. It is referred to in 2 peter 3:1. Papias evidently used it and there are clear traces of its language in Clement of Rome, Hermas and Polycarp. The old Latin and Syriac Versions contain it, while it is quoted in the Epistle of the churches of Vienne and Lyons, Irenaeus, Clement of Alexandria and Tertullian all quote it by name, and Eusebius classes it with the Homologoumena.

Some scholars objected to this Epistle that it was characterized by a want of distinctive character. But the objection is not well founded, since the letter certainly has a unique significance among the writings of the New Testament. It emphasizes the great importance which the hope of a blessed and eternal inheritance has in the life of God's children. Viewed in the light of their future glory, the present life of believers, with all its trials and sufferings, recedes into the background, and they realize that they are strangers and pilgrims in the earth. From that point of view they understand the significance of the sufferings of Christ as opening up the way to God, and they also learn to value their own hardships as these minister to the development of faith and to their everlasting glory. And then, living in expectation of the speedy return of their Lord, they realize that their sufferings are of short duration, and therefore bear them joyfully. In the midst of all her struggles the Church of God should never forget to look forward to her future glory,—the object of her living hope.

27

The Second General Epistle of Peter

CONTENTS

The contents of the Epistle can be divided into two parts:

I. The Importance of Christian Knowledge, 1:1-21. After the greeting, 1, 2, the author reminds the readers of the great blessings they received through the knowledge of Jesus Christ, and urges them to live worthy of that knowledge and thus to make sure their calling and election, 3-11. He says that he deemed it expedient to put them in mind of what they knew, and that he would see to it that they had a remembrance of these things after his decease, 12-15. This knowledge is of the greatest value, because it rests on a sure foundation, 16-21.

II. Warning against False Teachers, 2:1-3:18. The apostle announces the coming of false prophets, who shall deny the truth and mislead many, 2:1-3. Then he proves the certainty of their punishment by means of historical examples, 4-9, and gives a minute description of their sensual character, 10-22. Stating that he wrote the letter to remind them of the knowledge they had received, he informs them that the scoffers that will come in the last days, will deny the advent of Christ, 3:1-4. He refutes their arguments, assuring the readers that the Lord will come, and exhorting them to a holy conversation, 5-13. Referring to his agreement with Paul in this teaching, he ends his letter with an exhortation to grow in grace and in the knowledge of Jesus Christ, 14-18.

CHARACTERISTICS

1. Like the first Epistle this second one is also a letter of practical warning, exhortation and encouragement. But while in the former the dominant note is that of Christian hope, the controlling idea in the latter is that of Christian knowledge. It is the "ἐπίγνωσις χριστοῦ, which consists essentially in the acknowledgment of the δύναμις κὰι παρουσία of Christ. Advancement in this ἐπίγνωσις, as the ground and aim of the exercise of all

Christian virtues, is the prominent feature of every exhortation." Huther, Comm. p. 344. This knowledge, resting on a sure foundation, must be the mainstay of the readers, when false doctrines are propagated in their midst, and must be their incentive to holiness in spite of the seducing influences round about them.

2. This Epistle has great affinity with that of Jude, cf. 2:1–18; 3:1–3. The similarity is of such a character that it cannot be regarded as accidental, but clearly points to dependence of the one on the other. Though it cannot be said that the question is absolutely settled, the great majority of scholars, among whom there are some who deny the authorship of Peter (Holtzmann, Jülicher, Chase, Strachan, Barth e. a.), and others who defend the authenticity of the Epistle (Wiesinger, Brückner, Weiss, Alford, Salmon), maintain the priority of Jude. The main reasons that lead them to this conclusion, are the following: (1) The phraseology of Jude is simpler than that of Peter in the related passages. The language of the latter is more laborious and looks like an elaboration of what the former wrote. (2) Several passages in Peter can be fully understood only in the light of what Jude says, compare 2:4 with Jude 6; 2:11 with Jude 9; 3:2 with fade 17. (3) Though the similar passages are adapted to the subject-matter of both Epistles, they seem more natural in the context of Jude than in Peter; The course of thought is more regular in the Epistle of Jude.—The priority of Jude is quite well established, though especially Zahn, Spitta (who defends the second Epistle of Peter at the cost of the first) and Bigg put up an able defense for the priority of Peter.

3. The language of II peter has some resemblance to that of the first Epistle, cf Weiss, Introd. II p. 166, but the difference between the two is greater than the similarity. We need not call special attention to the ἅπαξ λεγόμενα found in this letter, since it contains but 48, while I Peter has 58. But there are other points that deserve our attention. Bigg says: "The vocabulary of I Peter is dignified; that of II peter inclines to the grandiose." Comm. p. 225. And according to Simcox, "we see in this Epistle, as compared with the first, at once less instinctive familiarity with Greek idiom and more conscious effort at elegant Greek composition." Writers of the N. T. p. 69.

There are 361 words in I Peter that are not found in this Epistle, and 231 in II Peter that are absent from the first letter. There is a certain fondness for the repetition of words, cf. Holtzmann, Einl. p. 322, which Bigg, however, finds equally noticeable in I Peter. The connecting particles, ἵνα, ὅτι, οὖν, μέν, found frequently in I Peter, are rare in this Epistle, where instead we find sentences introduced with τοῦτο or ταῦτα, cf. 1:8, 10; 3:11, 14. And while in the first Epistle there is a free interchange of prepositions, we often find a repetition of the same preposition in the second, f. i. διά, is found three times in 1:3-5 and ἐν seven times in 1:5-7. Different words are often used to express the same ideas; compare ἀποκάλυψις, 1 Pt. 1:7, 13; 4:13 with παρουσία, 2 Pt. 1:16; 3:4;—ῥαντισμός, 1 Pt. 1:2 with καθαρισμός, 2 Pt. 1:9;—κληρονομία, 1 Pt. 1:4 with ἀιώνος βασιλεία, 2 Pt. 1:11.

AUTHORSHIP

This Epistle is the most weakly attested of all the New Testament writings. Besides that of Jerome we do not find a single statement in the fathers of the first four centuries explicitly and positively ascribing this work to Peter. Yet there are some evidences of its canonical use, which indirectly testify to a belief in its genuineness. There are some phrases in Clement of Rome, Hermas, the Clementine Recognitions and Theophilus that recall II peter, but the coincidences may be accidental. Supposed traces of this Epistle are found in Irenaeus, though they may all be accounted for in another way, cf. Salmon, Introd. p. 324 f. Eusebius and Photius say that Clement of Alexandria commented on our Epistle, and their contention may be correct, notwithstanding the doubt cast on it by Cassiodorus, cf. Davidson, Introd. II p. 533 f. Origen attests that the book was known in his time, but that its genuineness was disputed. He himself quotes it several times without any expression of doubt. It is pointed out, however, that these quotations are found in those parts of his work that we know only in the Latin translation of Rufinus, which is not always reliable; though, according to Salmon, the presumption is that Rufinus did not invent them, Introd. p. 533 f. Eusebius classes this letter with the Antilegomena; and Jerome says: "Simon Peter wrote two Epistles, which are called catholic; the second of which most persons deny to be his, on account of its disagreement in style with the first." This difference he elsewhere explains by assuming that Peter employed a different interpreter. From that time the Epistle was received by Rufinus, Augustine, Basil, Gregory, Palladius, Hilary, Ambrose e. a. During the Middle Ages it was generally accepted, but at the time of the Reformation Erasmus and Calvin, though accepting the letter as canonical, doubted the direct authorship of Peter. Yet Calvin believed that in some sense the Petrine authorship had to be maintained, and surmised that a disciple wrote it at the command of Peter.

The Epistle itself definitely points to Peter as its author. In the opening verse the writer calls himself, "Simon Peter, a servant and an apostle
of Jesus Christ," which clearly excludes the idea of Grotius, that Symeon,
the successor of James at Jerusalem, wrote the letter. From 1:16–18 we learn
that the author was a witness of the transfiguration of Christ; and in 3:1 we
find a reference to his first Epistle. As far as style and expression are concerned there is even greater similarity between this letter and the speeches
of Peter in the Acts of the Apostles than between the first Epistle and those
addresses. Moreover Weiss concludes that, from a biblical and theological point of view, no New Testament writing is more like I Peter than this
Epistle, Introd. II p. 165. Besides the whole spirit of the Epistle is against
the idea that it is a forgery. Calvin maintained its canonicity, "because the
majesty of the Spirit of Christ exhibited itself in every part of the Epistle."

Notwithstanding this, however, the authenticity of the letter is subject
to serious doubt in modern times, such scholars as Mayerhoff, Credner,
Hilgenfeld, Von Soden, Hausrath, Mangold, Davidson, Volkmar, Holtzmann,
Jülicher, Harnack, Chase, Strachan e. a. denying that Peter wrote it. But
the Epistle is not without defenders; its authenticity is maintained among
others by Luthardt, Wiesinger, Guericke, Windischmann, Brückner,
Hofmann, Salmon, Alford, Zahn, Spitta, and Warfield, while Huther, Weiss,
and Kühl conclude their investigations with a non liquet.

The principle objections to the genuineness of II Peter are the following: (1) The Language of the Epistle is so different from that of I Peter as
to preclude the possibility of their proceeding from the same author. (2)
The dependence of the writer on Jude is inconsistent with the idea that
he was Peter, not only because Jude was written long after the lifetime of
Peter, but also since it is unworthy of an apostle to rely to such a degree
on one who did not have that distinction. (3) It appears that the author is
over-anxious to identify himself with the apostle Peter: there is a threefold allusion to his death, 1:13–15; he wants the readers to understand that
he was present at the transfiguration, 1:16–18; and he identifies himself
with the author of the first Epistle, 3:1. (4) In 3:2, where the reading ὑμῶν is
better attested than ἡμῶν, the writer by using the expression, τῆς τῶν ἀποστόλων ὑμῶν ἐντολῆς, seems to place himself outside of the apostolic circle.
Deriving the expression from Jude, the writer forgot that he wanted to
pass for an apostle and therefore could not use it with equal propriety. Cf.
Holtzmann, Einl. p. 321. (5) The writer speaks of some of Paul's Epistles as
Scripture in 3:16, implying the existence of a New Testament canon, and

thus betrays his second century standpoint. (6) The Epistle also refers to doubts regarding the second coming of Christ, 3:4 ff., which points beyond the lifetime of Peter, because such doubts could not be entertained before the destruction of Jerusalem. (7) According to Dr. Abbott (in the Expositor) the author of II peter is greatly indebted to the Antiquities of Josephus, a work that was published about A. D. 93.

We cannot deny that there is force in some of these arguments, but do not believe that they compel us to give up the authorship of Peter. The argument from style is undoubtedly the most important one; but if we accept the theory that Silvanus wrote the first Epistle under the direction of Peter, while the apostle composed the second, either with his own hand or by means of another amanuensis, the difficulty vanishes.—As far as the literary dependence of Peter on Jude is concerned, it is well to bear in mind that this is not absolutely proved. However, assuming it to be established, there is nothing derogatory in it for Peter, since Jude was also an inspired man, and because in those early days unacknowledged borrowing was looked at in a far different light than it is today.—That the author is extremely solicitous to show that he is the appostle Peter, is, even if it can be proved, no argument against the genuineness of this letter. In view of the errorists against which he warns the readers, it was certainly important that they should bear in mind his official position. But it cannot be maintained that he insists on this over-much. The references to his death, his experience on the Mount of Transfiguration, and his first Epistle are introduced in a perfectly natural way. Moreover this argument is neutralized by some of the others brought forward by the negative critics. If the writer really was so over-anxious, why does he speak of himself as Simon Peter, cf. 1 Pt. 1:1; why does he seemingly exclude himself from the apostolic circle, 3:2; and why did he not more closely imitate the language of I peter?—The difficulty created by 3:2 is not as great as it seems to some. If that passage really disproves the authorship of Peter, it certainly was a clumsy piece of work of a very clever forger, to let it stand. But the writer, speaking of the prophets as a class, places alongside of them another class, viz. that of the apostle's, who had more especially ministered to the New Testament churches, and could therefore as a class be called, "your apostle's," i. e. the apostle's who preached to you. The writer evidently did not desire to single himself out, probably, if for no other reasons, because other apostle's had labored more among the readers than he had.—The reference to the Epistles of Paul does not necessarily imply the existence of a New Testament canon; and it is a gratuitous assumption that they were not regarded as Scripture in the first century, so that the burden of proof rests on those who make it.—The same may be said of the assertion that no doubt could be entertain as the second coming of Christ before the destruction of Jerusalem. Moreover the author does not say that these were already expressed, but that they would be uttered by scoffers that would come in the last days.—The attempt to prove the dependence of II peter on Josephus, has been proved fallacious, especially by Salmon and by Dr. Warfield. The former says in conclusion: "Dr. Abbot has completely failed to establish his theory; but I must add that it was a theory never rational to try to establish." Introd. p. 536.

DESTINATION

The readers are simply addressed as those "that have obtained like precious faith with us through the righteousness of God and our Saviour Jesus Christ," 1:1. From 3:1 we gather, however, that they are identical with the readers of the first Epistle; and from 3:15, that they were also the recipients of some Pauline Epistle(s). It is vain to guess what Epistle(s) the writer may have had in view here. Zahn argues at length that our Epistle was written to Jewish Christians in and round about Palestine, who had been led to Christ by Peter and by others of the twelve apostle's. He bases his conclusion on the general difference of circumstances presupposed in the two letters of Peter, and on such passages as 1:1-4, 16-18; 3:2. But it seems to us that the Epistle does not contain a single hint regarding the Jewish character of its readers, while passages like 1:4 and 3:15 rather imply their Gentile origin. Moreover, in order to maintain his theory, Zahn must assume that both 3:1 and 3:15 refer to lost letters, cf. Einl. II p. 43 ff.

The condition of the readers presupposed in this letter is indeed different from that reflected in the first Epistle. No mention is made of persecution; instead of the affliction from without, internal dangers are now coming in view. The readers were in need of being firmly grounded in the truth, since they would soon have to contend with heretical teachers, who theoretically would deny the Lord'ship of Jesus Christ, 2:1, and his second coming, 3:4; and practically would disgrace their lives by licentiousness, ch. 2. These heretics have been described as Sadducees, as Gnostics, and as Nicolaitans, but it is rather doubtful, whether we can identify them with any particular sect. They certainly were practical Antinomians, leading careless, wanton and sinful lives, just because they did not believe in the

resurrection and in a future judgment. Their doctrine was, in all probability, an incipient Gnosticism.

Since the author employs both the future and the present tense in
describing them, the question arises, whether they were already present or were yet to come. The most natural explanation is that the author
already knew such false teachers to be at work in some places (cf. especially I Corinthians and the Epistles to the Thessalonians), so that he could
consequently give a vivid description of them; and that he expected them
to extend their pernicious influence also to the churches of Asia Minor.

COMPOSITION

1. Occasion and Purpose. The occasion that led to the composition of this
Epistle must be found in the dangerous heresies that were at work in
some of the churches, and that also threatened the readers.

In determining the object of the writer the Tübingen school emphasized 3:15, and found it in the promotion of harmony and peace between
the Petrine and Pauline parties (Baur, Schwegler, Hausrath). With this
end in view, they say, the writer personating Peter, the representative of
Jewish Christendom, acknowledges Paul, who represents the more liberal
tendency of the Church. But it is unwarranted to lay such stress on that
particular passage. Others regarded the Epistle as primarily a polemic
against Gnosticism, against the false teachers depicted in the letter. Now
it cannot be denied that the Epistle is in part controversial, but it is only its
secondary character. The main object of the letter, as indicated in 1:16 and
3:1, 2, was to put the readers in mind of the truth which they had learned,
in order that they might not be led astray by the theoretical and practical libertines that would soon make their influence felt, and especially to
strengthen their faith in the promised parousia of Jesus Christ.

2. Time and Place. The Epistle contains no certain data as to the time
of its composition. We can only infer from 3:1 that it was written after I
peter, though Zahn, who is not bound by that passage, places it before the
first Epistle, about A. D. 60–63. The fact that the condition of the churches,
which is indicated in this letter, is quite different from that reflected in
the earlier writing, presupposes the lapse of some time, though it does not
require many years to account for the change. A short time would suffice
for the springing up of the enemies to which the Epistle refers. Can we not
say, in view of the tendencies apparent at Corinth that their doctrines had
already been germinating for some time? Moreover, according to 1:14 the

writer felt that his end was near. Hence we prefer to date the letter about the year 66 or 67.

They who deny the authenticity of the Epistle generally place it somewhere between the years 90 and 175, for such reasons as its dependence on Jude and on the Apocalypse of Peter, its reference to Gnosticism, and its implication respecting the existence of a New Testament canon.

Since a trustworthy tradition informs us that Peter spent the last part of his life at Rome, the Epistle was in all probability composed in the imperial city. Zahn points to Antioch, and Jülicher suggests Egypt as the place of composition.

CANONICAL SIGNIFICANCE

For the reception of this Epistle in the early church, we refer to what has been said above.

Like all the canonical writings this one too has abiding significance. Its importance is found in the fact that it emphasizes the great value of true Christian knowledge, especially in view of the dangers that arise for believers from all kinds of false teachings, and from the resultant example of a loose, a licentious, an immoral life. It teaches us that a Christianity that is not well founded in the truth as it is in Christ, is like a ship without a rudder on the turbulent sea of life. A Christianity without dogma cannot maintain itself against the errors of the day, but will go down before the triumphant forces of darkness; it will not succeed in cultivating a pure, noble spiritual life, but will be conformed to the life of the world. In particular does the Epistle remind us of the fact that faith in the return of Christ should inspire us to a holy conversation.

28

The First General Epistle of John

CONTENTS

It is impossible to give a satisfactory schematic representation of the contents of this letter. After the introduction, 1:1-4, in which the apostle declares that the purpose of his ministry is to manifest the life-giving divine Word, in order that the readers may have fellowship with him and the other apostle's, and through them with God and Christ, he defines the character of this fellowship and points out that, since God is light, believers also should be and walk in the light, 5-10, i. e. they should guard against sin and keep Gods commandments, 2:1-6. He reminds the readers of the great commandment, which is at once old and new, that they should love the brethren, 7-14; and in connection with this warns them not to love the world, and to beware of the false teachers that deny the truth, 15-27.

The representation of God as light now passes over into that of God as righteous, and the writer insists that only he that is righteous can be a child of God, 2:28-3:6. He reminds the readers of the fact that to be righteous is to do righteousness, which in turn is identical with love to the brethren, 7-17. Once more he warns the readers against the love of the world, and points out that the commandment of God includes two things, viz. belief in Christ and love to the brethren, 18-24.

In view of the false teachers he next reminds the readers that the test of having the Spirit of God, is to be found in the true confession of Christ, in adherence to the teaching of the apostle's, and in that faith in Jesus that is the condition of love and of true spiritual life, 4:1-5:12. Finally he states the object of the Epistle once more, and gives a brief summary of what he has written, 13-21.

CHARACTERISTICS

1. The literary form of this Epistle is different from that of all the other New Testament letters, the Epistle to the Hebrews and that of James resembling it most in this respect. Like the Epistle to the Hebrews it does not name its author nor its original readers, and contains no apostolic blessing at the beginning; and in agreement with that of James it has no formal conclusion, no greetings and salutations at the end. This feature led some to deny its epistolary character; yet, taking everything into consideration, the conclusion is inevitable that it is an Epistle in the proper sense of the word, and not a didactic treatise. "The freedom of the style, the use of such direct terms as, 'I write unto you,' 'I wrote unto you,' and the footing on which writer and readers stand to each other all through its contents, show it to be no formal composition." (Salmond) Moreover it reveals no such plan as would be expected in a treatise. The order found in it is determined by association rather than by logic, the thoughts being grouped about certain clearly related, ruling ideas.

2. The great affinity of this Epistle with the Gospel of John naturally attracts attention. The two are very similar in the general conception of the truth, in the specific way of representing things, and in style and expression. Besides there are several passages in both that are mutually explanatory, as f. i.:

1:1, 2	John 1:1, 2, 4, 14
2:1	John 14:16
2:2	John 11:51, 52
2:8	John 13:34; 15:10, 12
2:10	John 11:9, 10; 12:35
2:23	John 15:23, 24
2:27	John 14:26; 16:13
3:8, 15	John 8:44
3:11, 16	John 15:12, 13
4:6	John 8:47
5:6	John 19:34, 35
5:9	John 5:32, 34, 36; 8:17, 18
5:12	John 3:36
5:13	John 20:31

5:14	John 14:13, 14; 16:23
5:20	John 17:3

Hence many scholars assume a very intimate connection of the Epistle with the Gospel, regarding it as a kind of introduction (Lightfoot), a sort of dedicatory writing (Hausrath, Hofmann), or a practical companion (Michaelis, Storr, Eichhorn), destined to accompany the Gospel. At the same time there are differences of such a kind between the two writings, as make it seem more likely that the Epistle is an independent composition. Cf. Holtzmann, Einl. p. 478; Salmond, Hastings D. B. Art. I John, 5.

3. The truth is represented in this Epistle ideally rather than historically. This important fact is stated by Salmond concisely as follows: "The characteristic ideas of the Epistle are few and simple, they are of large significance, and they are presented in new aspects and relations as often as they occur. They belong to the region of primary principles, realities of the intuition, certainties of the experience, absolute truths. And they are given in their absoluteness. (Italics are ours). The regenerate man is one who cannot sin; Christian faith is presented in its ideal character and completeness; the revelation of life is exhibited in its finality, not in the stages of its historical realization." Cf. especially Weiss, Biblical Theology of the N. T. II p. 311 ff. Stevens, Johannine Theology, p. 1 ff.

4. The style of the Epistle is very similar to that of the Gospel. Fundamental words and phrases are often repeated, such as "truth," "love," "light," "In the light," "being born of God," "abiding in God," etc.; and the construction is characterized by utter simplicity, the sentences being coordinated rather than subordinated, and involved sentences being avoided by the repetition of part of a previous sentence. There is a remarkable paucity pf connecting particles, f. i. γάρ occurs only three times; δέ but nine times; μέν τε and οὖν are not found at all (while the last is of frequent occurrence in the Gospel). On the other hand ὅτι is often used, and καί is the regular connective. In many cases sentences and clauses follow one another without connecting particles, e. g. 2:22–24; 4:4–6, 7–10, 11–13.

AUTHORSHIP

The authorship of John is clearly attested by external testimony. Eusebius says that Papias employed this Epistle, and also that Irenaeus often quoted from it. The last assertion is borne out by the work against heresies, in which Irenaeus repeatedly quotes the letter and ascribes it to John. Clement of Alexandria, Tertullian, Cyprian and Origen all quote it by name; it is contained in the Muratorian Fragment and in the old Latin and Syriac Versions; and Eusebius classes it with the writings universally received by the churches. This testimony may be regarded as very strong, especially in view of the fact that the author is not named in the Epistle.

That conviction of the early church is corroborated by what internal evidence we have. All the proofs adduced for the Johannine authorship of the fourth Gospel also apply in the case of this Epistle, cf. p. 106 above. The two writings are so similar that they evidently were composed by the same hand. It is true, there are some points of difference, but these divergencies are of such a kind that they altogether preclude the idea that the Epistle is the product of a forger trying to imitate John. The almost general verdict is that he who wrote the one, also wrote the other. From 1:1–3 it is evident that the author has known Christ in the flesh; and the whole Epistle reveals the character of John as we know it from the Gospel and from tradition.

But the authenticity of the letter did not go unchallenged. In the second century the Alogi and Marcion rejected it, but only for dogmatical reasons. The truth presented in it did not fit their circle of ideas. The next attack on it followed in the sixteenth century, when Joseph Scaliger declared that none of the three Epistles that bear the name of John, were written by him; and S. G. Lange pronounced our letter unworthy of an apostle. It was not until 1820, however, that an important critical assault was made on the Epistle by Bretschneider. He was followed by the critics of the Tübingen school who, however they may differ in the details of their arguments, concur in denying the Johannine authorship and in regarding the Epistle as a second century production. Some of them, such as Köstlin, Georgii, and Hilgenfeld maintain that this Epistle and the fourth Gospel were composed by the same hand, while others, as Volkmar, Zeller, Davidson, Scholten e. a. regard them as the fruit of two congenial spirits.

The main arguments against the Johannine authorship are the following: (1) The Epistle is evidently directed against second century Gnosticism, which separated in a dualistic manner knowledge and conduct, the divine Christ and the human Jesus, cf. 2:4, 9, 11; 5:6, etc. (2) The letter also seems to be a polemic against Docetism, another second century heresy, cf. 4:2, 3. (3) There are references to Montanism in the Epistle, as f. i. where the writer speaks of the moral perfection of believers, 3:6, 9, and distinguishes between sins unto death and sins not unto death, 3:16, 17, a distinction which, Tertullian says, was made by the Montanists. (4) The difference between this Epistle and the Apocalypse is so great that it is impossible that one man should have written both.

We need not deny that the Epistle is partly an indirect polemic against Gnosticism, but we maintain that this was an incipient Gnosticism that made its appearance before the end of the first century in the heresy of Cerinthus, so that this does not argue against the authorship of John.— The supposed references to Docetism are very uncertain indeed; but even if they could be proved they would not point beyond the first century, for most of the Gnostics were also Docetæ, and the Cerinthian heresy may be called a species of Docetism.—The representations of John have nothing in common with those of the Montanists. When he speaks of the perfection of believers, he speaks ideally and not of a perfection actually realized in this life. Moreover the "sin unto death" to which he refers, is evidently a complete falling away from Christ, and is not to be identified with the sins to which Tertullian refers, viz. "murder, idolatry, fraud, denial of Christ, blasphemy, and assuredly also adultery and fornication."—With reference to the last argument we refer to what we have said above p. 111, and to the explanation given of the difference between the Apocalypse and the other Johannine writings below p. 321.

DESTINATION

There is very little in the letter that can help us to determine the location of the original readers. Because there is no local coloring whatever, it is not likely that the Epistle was sent to some individual church, as Ephesus (Hug) or Corinth (Lightfoot); and since the letter favors the idea that it was written to Gentile, rather than to Jewish Christians, it is very improbable that it was destined for the Christians of Palestine (Benson). There is not a single Old Testament quotation in the Epistle, nor any reference to the Jewish nationality or the Jewish tenets of the readers. The statement of Augustine that this is John's letter "ad Parthos" is very obscure. Some, as f. i. Grotius, inferred from it that the Epistle was written for Christians beyond the Euphrates; but most generally it is regarded as a mistaken reading for some other expression, the reading πρός παρθένους, finding most favor, which, Gieseler suggests, may in turn be a corruption of the title τόυ παρθένου, which was commonly given to John in early times.

In all probability the correct opinion respecting the destination of this Epistle is that held by the majority of scholars, as Bleek, Huther, Davidson, Plummer, Westcott, Weiss, Zahn, Alford e. a., that it was sent to the Christians of Asia Minor generally, for (1) that was John's special field of labor during the latter part of his life; (2) the heresies referred to and combated were rife in that country; and (3) the Gospel was evidently written for the Christians of that region, and the Epistle presupposes similar circumstances.

We have no definite information retarding the condition of the original readers. They had evidently left behind the Church's early struggles for existence and now constituted a recognized κοινωνία of believers, a community that placed its light over against the darkness of the world, and that distinguished itself from the unrighteous by keeping the commandments of God. They only needed to be reminded of their true character, which would naturally induce them to a life worthy of their fellowship with Christ. There are dangerous heresies abroad, however, against which they must be warned. The pernicious doctrine of Cerinthus, that Jesus was not the Christ, the Son of God, threatened the peace of their souls; and the subtle error, that one could be righteous without doing righteousness, endangered the fruitfulness of their Christian life.

COMPOSITION

1. Occasion and Purpose. Although the Epistle is not primarily and directly polemical, yet it was most likely occasioned by the dangers to which we already referred.

As to the object of the letter the author himself says: "that which we have seen and heard declare we unto you also, that ye also may have fellowship with us; yea, and our fellowship is with the Father and with his Son Jesus Christ," 1:3; and again in 5:13: "These things have I written unto you, that ye may know that ye have eternal life, even unto you that believe in the Name of the Son of God." The direct purpose of the author is to give his readers authentic instruction regarding the truth and reality of the things which they, especially as believers in Jesus Christ, accepted by faith; and to help them to see the natural issues of the fellowship to which they had been introduced, in order that they might have a full measure of peace and joy and life. The purpose of the writer is therefore at once theoretical and practical.

2. Time and Place. What we said above, pp. 113, 114, respecting the date of the fourth Gospel and the place of its composition, also favors the idea that this Epistle was written between the years 80–98, and at Ephesus. It is impossible to narrow down these time-limits any more. The only remaining

question is, whether the Epistle was written prior to the Gospel, (Bleek, Huther, Reuss, Weiss), or the Gospel prior to the Epistle (DeWette, Ewald, Guericke, Alford, Plummer). It appears to us that the grounds adduced for the priority of the Epistle, as f. i. that a writing of momentary design naturally precedes one of permanent design; a letter of warning to particular churches, a writing like the Gospel addressed to all Christendom,—are very weak. And the arguments for the other side are almost equally inconclusive, although there is some force in the reasoning that the Epistle in several places presupposes a knowledge of the Gospel, cf. the points of resemblance referred to on p. 311 above. But even this does not carry conviction, for Reuss correctly says: "For us, the Epistle needs the Gospel as a commentary; but inasmuch as at the first it had one in the oral instruction of the author, it is not thereby proved that it is the later." History of the N. T. I p. 237. Salmond and Zahn wisely conclude their discussion of this point with a non liquet.

CANONICAL SIGNIFICANCE

The canonicity of this letter was never doutbed by the Church. Polycarp and Papias, both disciples of John, used it, and Irenaeus, a disciple of Polycarp, directly ascribes it to John. Clement of Alexandria, Tertullian, Cyprian, Origen and Dionysius of Alexandria all quote it by name, as a writing of the apostle John. It is referred to as John's in the Muratorian Fragment, and is contained in the old Latin and Syriac Versions.

The abiding significance of this important Epistle is, that it pictures us ideally the community of believers, as a community of life in fellowship with Christ, mediated by the word of the apostle's, which is the Word of life. It describes that community as the sphere of life and light, of holiness and righteousness, of love to God and to the brethren; and as the absolute antithesis to the world with its darkness and death, its pollution and unrighteousness, its hatred and deception. All those who are introduced into that sphere should of necessity be holy and righteous and filled with love, and should avoid the world and its lusts. They should test the spirits, whether they be of God, and shun all anti-Christian error. Thus the Epistle describes for the Church of all ages the nature and criteria of heavenly fellowship, and warns believers to keep themselves unspotted from the world.

29

The Second and Third General Epistles of John

CONTENTS

The Second Epistle. After the address and the apostolic blessing, 1–3, the writer expresses his joy at finding that some of the children of the addressee walk in the truth, and reiterates the great commandment of brotherly love, 4–6. He urges the readers to exercise this love and informs them that there are many errorists, who deny that Jesus Christ is come in the flesh, admonishing them not to receive these, lest they should become partakers of their evil deeds, 7–11. Expressing his intention to come to them, he ends his Epistle with a greeting, 12, 13.

The Third Epistle. The writer, addressing Gajus, sincerely wishes that he may prosper, as his soul prospereth, 1–3. He commends him for receiving the itinerant preachers, though they were strangers to him, 5–8. He also informs the brother that he has written to the church, but that Diotrephes resists his authority, not receiving the brethren himself and seeking to prevent others from doing it, 9, 10. Warning Gajus against that evil example, he commends Demetrius, mentions an intended visit, and closes the Epistle with greetings, 11–14.

CHARACTERISTICS

1. These two Epistles have rightly been called twin-epistles, since they reveal several points of similarity. The author in both styles himself the elder; they are of about equal length; each one of them, as distinguished from the first Epistle, begins with an address and ends with greetings; both contain an expression of joy; and both refer to itinerant preachers and to an intended visit of the writer.

2. The letters show close affinity to I John. What little they contain of doctrinal matter is closely related to the contents of the first Epistle, where we can easily find statements corresponding to those in 2 John 4–9 and 3 John 11. Several concepts and expressions clearly remind us of I John, as f. i.

"love," "truth," "commandments," "a new commandment," one "which you had from the beginning," "loving truth," "walking in the truth," "abiding in" one, "a joy that may be fulfilled," etc. Moreover the aim of these letters is in general the same as that of the first Epistle, viz. to strengthen the readers in the truth and in love; and to warn them against an incipient Gnosticism.

AUTHORSHIP

Considering the brevity of these Epistles, their authorship is very well attested. Clement of Alexandria speaks of the second Epistle and, according to Eusebius, also commented on the third. Irenaeus quotes the second Epistle by name, ascribing it to "John the Lord's disciple." Tertullian and Cyprian contain no quotations from them, but Dionysius of Alexandria, Athanasius and Didymus received them as the work of the apostle. The Muratorian Canon in a rather obscure passage mentions two Epistles of John besides the first one. The Peshito does not contain them; and Eusebius, without clearly giving his own opinion, reckons them with the Antilegomena. After his time they were generally received and as such recognized by the, councils of Laodicea (363), Hippo (393) and Carthage (397).

Internal evidence may be said to favor the authorship of John. One can scarcely read these letters without feeling that they proceeded from the same hand that composed I John. The second Epistle especially is very similar to the first, a similarity that can hardly be explained, as Baljon suggests, from an acquaintance of the author with I John, Inl. p. 237, 239. And the third Epistle is inseparably linked to the second. The use of a few Pauline terms, προπέμπειν, εὐοδοῦσθαι and ὑγιαίνειν, and of a few peculiar words, as φλυαρεῖν, φιλοπρωτεύειν ὑπολαμβάνειν, prove nothing to the contrary.

The great stumbling block, that prevents several scholars from accepting the apostolic authorship of these Epistles, is found in in the fact that the author simply styles himself ὁ πρεσβύτερος. This appellation led some, as Erasmus, Grotius, Beck, Bretschneider, Hase, Renan, Reuss, Wieseler e. a., to ascribe them to a certain well-known presbyter John, distinct from the apostle. This opinion is based on a passage of Papias, as it is interpreted by Eusebius, The passage runs thus: "If I met anywhere with anyone who had been a follower of the elders, I used to inquire what were the declarations of the elders; what was said by Andrew, by Peter, by Philip, what by Thomas or James, what by John or Matthew, or any other of the disciples of our Lord; and the things which Aristion and the presbyter John, the disciples of the Lord say; for I did not expect to derive so much benefit from the contents of books as from the utterances of a living and abiding voice." From this statement Eusebius infers that among the informants of Papias there was besides the apostle John also a John the presbyter, Church Hist. III 39. But the correctness of this inference is subject to doubt. Notice (1) that Papias first names those whose words he received through others and then mentions two of whom he had also received personal instruction, cf. the difference in tense, εἶπεν and λέγουσιν; (2) that it seems very strange that for Papias, who was himself a disciple of the apostle John, anyone but the apostle would be ὁ πρεσβύτερος; (3) that Eusebius was the first to discover this second John in the passage of Papias: (4) that history knows nothing of such a John the presbyter; he is a shadowy person indeed; and (5) that the Church historian was not unbiased in his opinion; being averse to the supposed Chiliasm of the Apocalypse, he was only too glad to find another John to whom he could ascribe it.

But even if the inference of Eusebius were correct, it would not prove that this presbyter was the author of our Epistles. The same passage of Papias clearly establishes the fact that the apostle's were also called elders in the early Church. And does not the appellation, ὁ πρεσβύτερος, admirably fit the last of the apostle's, who for many years was the overseer of the churches in Asia Minor? He stood preeminent above all others; and by using this name designated at once his official position and his venerable age.

DESTINATION

The second Epistle is addressed to "ἐκλεκτῇ κυρίᾳ and her children, whom I love in truth, and not only I, but all those that know the truth," 1:1. There is a great deal of uncertainly about the interpretation of this address. On the assumption that the letter was addressed to an individual, the following renderings have been proposed: (1) to an elect lady; (2) to the elect lady; (3) to the elect Kuria; (4) to the Lady Electa; (5) to Electa Kuria.

The first of these is certainly the simplest and the most natural one, but considered as the address of an Epistle, it is too indefinite. To our mind the second, which seems to be grammatically permissible, is the best of all the suggested interpretations. As to the third, it is true that the word κυρία does occur as a proper name, cf. Zahn, Einl. II p. 584; but on the supposition that this is the case here also, it would be predicated of a single individual, which in Scripture is elsewhere done only in Rom. 16:13, a case that is not altogether parallel; and the more natural construction would be κυρίᾳ τῇ ἐκλεκτῇ. Cf. 3 John 1:1; the case in 1 Pet. 1:1 does not offer a parallel, because παρεπιδήμοις is not a proper noun. The fourth must be ruled out, since ἐκλεκτά is not known to occur as a nomen proprium; and if this were the name of the addressee, her sister, vs. 13, would strangely bear the same name. The last rendering is the least likely, burdening the lady, as it does, with two strange names. If the letter was addressed to an individual, which is favored by the analogy of the third Epistle, and also by the fact that the sister's children are spoken of in vs. 13, while she herself is not mentioned, then in all probability the addressee was a lady well known and highly esteemed in the early church, but not named in the letter. Thus Salmond (Hastings D. B.), while Alford and D. Smith regard Kuria as the name of the lady.

In view of the contents of the Epistle, however, many from the time of Jerome on have regarded the title as a designation of the Church in general (Jerome, Hilgenfeld, Lunemann, Schmiedel), or of some particular church (Huther, Holtzmann, Weiss, Westcott, Salmon, Zahn, Baljon). The former of these two seems to be excluded by vs. 13, since the Church in general can hardly be represented as having a sister. But as over against the view that the Epistle was addressed to an individual, the latter is favored by (1) the fact that everything of a personal nature is absent from the Epistle; (2) the plurals which the apostle constantly uses, cf. 6, 8, 10, 12; (3) the way in which he speaks to the addressee in vss. 5, 8; (4) the expression, "and not I only, but also all they that have known the truth," 1, which is more applicable to a church than to a single individual; and (5) the greeting, 13, which is most naturally understood as the greeting of one church to another. If this view of the Epistle is correct, and we are inclined to think it is, κυρία is probably used as the feminine of κύριος, in harmony with the Biblical representation that the Church is the bride of the Lamb. It is useless to guess, however, what particular church is meant. Since the church of Ephesus is in all probability the sister, it is likely that one of the other churches of Asia Minor is addressed.

The third Epistle is addressed to a certain Gajus, of whom we have no knowledge beyond that gained from the Epistle, where he is spoken of as a beloved friend of the apostle, and as a large-hearted hospitable man, who with a willing heart served the cause of Christ. There have been some attempts to identify him with a Gajus who is mentioned in the Apostolic Constitutions as having been appointed bishop of Pergamum by John, or with some of the other persons of the same name in Scripture, Acts 19:29;

20:4, especially with Paul's host at Corinth, Rom. 16:23; 1 Cor. 1:14; but these efforts have not been crowned with success.

COMPOSITION

1. Occasion and Purpose. In all probability the false agitators to whom the apostle refers in the Second Epistle, 7-12, gave him occasion to write this letter. His aim is to express his joy on account of the obedience of some of the members of the church, to exhort all that they love one another, to warn them against deceivers who would pervert the truth, and to announce his coming.

The third Epistle seems to have been occasioned by the reports of certain brethren who traveled about from place to place and were probably engaged in preaching the Gospel. They reported to the apostle that they had enjoyed the hospitality of Gajus, but had met with a rebuff at the hands of Diotrephes, an ambitious fellow (probably, as some have thought, an elder or a deacon in the church), who resisted the authority of the apostle and refused to receive the brethren. The authors purpose is to express his satisfaction with the course pursued by Gajus, to condemn the attitude of Diotrephes, to command Demetrius as a worthy brother, and to announce an intended visit.

2. Time and Place. The assumption seems perfectly warranted that John wrote these Epistles from Ephesus, where he spent perhaps the last twenty-five years of his life. We have no means for determining the time when they were composed. It may safely be said, however, that it was after the composition of I John. And if the surmise of Zahn and Salmon is correct, that the letter referred to in 3 John 9 is our second Epistle, they were probably written at the same time. This idea is favored somewhat by the fact that the expression, "I wrote somewhat (ἔγραψά τι) to the church," seems to refer to a short letter; and by the mention of an intended visit at the end of each letter. But from the context it would appear that this letter must have treated of the reception or the support of the missionary brethren, which is not the case with our second Epistle.

CANONICAL SIGNIFICANCE

There was some doubt at first as to the canonicity of these Epistles. The Alexandrian church generally accepted them, Clement, Dionysius and Alexander of Alexandria all recognizing them as canonical, though Origen had doubts. Irenaeus cites a passage from the second Epistle as John's. Since neither Tertullian nor Cyprian quote them, it is uncertain, whether they were accepted by the North African church. The Muratorian Fragment mentions two letters of John in a rather obscure way. In the Syrian church they were not received, since they were not in the Peshito, but in the fourth century Ephrem quotes both by name. Eusebius classed them with the Antilegomena, but soon after his time they were universally accepted as canonical.

The permanent significance of the second Epistle is that it emphasizes the necessity of abiding in the truth and thus exhibiting one's love to Christ. To abide in the doctrine of Christ and to obey his commandments, is the test of sonship. Hence believers should not receive those who deny the true doctrine, and especially the incarnation of Christ, lest they become partakers of their evil deeds.

The third Epistle also has its permanent lesson, in that it commends the generous love that reveals itself in the hospitality of Gajus, shown to those who labor in the cause of Christ, and denounce the self-centered activity of Diotrephes; for these two classes of men are always found in the Church.

30

The General Epistle of Jude

CONTENTS

The writer begins his Epistle with the regular address and apostolic blessing, 1, 2. He informs his readers that he felt it incumbent on him to warn them against certain intruders, who deny Christ, lead lascivious lives and will certainly be punished like the people delivered from Egypt, the fallen angels and the cities of the plain, 3-7. These intruders are further described as defilers of the flesh and as despisers and blasphemers of heavenly dignities, and the woe is pronounced on them, 8-11. After giving a further description of their debauchery, the author exhorts the readers to be mindful of the words of the apostle's, who had spoken of the appearance of such mockers, 12-19. Admonishing them to increase in faith and to keep themselves in the love of God, and giving them directions as to the correct behaviour towards others, he concludes his Epistle with a doxology, 20-25.

CHARACTERISTICS

1. This Epistle is characterized by its very close resemblence to parts of II peter. Since we have already discussed the relation in which the two stand to each other (cf. p. 307 above), we now simply refer to that discussion.

2. The letter is peculiar also in that it contains quotations from the apocryphal books. The story in verse 9 is taken from the Assumption of Moses, according to which Michael was commissioned to bury Moses, but Satan claimed the body, in the first place because he was the lord of matter, and in the second place since Moses had committed murder in Egypt. The falsity of the first ground is brought out by Michael, when he says: "The Lord rebuke thee, for it was God's Spirit which created the word and all mankind." He does not reflect on the second. The prophecy in verses 14, 15 is taken from the Book of Enoch, a book that was highly esteemed by the early church. According to some the statement regarding the fallen

angels, verse 6, is also derived from it. The latest editor of these writings, R. H. Charles, regards the first as a composite work, made up of two distinct books, viz. the Testament and the Assumption of Moses, of which the former, and possibly also the latter was written in Hebrew between 7 and 29 A. D. With respect to the Book of Enoch he holds, "that the larger part of the book was written not later than 160 B. C., and that no part of it is more recent than the Christian era." Quoted by Mayor, Exp. Gk. Test. V p. 234.

3. The language of Jude may best be likened to that of his brother James. He speaks in a tone of unquestioned authority and writes a vigorous style. His Greek, though it has a Jewish complexion, is fairly correct; and his descriptions are often just as picturesque as those of James, f. i. when he compares the intruders to "spots (R. V. 'hidden rocks') in the feasts of charity;" "clouds without water, carried along by winds," "autumn trees without fruit, twice dead, plucked up by the roots," "wild waves of the sea, foaming out their own shame;" etc., 12, 13. Like James also he employs some words that are otherwise exclusively Pauline, as ἀΐδιος, κυριότης, οἰκητήριον, προγράφειν. Moreover the letter contains a few ἅπαξ λεγόμενα.

AUTHORSHIP

The Muratorian Canon accepts Jude, but indicates that it was doubted by some. Clement of Alexandria commented on it, and Tertullian quotes it by name. Origen acknowledges that there were doubts as to the canonicity of Jude, but does not seem to have shared them. Didymus of Alexandria defends the Epistle against those who questioned its authority on account of the use made in it of apocryphal books. Eusebius reckoned it with the Antilegomena; but it was accepted as canonical by the third council of Carthage in 397 A. D.

The author designates himself as "Jude the servant of Jesus Christ, and brother of James." There are several persons of that name mentioned in the New Testament, of which only two can come in consideration here, however, viz. Jude, the brother of the Lord, Mt. 13:55; Mk. 6:3, and Jude the apostle, Lk. 6:16; Acts 1:13, also called Lebbeus, Mt. 10:3, and Thaddeus, Mk. 3:18. It appears to us that the author was Jude, the brother of the Lord, because: (1) He seeks to give a clear indication of his identity by calling himself, "the brother of James." This James must have been so well known, therefore, as to need no further description; and there was but one James at that time of whom this could be said, viz. James the brother of the Lord. (2) It is inconceivable that an apostle, rather than name his official position, should make himself known by indicating his relationship to another person, whoever that person might be. (3) Though it is possible that the writer, even if he were an apostle, should speak as he does in the 17th verse, that passage seems to imply that he stood outside of the apostolic circle.—In favor of the view that the author was the apostle Jude, some have appealed to Lk. 6:16; Acts 1:13, where the apostle is called Ἰούδας Ἰακώβου but it is contrary to established usage to supply the word brother in such a case.

Very little is known of this Jude. If the order in which the brethren of the Lord are named in Scripture is any indication of their age, he was the youngest or the youngest but one of the group; compare Mt. 13:55 with Mk. 6:3. With his brothers he was not a believer in Jesus during the Lord's public ministry, John 7:5, but evidently embraced him by faith after the resurrection, Acts 1:14. For the rest we can only gather from 1 Cor. 9:5 respecting the brethren of the Lord in general, undoubtedly with the exception of James, who resided at Jerusalem, that they traveled about with their wives, willing workers for the Kingdom of God, and were even known at Corinth.

The authenticity of the Epistle has been doubted, because: (1) The author speaks of faith in the objective sense, as a fides quae creditur, 3, 20, a usage that points to the post-apostolic period; (2) He mentions the apostle's as persons who lived in the distant past, 17; and (3) he evidently combats the second century heresy of the Carpocratians. But these grounds are very questionable indeed. The word faith is employed in the objective sense elsewhere in the New Testament, most certainly in the Pastorals, and probably also in Rom. 10:8; Gal. 1:23; Phil. 1:27. And there is nothing impossible in the assumption that that meaning should have become current in the time of the apostle's. The manner in which Jude mentions the apostle's does not necessarily imply that they had all passed away before this letter was composed. At most the death of a few is implied. But we agree with Dr. Chase, when he judges that the supposition that the apostle's were dispersed in such a way that their voice could not at the time reach the persons to whom this letter is addressed, meets all the requirements of the case. Hastings D. B. Art. Jude. The assumption that the heretics referred to were second century Carpocratians, is entirely gratuitous; it rests on a mistaken interpretation of three passages, viz. the verses 4b, 8, 19.

DESTINATION

Jude addresses his Epistle to "those that are sanctified by God the Father, and preserved in Jesus Christ, and called." On account of the very general character of this designation some, as Ewald, regard the Epistle as a circular letter; but the contents of the Epistle are against this assumption. Yet we are left entirely to conjecture as to the particular locality in which the readers dwelt. Some scholare, e. g. Alford and Zahn, believe that the Epistle was written to Jewish readers, but we are inclined to think with Weiss, Chase, Bigg, Baljon e. a. that the recipients of the letter were Gentile Christians, (1) because the letter is so closely related to II Peter, which was sent to the Christians of Asia Minor; and (2) since the heresies to which it refers are known to have arisen in Gentile churches. Cf. especially I Corinthians and the letters to the seven churches in the Apocalypse.

Many expositors are inclined to look for the first readers in Asia Minor on account of the resemblance of the heresies mentioned in the Epistle to those referred to in II Peter. But possibly it is better to hold with Chase that the letter was sent to Syrian Antioch and the surrounding district, since they had evidently received oral instruction from the apostle's generally, and were therefore most likely in the vicinity of Palestine. Moreover Jude may have felt some special responsibility for the church in that vicinity since the death of his brother James.

In the condition of the readers there was cause for alarm. The danger that Peter saw as a cloud on the distant horizon, Jude espied as a leaven that was already working in the ranks of his readers. False brethren had crept into the church who were, it would seem, practical libertines, enemies of the cross of Christ, who abused their Christian liberty (Alford, Salmon, Weiss, Chase), and not at the same time heretical teachers (Zahn, Baljon). Perhaps they were no teachers at all. Their life was characterized by lasciviousness, 4, especially fornication, 7, 8, 11, mockery, 10, ungodliness, 15, murmuring, complaining, pride and greed, 16. Their fundamental error seems to have been that they despised and spoke evil of the authorities that were placed over them. They were Antinomians and certainly had a great deal in common with the Nicolaitans of the Apocalypse.

COMPOSITION

1. Occasion and Purpose. The danger to which these Christians were thus exposed, led to the composition of this Epistle. Apparently Jude intended to write to them of the common salvation, when he suddenly heard of the grave situation and found it necessary to pen a word of warning, 3. In the verse from which we draw this conclusion, the author also clearly states his aim, when he says that he deemed it imperative to write to them that

they should earnestly contend for the faith which was once delivered to the saints. In order to do this, he pictures to them the disobedient and immoral character of the ungodly persons that had unawares crept into the fold and endangered their Christian faith and life; reminds them of the fact that God would certainly punish those wanton libertines, just as He had punished sinners in the past; and exhorts them to stand in faith and to strive after holiness.

2. Time and Place. We have absolutely no indication of the place where this Epistle was written; it is not unlikely, however, that it was at Jerusalem.

With respect to the time of its composition we have a terminus ad quem in the date of II Peter, about A. D. 67, since that Epistle is evidently dependent on Jude. On the other hand it does not seem likely that Jude would write such a letter, while his brother James was still living, so that we have a terminus a quo in A. D. 62. A date later than 62 is also favored by the Pauline words employed in this letter, in some of which we seem to have an echo of Ephesians and Colossians. Moreover the great similarity between the conditions pictured in this letter and those described in II Peter is best explained, if we date them in close proximity to each other. We shall not go far wrong in dating the Epistle about the year 65.

The older critics of the Tübingen school dated the Epistle late in the second century, while more recent critics, as Pfleiderer, Holtzmann, Jülicher, Harnack, Baljon, think it originated about the middle or in the first half of the second century. They draw this conclusion from, (1) the way in which the writer speaks of faith, 3, 20; (2) the manner in which he refers to the apostle's, 17; (3) the use of the apocryphal books; and (4) the supposed references to the doctrines of the Carpocratians. But these arguments can all be met by counter-arguments, cf. above.

CANONICAL SIGNIFICANCE

In the early Church there was considerable doubt as to the canonicity of this Epistle, especially because it was not written by an apostle, and contained passage from apocryphal books. There are allusions more or less clear to the Epistle in II Peter, Polycarp, Athenagoras and Theophilus of Antioch. The Muratorian Canon mentions it, but in a manner which implies that it was doubted by some. It is found in the old Latin Version, but not in the Peshito. Clement of Alexandria, Tertullian and Origen recognized it, though Origen intimates that there were doubts regarding its canonicity. Eusebius doubted its canonical authority, but the council of Carthage (397) accepted it.

In the Epistle of Jude we have the Christian war-cry, resounding through the ages: Contend earnestly for the faith that was once delivered unto the saints! This letter, the last of the New Testament, teaches with great emphasis that apostacy from the true creed with its central truths of the atonement of Christ and the permanent validity of the law as the rule of life, is assured perdition; and clearly reveals for all generations the inseparable connection between a correct belief and a right mode of living.

— CHAPTER

31

The Revelation of John

CONTENTS

After the introduction and the apostolic blessing, 1:1-8, the book contains seven visions or series of visions, extending from 1:9-22:7, followed by a conclusion, 22:8-21.

I. The first Vision, 1:9-3:22, is that of the glorified Christ in the midst of the Church, directing John to write letters of reproof, of warning, of exhortation and of consolation to seven representative churches of proconsular Asia, viz. to Ephesus, Smyrna, Pergamus, Thyatire, Sardis, Philadelphia and Laodicea.

II. The second Vision, 4:1-8:1, reveals God as ruling the world's destiny, and the Lamb as taking the book of the divine decrees and breaking the seven seals of which each one represents a part of God's purpose, the first four referring to the terrestrial, and the last three to the celestial sphere. Between the sixth and seventh seals an episode is introduced to show the safety of the people of God amid the judgments that are inflicted on the world.

III. The third Vision, 8:2-11:19, shows us seven angels, each one having a trumpet. After an angel has offered up the prayers of the saints to God, the seven angels blow their trumpets, and each trumpet is followed by a vision of destruction on the sinful world, the destruction of the last three being more severe than that of the first four. Between the sixth and seventh trumpets there is again an episode describing the preservation of the Church.

IV. The fourth Vision, 12:1-14:20, describes the conflict of the world with the Church of God. The Church is represented as a woman bringing forth the Christ, against whom the dragon representing satan wages war. In successive visions we behold the beasts which satan will employ as his agents, the militant Church, and the advancing stages of Christ's conquest.

V. The fifth Vision, 15:1–16:21, once more reveals seven angels, now having seven vials or bowls containing the last plagues or judgments of God. First we have a description of the Church that triumphed over the beast, glorifying God; and this is followed by a picture of the sevenfold judgment of God on the world, represented by the seven vials.

VI. The sixth Vision, 17:1–20:15, reveals the harlot city Babylon, the representative of the world, and the victory of Christ over her and over the enemies that are in league with her, the great conflict ending in the last judgment.

VII. The seventh Vision, 21:1–22:7, discloses to the eye the ideal Church, the new Jerusalem, and pictures in glowing colors her surpassing beauty and the everlasting, transcendent bliss of her inhabitants.

The book closes with an epilogue in which the seer describes its significance and urges the readers to keep the things that are written on its pages, 22:7–21.

CHARACTERISTICS

1. The Revelation of John is the only prophetic book in the New Testament. It is called a prophecy in 1:3, 22:7, 10, 18, 19. A nearer description of the book is given, however, in the name Apocalypse, for there is a difference between the prophetic books of the Bible in general and that part of them that may be said to belong to the Apocalyptic literature. Naturally the two have some elements in common: they both contain communications, mediated by the Holy Spirit, of the character, will and purposes of God; and the one as well as the other looks to the future of the Kingdom of God. But there are also points of difference. Prophecy, while it certainly has reference also to the future of God's Kingdom, is mainly concerned with a divine interpretation of the past and the present, while the chief interest of Apocalyptic lies in the future. Prophecy again, where it does reveal the future, shows this in its organic relation with principles and forces that are already working in the present, while Apocalyptic pictures the images of the future, not as they develop out of existing conditions, but as they are shown directly from heaven and to a great extent in supernatural forms.

2. A characteristic feature of the book is that its thought is largely clothed in symbolic language derived from some of the prophetic books of the Old Testament. Hence its correct understanding is greatly facilitated by studying the writer's Old Testament sources. Yet we must constantly

bear in mind that he does not always employ the language so derived in its original significance. Compare ch. 18 with Is. 13, 14; Jer. 50, 51;—21:1-22:5 with various parts of Is. 40-66; Ezek. 40-48;—1:12-20 with Dan. 7, 10;—ch. 4 with Is. 6; Ezek. 1, 10. But however dependent the author may be on the prophets, he does not slavishly follow them, but uses their language with great freedom. The symbolic numbers 3, 4, 7, 10, 12 and their multiples also play an important part in the book.

3. The language of the Apocalypse differs from that of all the rest of the New Testament. It is very decidedly Hebraistic Greek. According to Simcox its vocabulary is far less eccentric than its style and grammar. This author in his, Writers of the New Testament pp. 80-89 classifies the most import- ant peculiarities of the language of Revelation under several heads: (1) As in Hebrew the copula is generally omitted, cf. 4:1, 3; 5:2; 6:8; 9:7, 10, 16, 17; 10:1; 11:8; 19:1, 12; 21:8, 13, 19. (2) Apparently the writer, at least in several instances, does not use the Greek tenses in their purely temporal sense, but more like the Hebrew perfect and imperfect, cf. 2:5, 22, 24; 4:10; 10:7; 12:4. (3) The use of a redundant pronoun or pronominal adverb is very frequent, cf. 3:8; 7:2, 9; 12:6, 14; 13:12; 17:9; 20:8. (4) When two nouns are in opposi- tion, the second is usually put in the nominative, whatever be the case of the first, cf. 1:5; 2:13, 20; 3:12; 7:4; 8:9; 9:14; 14:12, 14; 17:3; 20:2. (5) There are some irregularities which, considered abstractly are perfectly legitimate, but are contrary to established Greek usage, as f. i. the use of the dative instead of the double accusative in 2:14; and the use of the plural of verbs with a subject in the neuter nominative, as in 3:4; 4:5; 11:13. (6) False con- cords in gender, constructions ad sensum are also frequently found, 4:7, 8; 7:4, 8; 9:5, 6, etc.

AUTHORSHIP

The external testimony for the authorship of the apostle John is quite strong. Justin Martyr clearly testifies that the book was written by "John one of the apostle's of the Lord." Irenaeus, whose teacher was Polycarp, the disciple of John, gives very decisive and repeated testimony for the authorship of the apostle. The Muratorian Canon mentions John as the author of the book, and the context shows that the son of Zebedee is meant. Hippolytus quotes the Apocalypse several times as a work of John; and that the John which he has in mind is the apostle, is clear from a pas- sage in which he speaks of him as "an apostle and disciple of the Lord." Clement of Alexandria names the apostle as the author of the book, as do also Origen, Victorinus, Ephrem the Syrian, Epiphanius e. a. In the West Ambrose and Augustine repeatedly quote the Apocalypse as written by John the apostle, and Jerome speaks of the apostle John as also being a prophet.

This strong external testimony is corroborated by internal evidence: (1) The author repeatedly calls himself John, 1:1, 4, 9; 22:8, and there is but one person who could use the name thus absolutely to designate himself without fear of being misunderstood, viz. John the apostle. (2) The writer evidently stood in some special relation to the churches of proconsular Asia (i. e. Mysia, Lydia, Caria and a part of Phrygia), which is in perfect harmony with the fact that John spent the later years of his life at Ephesus. (3) The author was evidently banished to the island called Patmos in the Aegean sea, one of the Sporades to the South of Samos. Now a quite consistent tradition, which is, however, discredited by some scholars, says that this happened to the apostle John; and there are some features that seem to mark this as an independent tradition. (4) There are also notes of identity between the writer and the author of the fourth Gospel and of I John. Like in John 1:1 ff. and 1 John 1:1, so also in Rev. 19:13 the name ὁ λόγος is given to our Lord. He is called ἀρνίον twenty-nine times in this book, a word that is used elsewhere only in John 21:15, as a designation of the disciples of the Lord. It is remarkable also that the only place, where Christ is called a Lamb outside of this book, is in John 1:29, the word ἀμνός being used. The term ἀληθινός, found but once in Luke, once in Paul and three times in Hebrews, is employed nine times in the gospel of John, four times in the first Epistle, and ten times in the Apocalypse, though not always in exactly the same sense. Compare also with the repeated expression ὁ νιχῶν, 2:7, 11, 17, etc.; John 16:33; 1 John 2:13, 14; 4:4; 5:4, 5.

Still there have been dissentient voices from the beginning. The Alogi for dogmatical reasons impugned the authorship of John and ascribed the book to Cerinthus. Dionysius of Alexandria for more critical reasons, but also laboring with a strong anti-chiliastic bias, referred it to another John of Ephesus. Eusebius wavered in his opinion, but, led by considerations like those of Dionysius, was inclined to regard that shadowy person, John the presbyter, as the author. And Luther had a strong dislike for the book, because, as he said, Christ was neither taught nor recognized in it; and because the apostle's did not deal in visions, but spoke in clear words, he declared that it was neither apostolic nor prophetic.

The Tübingen school accepted the Johannine authorship of the Apocalypse, while it denied that the apostle had written any of the other books that are generally ascribed to him. A great and increasing number of critical scholars, however, do not believe that the apostle John composed the Apocalypse. Some of them, as Hitzig, Weiss and Spitta, suggest John Mark as the author, while many others, such as Bleek, Credner, Düsterdieck, Keim, Ewald, Weizsäcker e. a., regard it as the work of John the presbyter. The principal objections urged against the authorship of the apostle are the following: (1) While the apostle in the gospel and in the first Epistle does not mention his name, the writer of this book names himself both in the first and in the third person. (2) The genius of the two writers is quite different: the one is speculative and introspective, the other, imaginative, looking especially to the external course of events; the one is characterized by mildness and love, the other is stern and revengeful; the views of the one are spiritual and mystic, those of the other are sensuous and plastic. (3) The type of doctrine found in the Apocalypse has a Jewish stamp and is very unlike that of the gospel of John, which is idealizing and breaks away from the Mosaic basis. In this book we find the Old Testament conception of God as a fearful Judge, of angels and demons, and of the Church as the new Jerusalem. There are twenty-four elders round about the throne, twelve thousand of each tribe that are sealed, and the names of the apostle's are engraved on the foundation stones of the heavenly city. Moreover the necessity of good works is strongly emphasized, cf. chs. 2, 3 and also 14:13. (4) The style of the book is of a very distinct Hebraic type, different from anything that is found in the other writings of John. Instead of the regular and comparatively faultless construction of the Gospel, we here find a language full of irregularities.

But we do not believe that these considerations necessitate the assumption that the author of the book cannot be identified with the writer of the fourth gospel. It is in perfect harmony with the usage of the historical and the prophetical writers of the Bible throughout that the writer conceals his name in the Gospel and mentions it in the Apocalypse. The different light in which we see him in his various books is the natural result of the vastly different character of these writings. We should also remember that a prophetic book naturally reflects far less of the personal character of its author than epistolary writings do. The alleged Judæistic type of the teachings found in the Apocalypse does not militate against the authorship of John. In a symbolic description of the future condition of the Church it is perfectly natural and indeed very fitting that the author should derive his symbolism from Old Testament sources, since the Old Testament is symbolically and typically related to the New. It cannot be maintained that the Christological and Soteriological teaching of the Apocalypse is essentially Jewish. The Jews that oppose Jesus are denounced, 3:9; the Church is composed of people out of every nation, 7:9; salvation is the free gift of grace, 21:6; 22:17; and though the necessity of good works is emphasized, those are not regarded as meritorious, but as the fruits of righteousness, and are even called the works of Jesus, 2:26. The strongest argument against the authorship of John is undoubtedly that derived from the style and language of the book. There has been an attempt on the part of some scholars, as Olshausen and Guericke, to explain the linguistic differences between the Apocalypse and the Gospel of John by assuming that the former preceded the latter by about 20 or 25 years, in which time the authors knowledge of Greek gradually matured. But the differences are of such a kind that it may be doubted, whether the lapse of a few years can account for them. The language of the fourth Gospel is not that of the Apocalypse in a more developed form. While it is questionable, whether an altogether satisfactory explanation can be given with the data at hand, it seems certain that the solution must be found, at least in part, in the transcendent nature of the subject-matter and in the symbolic character of the book. The fact that the author so often violates the rules of Greek grammar, does not necessarily mean that he did not know them, but may also indicate that under the stress of the lofty ideas that he wished to express, he naturally resorted to Aramaic usage, which was easier for him. The facts in the case do not prove that the Greek of the Gospel is superior to that of the Apocalypse. In the former writing the author does not attempt so much as in the latter; the language of the one is far simpler than that of the other.

DESTINATION

The apostle addresses the Apocalypse to "the seven churches which are in Asia," 1:4. Undoubtedly this number is not exhaustive but representative of the Church in general, the number seven, which is the number of completeness, forming a very important element in the texture of this prophetic writing. These churches are types that are constantly repeated in history. There are always some churches that are predominantly good and pure like those of Smyrna and Philadelphia, and therefore need no reproof but only words of encouragement; but there are also constantly

others like Sardis and Laodicea in which evil preponderates, and that
deserve severe censure and an earnest call to repentance. Probably the
greater number of churches, however, will always resemble those of
Ephesus, Pergamus and Thyatire in that good and evil are about equally
balanced in their circle, so that they call for both commendation and
censure, promise and threatening. But while there is a great difference
both in the outward circumstances and in the internal condition of these
churches, they all form a part of the militant Church that has a severe
struggle on earth in which it must strive to overcome by faith (notice the
constantly repeated ὁ νικῶν) and that may expect the coming of the Lord
to reward her according to her works.

COMPOSITION

1. Occasion and Purpose. The historical condition that led to the composition of the Apocalypse was one of increasing hardships for the Church
and of an imminent life and death struggle with the hostile world, represented by the Roman empire. The demand for the deification of the
emperor became ever more insistent and was extended to the provinces.
Domitian was one of the emperors who delighted to be styled dominus
et deus. To refuse this homage was disloyalty and treason; and since the
Christians as a body were bound to ignore this demand from the nature
of their religion, they stood condemned as constituting a danger to the
empire. Persecution was the inevitable result and had already been suffered by the churches, when this book was written, while still greater
persecution was in store for them. Hence they needed consolation and
the Lord directed John to address the Apocalypse to them. Cf. especially
Ramsay, The Church in the Roman Empire pp. 252-319.

It is but natural therefore that the contents of the book are mainly con-
solatory. It aims at revealing to the servants of Christ, i. e. to Christians in
general the things that must shortly (not quickly, but before long) come
to pass. This note of time is to be considered as a prophetic formula, in
connection with the fact that one day is with the Lord as a thousand years
and thousand years as one day. The central theme of the book is, "I come
quickly," and in the elaboration of this theme Christ is pictured as coming
in terrible judgments on the world, and in the great final struggle in which
He is conqueror, and after which the ecclesia militans is transformed into
the ecclesia triumphans.

2. Time and Place. There are especially two opinions as to the composition of the Apocalypse, viz. (1) that it was written toward the end of Domitian's reign, about A. D. 95 or 96; and (2) that it was composed between the death of Nero in the year 68 and the destruction of Jerusalem.

(1). The late date was formerly the generally accepted time of composition (Hengstenberg, Lange, Alford, Godet e. a.) and, although for a time the earlier date was looked upon with great favor, there is now a noticeable return to the old position (Holtzmann, Warfield, Ramsay, Porter (Hastings D. B.), Moffat (Exp. Gk. Test.) e. a. This view is favored by the following considerations: (a) The testimony of antiquity. While there are a few witnesses that refer the book to an earlier date, the majority, and among them Irenaeus whose testimony should not lightly be set aside, point to the time of Domitian. (b) The antithesis of the Roman empire to the Church presupposed in the Apocalypse. The persecution of Nero was a purely local and somewhat private affair. The Church did not stand opposed to the empire as representing the world until the first century was approaching its close; and the Apocalypse already looks back on a period of persecution. Moreover we know that banishment was a common punishment in the time of Domitian. (c) The existence and condition of the seven churches in Asia. The utter silence of Acts and of the Epistles regarding the churches of Smyrna, Philadelphia, Sardis, Pergamus and Thyatira favors the supposition that they were founded after the death of Paul. And the condition of these churches presupposes a longer period of existence than the earlier date will allow. Ephesus has already left her first love; in Sardis and Laodicea spiritual life has almost become extinct; the Nicolaitans, who are not mentioned elsewhere in the New Testament, have already made their pernicious influence felt in the churches of Ephesus and Pergamus, while similar mischief was done in Thyatira by the woman Jesebel. Moreover Laodicea, which was destroyed by an earthquake in the 6th (Tactitus) or in the 10th (Eusebius) year of Nero, is here described as boasting of her wealth and self-sufficiency.

(2). Against this and in favor of the earlier date, defended by Dusterdieck, Weiss, Guericke, Schaff, are urged: (a) The late testimony of the Syrian Apocalypse that John was banished in the time of Nero, and the obscure and self-contradictory passage in Epiphanius that places the banishment in the time of Claudius. Cf. Alford, Prolegamena Section II. 14, where the weakness of this testimony is pointed out. (b) The supposed references in the Apocalypse to the destruction of the Holy City as still future in 11:1, 2,

13. But it is quite evident that these passages must be understood symbolically. Regarded as historical predictions of the destruction of Jerusalem they did not come true, for according to 11:2 only the outer court would be abolished, and according to vs. 13 merely the tenth part of the city would be destroyed, and that not by Rome but by an earthquake, (c) The supposed indications of the reigning emperor in 13:1 ff., especially in connection with the symbolical interpretation of the number 666 as being equal to the Hebrew form of Nero Ceasar. But the great diversity of opinion as to the correct interpretation of these passages, even among the advocates of the early date, proves that their support is very questionable. (d) The difference between the language of this book and that of the Gospel of John is thought to favor an early date, but, as we have already pointed out, this is not necessarily the case.

It is impossible to tell, whether John wrote the Apocalypse while he was still on the island of Patmos, or after his return from there. The statement in 10:4 does not prove the former theory, nor the past tenses in 1:2, 9, the latter.

3. Method. Of late several theories have been broached to explain the origin of the Apocalypse in such a manner as to account satisfactorily for the literary and psychological features of the book. (1) The Incorporation-hypothesis holds to the unity of the Apocalypse, but believes that several older fragments of Jewish or Christian origin are incorporated in it (Weizsäcker, Sabatier, Bousset, McGiffert, Moffat, Baljon). (2) The Revision-hypothesis assumes that the book has been subject to one or more revisions, (Erbes, Briggs, Barth). The last named author is of the opinion that John himself in the time of Domitian revised an Apocalypse which he had written under Nero. (3) The Compilation-hypothesis teaches that two or more sources fairly complete in themselves have been pieced together by a redactor or redactors, (Weyland, Spitta, Völter at least in part). (4) The Jewish and Christian hypothesis maintains that the groundwork of the Apocalypse was a Jewish writing in the Aramaic language, written about 65–70, that was later translated and edited by a Christian (Vischer, Harnack, Martineau). In connection with these we can only say that to us these theories seem unnecessary and in the majority of cases very arbitrary. There is every reason to maintain the unity of the Apocalypse. The use of written sources in its composition is an unproved assumption; but the author was evidently impregnated with Old Testament ideas and modes of expression,

and drew largely on the storehouse of his memory in the symbolic description of the supernatural scenes that were presented to his vision.

INTERPRETATION

Various principles of interpretation have been adopted with reference to this book in the course of time:

1. The older expositors and the majority of orthodox Protestant commentators adopted the Continuïst (kirchengeschichtliche) interpretation, which proceeds on the assumption that the book contains a prophetic compendium of Church history from the first Christian century until the return of Christ, so that some of its prophecies have now been realized and others still await fulfilment. This theory disregards the contemporaneous character of the seven series of visions and has often led to all sorts of vain speculations and calculations as to the historical facts in which particular prophecies are fulfilled.

2. In course of time the Futurist (endgeschichtliche) interpretation found favor with some, according to which all or nearly all the events described in the Apocalypse must be referred to the period immediately preceding the return of Christ. (Zahn, Kliefoth) Some of the Futurists are so extreme that they deny even the past existence of the seven Asiatic churches and declare that we may yet expect them to arise in the last days. As a matter of course this interpretation fails to do justice to the historical element in the book.

3. Present day critical scholars are generally inclined to adopt the Præterist (zeitgeschichtliche) interpretation, which holds that the view of the Seer was limited to matters within his own historical horizon, and that the book refers principally to the triumph of Christianity over Judæism and Paganism, signalized in the downfall of Jerusalem and Rome. On this view all or almost all the prophecies contained in the book have already been fulfilled. (Bleek, Düisterdieck, Davidson, F. C. Porter e. a.). But this theory does not do justice to the prophetic element in the Apocalypse.

Though all these views must be regarded as one-sided, each one contains an element of truth that must be taken in consideration in the interpretation of the book. The descriptions in it certainly had a point of contact in the historical present of the Seer, but they go far beyond that present; they certainly pertain to historical conditions of the Church of God, and conditions that will exist in all ages, but instead of arising successively in the order in which they are described in the Apocalypse, they make their appearance in every age contemporaneously; and finally they will certainly issue in a terrific struggle immediately preceding the parousia of Christ and in the transcendent glory of the bride of the Lamb.

INSPIRATION

The particular form of inspiration in which the writer shared was the prophetic, as is perfectly evident from the book itself. The author, while in the Spirit, was the recipient of divine revelations, 1:1, 10, and received his intelligence by means of visions, in part at least mediated and interpreted by angels, 1:10, 19; 4:1, 2; 5:1; 6:1; 17:7-18; 21:9. He received the command to write and to prophecy from God himself, 1:19; 10:4, 11; 14:13. And the "I" speaking in the book is sometimes that of the Lord himself and sometimes that of the prophet, which is also a characteristic mark of the prophetic inspiration. In chapters 2 and 3 f. i. the Lord speaks in the first person, and again in 16:15 and 22:7.

CANONICAL SIGNIFICANCE

The canonical authority of the Apocalypse has never been seriously doubted by the Church. Hermas, Papias and Melito recognized its canonicity, and according to Eusebius Theophilus cited passages from it. The three great witnesses of the end of the second century all quote it by name and thus recognize its authority. Hippolytus and Origen also regarded it as canonical. Similarly Victorinus, Ambrose, Jerome and Augustine. Gradually, however, the fact that Millenarians found their chief support in the book, made it obnoxious to some of the Church fathers, who deemed it inexpedient to read it in the churches. This explains, why it is absent from some MSS. and from some of the catalogues of the ancient councils.

The book is primarily a book of consolation for the militant Church in its struggles with the hostile world and with the powers of darkness. It directs the glance of the struggling, suffering, sorrowing and often persecuted Church toward its glorious future. Its central teaching is, "I come quickly!" And while it reveals the future history of the Church as one of continual struggle, it unfolds in majestic visions the coming of the Lord, which issues in the destruction of the wicked and of the evil One, and in the everlasting bliss of the faithful witnesses of Jesus Christ. Hence the book comes to the enemies of God's Kingdom with words of solemn warning and with threatenings of future punishment, while it encourages the followers of the Lord to ever greater faithfulness, and opens up to them bright visions of the future, thus inspiring the Church's constant prayer: "Even so, come, Lord Jesus!"